Breaking the China-Taiwan Impasse

Breaking the China-Taiwan Impasse

Edited by Donald S. Zagoria with the assistance of Chris Fugarino

A Publication of the National Committee on American Foreign Policy

Westport, Connecticut
London

Library of Congress Cataloging-in-Publication Data

Breaking the China-Taiwan impasse / edited by Donald S. Zagoria with the assistance of Chris Fugarino.

p. cm.

ISBN 0-275-98011-1 (alk. paper)—ISBN 0-275-98022-7 (pbk. : alk. paper)

1. Taiwan—Relations—China. 2. China—Relations—Taiwan. 3. Chinese reunification question, 1949– I. Zagoria, Donald S. II. Fugarino, Chris.

DS799.63.C6B74 2003

327.5105124'09049—dc21 2003042859

British Library Cataloguing in Publication Data is available.

Library of Congress Catalog Card Number: 2003042859

ISBN: 0-275-98011-1

0-275-98022-7 (pbk.)

First published in 2003

Praeger Publishers, 88 Post Road West, Westport, CT 06881

An imprint of Greenwood Publishing Group, Inc.

www.praeger.com

Printed in the United States of America

The paper used in this book complies with the Permanent Paper Standard issued by the National Information Standards Organization (Z39.48–1984).

10 9 8 7 6 5 4 3 2 1

Contents

Acknowledgments

I would like to take this opportunity to thank a number of people who made this volume possible. First, the National Committee on American Foreign Policy (NCAFP), led by its chairman, William J. Flynn, and its president, George D. Schwab, have offered outstanding support for the project on U.S.-China Policy and Cross-Strait Relations since it began in 1996. Also, William M. Rudolf, executive vice president, and Donald S. Rice, Esq., senior vice president, have been unstinting in their support. C. Kay Larson and Marcie Rudell of the NCAFP staff have been instrumental in organizing the various roundtables. And Xi Chen and Chris Fugarino have played a critical role in helping me organize the material included.

I also want to thank three foundations that have supported these roundtables: Smith Richardson, W. Alton Jones, and Ford. Marin Strmecki of Smith Richardson, George Perkovich of W. Alton Jones, and Andrew Watson of Ford have all been extraordinarily supportive and generous. I also want to thank the Mutual of America Life Insurance Company for their generous support.

I want to thank, too, the many hosts we have had in China and Taiwan during the past several years. In China, the list includes the Taiwan Institute of the Chinese Academy of Social Sciences, the Chinese Institute of Contemporary International Relations, and the Shanghai Institute of International Studies. We are particularly indebted to Xu Shiquan, Lu Zhongwei, and Yang Jiemian. In Taiwan, our host was usually the foreign ministry, and we want to express our appreciation to Hung mao Tien, Taiwan' s former foreign minister, and to Eugene Chen, the current foreign minister, as well as to their staff. We also could not have functioned effectively without the support in New

York of Andrew Hsia, director general of the Taipei Economic and Cultural Office (TECO) in New York, and Corinna Hu, also of TECO.

I will not list the names of all the officials and scholars in the People's Republic of China and Taiwan who we have met with over the past several years. But we owe them a debt of appreciation for helping us understand the issues. I also want to thank the many U.S. government officials in Washington, Beijing, and Shanghai, who took the time to meet with us.

Introduction

Donald S. Zagoria

Since 1997, the National Committee on American Foreign Policy (NCAFP) has been sponsoring regular roundtables with American, Chinese, and Taiwan participants to analyze the state of play in the complex and dangerous United States-China-Taiwan relationship. It has been our intention to try to clarify the position of each side for the other two sides, to increase mutual understanding, and, we hope, to promote a peaceful resolution of the issue.

The chapters included in this book were, with the exception of the one by Wilson Tien, all originally presented as essays to one of the roundtables.

The first two chapters examine U.S. policy on the cross-strait issue. Robert A. Scalapino argues that the central problem lies in the fact that no mutually acceptable formula for a long-term or interim political relationship between China and Taiwan has yet been found. The People's Republic of China (PRC) insists that Taiwan must accept the one country, two systems formula, with the proviso that the system for Taiwan can allow greater self-governance than that applicable to Hong Kong or Macao. Taiwan authorities, however, have rejected that formula under any condition, and in this position, they have the support of a strong majority of the Taiwan citizens who support maintaining the status quo, broadly defined. Scalapino says that the risk of conflict, at least in the short run, is slight, but the more distant future is more dangerous. In discussing U.S. policy options, he concludes that the United States should continue its present policy of refusing to support or recognize any de jure declaration of independence by Taiwan while asserting that any use of force by China would be regarded with the utmost gravity. Also, the United States should continue to express its view that any resolution of the impasse must have the support of the Taiwan people, a thesis that is strongly in accord with American principles and not likely to be altered.

Richard Bush contends that the principal U.S. effort should be to create an environment that will foster a relaxation of tension in the Taiwan Strait. He also makes the important argument that within Taiwan there is a consensus cutting across the political spectrum on two points: the governing authorities in Taiwan possess sovereignty within the context of one China, and Taiwan deserves a greater international role within the context of one China. This consensus, says Bush, is not inconsistent with the principle that Taiwan is a part of China, as broadly defined. Nor is it inconsistent with the goal of the reunification of China, as broadly defined. The implication of this analysis is that the challenge for both sides, but particularly for the PRC, is to find a formula for defining one China that is sufficiently broad to be mutually satisfactory. A formula such as confederation might be one such idea.

In chapter 3, Alan D. Romberg argues that the cross-strait relationship is far less tense today than it was two years ago when Chen Shui-bian was elected or even than it was during most of the five years before that when Lee Teng-hui sought to push the envelope on Taiwan's status. Romberg says this is so because both sides of the strait are currently focused on creating stronger economic relations, Taiwan out of economic necessity and Beijing out of a desire to reap the economic rewards of greater trade and investment and to create a more favorable climate for political negotiations later on.

In chapter 4, Dr. Ying-jeou Ma, mayor of Taipei and a prominent leader of the Kuomintang, argues that Taiwan's president Chen Shui-bian, although a past supporter of Taiwan independence, has consistently demonstrated much flexibility and pragmatism in handling cross-strait issues. According to Ma, this flexibility has been evident in Chen's Five No's and in the Taiwan president's acknowledgment that the Republic of China (ROC) Constitution is a one-China constitution. According to Ma, Chen's call for political integration with the mainland signals his willingness to explore the possibility of a "permanent association with the PRC short of outright unification."

Ma also contends that the 1992 Consensus on one China did exist. Although no written agreement was signed at the time, correspondence between the two sides following the November 1992 meeting attested to the existence of such a consensus. Finally, Ma urges the Taiwan government to try to break the stalemate with the mainland by bringing the opposition parties on Taiwan into a consensus-building process and then to take an appropriate initiative in a concrete form at a proper time.

Wilson Tien, the director of international affairs for the Democratic Progressive Party (DPP), spells out the DPP position on cross-strait issues with much clarity in chapter 5. He argues, like Ma, that Chen Shui-bian has demonstrated considerable flexibility on cross-strait issues. He says also that the DPP has concluded that there is no need for Taiwan to declare formal independence because Taiwan is already a sovereign state and a declaration of independence is not necessary. He points out, too, that the DPP understands that Taiwan's geopolitical position cannot be changed and that China is a powerful neighbor that strongly advocates unification. Taking into account these geographic and power realities, the DPP is prepared to enter political negotiations with the PRC, including "some negotiation on sovereignty issues." Moreover, he says that "we believe that Taiwan might be able to set up a deal in which Taiwan sacrifices a part of its sovereignty in exchange for permanent peace across the strait, as long as the proposed political arrangement is reasonable, worthwhile, and acceptable to the Taiwan people." Among the possible outcomes of such a deal he mentions are commonwealth, confederation, or a European Union–type arrangement.

In chapter 6, Julian Kuo, director of the policy council of the DPP, recently elected to the Legislative Yuan, and a member of the NCAFP's roundtable, argues that the PRC's "relentless dogmatism about the 'one-China' myth'" remains the most difficult barrier to normalizing cross-strait relations. He contends that the Chen Shui-bian government has made a number of gestures to the PRC in an effort to stabilize cross-strait relations, but that these overtures have been rejected by the mainland, thereby weakening the moderate elements in the DPP.

In chapter 7, Xu Shiquan, president of the Taiwan Institute of the Chinese Academy of Social Sciences, makes the case that the one-China principle is the cornerstone of the PRC government's policy toward Taiwan and that it is only on the basis of the one-China principle that any breakthrough in the political deadlock between the two sides will be possible.

In chapter 8, David Lampton argues that although it is unlikely that there will be a breakthrough on the critical sovereignty issue in the next few years, economic ties and interdependencies are likely to grow, and this will necessitate both sides developing cooperative frameworks and legal mechanisms to manage these ties.

Ralph Clough also emphasizes the significance of growing cross-strait economic relations. In chapters 9 and 10, he details the growing economic as well as academic and cultural ties. He highlights the fact that the Chen Shui-bian government has abandoned the go slow, be patient policy of its predecessor in favor of a policy of active opening, effective management.

In chapter 11, Yu Xintian, the president of the Shanghai Institute for International Studies, also discusses the deepening of cross-strait economic ties, and she urges the United States to promote the cross-strait economic relations and the move toward economic integration.

In chapter 12, David Shlapak discusses the cross-strait military balance. He concludes that the PRC's People's Liberation Army (PLA) is unlikely to achieve the degree of air and maritime superiority required to lay Taiwan open for invasion. And, in the event of war, he says that the United States could play a crucial role in helping Taiwan defend itself by adding only modest amounts of U.S. air and naval power. He notes, too, that although both China and Taiwan are working hard to upgrade their military capabilities, neither side is embarked on the kind of crash program that could upset the cross-strait balance in the near to midterm. He also thinks that the United States will eventually need to make a decision regarding how to deal with China's missile buildup opposite Taiwan.

In chapter 13, Bonnie Glaser makes the case for the opening of a dialogue between China and Taiwan on cross-strait military confidence-building measures. Such a dialogue should begin with informal exchanges between the two sides to discuss security issues.

In chapter 14, Nancy Bernkopf Tucker writes that the results of the Taiwan elections in December 2001 are both reassuring and disturbing in promising more of the same in Taiwan's relations with China. She concludes that we are entering a period of quietude as all three actors—Taiwan, China, and the United States—become ever more preoccupied with their separate agendas.

In chapter 15, Xu Shiquan analyzes the impact of the recent elections in Taiwan on cross-strait relations. He says that Chen Shui-bian is faced by conflicting pressures inside Taiwan and that he is unlikely to accept either the one-China principle or the 1992 Consensus. Under these circumstances, the political gridlock will continue with added potential dangers.

In chapter 16, Jiemian Yang, of Shanghai's Institute for International Studies, concludes that although the United States and China cannot remove the root causes of their fundamental differences, especially over Taiwan, they can control them. The differences over Taiwan, he says, were not made in one day nor can they be solved overnight. But it is in the fundamental interests of both sides not to let that issue divert their attention, let alone to make them confront each other.

Part I

Policy Positions: United States, Taiwan, and China

CHAPTER 1

Cross-Strait Relations and the United States

Robert A. Scalapino

Relations between mainland China and Taiwan are presently marked by a seeming paradox that has become more pronounced in the recent past. On the one hand, economic intercourse between the two parties has grown explosively. On the other hand, the political impasse continues, with the December 2001 elections signaling the likelihood that the deep political gulf is likely to remain for the foreseeable future.

Certain details concerning this situation are warranted. Investment in China from Taiwan now totals some U.S. $60 billion, and certain sources regard the accurate figure as being larger. Approximately one-half of Taiwan's business establishments are now engaged in production in China. Moreover, cross-strait trade was nearly U.S. $15 billion for the first six months of 2001, and although that represented a 6 percent decline from the previous year, it is still a major factor in the Taiwan economy, since some 50 percent of gross domestic product comes from exports, with the information technology (IT) industry accounting for 35 percent of all exports.

The great bulk of Taiwan's economic activity on the mainland has been concentrated in the coastal regions and especially Shanghai. In the latter region, it is estimated that there are presently 250,000–300,000 Taiwan residents. Symbolic of the trends is the agreement between the government-owned oil companies of the two sides to undertake a joint venture in gas and oil drilling in the strait that began in early 2002, upon approval by the Taiwan Mainland Affairs Council.

The change in the official Taiwan government exhortation regarding cross-strait economic activities from "go slow, be patient" to "active opening, effective management" clearly signals the major shift. The Chen government, contrary to expectations, has initiated a number of changes in existing laws and edicts, from the mini-three links to the liberalization of regulations governing investment. Behind these economic developments lies the fact that with the Taiwan economy in serious trouble, the business community has put intensive pressure on the government to make major policy changes. Strong objections from certain Democratic Progressive Party (DPP) figures, such as Annette Lu, have not prevented the inauguration of the new course.

As noted, adverse economic conditions were the dominant influence. After years of rapid growth, the Taiwan economy declined by slightly more than 2 percent in 2001. The level of unredeemable loans held by Taiwan banks is estimated to be approximately U.S. $28 billion, unemployment has topped 5 percent, and Taiwan's exports fell 28 percent in the first six months of 2001 from the same period the previous year, with imports declining by a slightly smaller percentage. The factors involved are well known: the sagging competitiveness of Taiwan's manufacturing sector, together with the sharp decline of the global IT market; the decline of the American and Japanese economies; irresponsible banking practices; and a damaging typhoon. Optimists see the Taiwan economy growing over 2 percent in 2002 if the U.S. economy turns upward, but the recent period has been painful.

If China-Taiwan economic relations have flourished in the recent past, however, this has had little impact upon political relations. To be sure, cultural relations have moved forward, with increased visitations on both sides at various levels. Beijing authorities have also pursued a united front strategy, cultivating the Taiwan opposition parties, especially the Kuomintang (KMT) and the New Party, both regarded as more favorable to the one-China principle. On the other hand, Chen Shui-bian and his DPP continued to be shunned. Despite Chen's efforts to present a cautious demeanor, moving away from any statements signaling support for independence and holding to the designation the Republic of China, there remains a total lack of trust between Beijing and Chen. Moreover, until recently, given conditions in Taiwan, the People's Republic of China (PRC) authorities felt that time was on their side.

Thus, the legislative elections of December 1, 2001, were a rude shock. The DPP, winning 87 seats in the 225-member body, became the largest party in the legislative assembly. The KMT dropped 42 seats, obtaining only 68 victories and losing its majority status, one held for 52 years. Former President Lee Teng-hui's new party, the Taiwan Solidarity Union, staunchly opposed to unification, obtained 13 seats, and James Soong's People First Party won 46 seats. The New Party, strongest proponent of early unification, was virtually eliminated, winning only 1 seat.

Clearly, the KMT is in disarray. With numerous splits having occurred and the aura of corruption and weak leadership hovering over it, Chen will still have a formidable task in constructing and maintaining a workable coalition. Taiwan politics may continue to be contentious, but the DPP victory despite the troubled economy is a tribute to the support given Chen and his party by the electorate.

The response of Beijing authorities to the election has been muted, but disappointment is manifest. Only four days after the election, Zhang Mingqing of the State Council's Taiwan Affairs Office, asserted, "It is impossible at present for us to have contact with them, because the DPP still upholds its pro-independence platform, refuses to accept the one-China principle and denies the 1992 Consensus." Action followed words. Taiwan was barred from the Asia-Pacific Cooperation Forum (APEC) meeting in mid-December in Shanghai by China because Taipei had sent a former official, Li Yuan-tsu, as representative.

Earlier, in mid-July, Vice President Qian Qichen had introduced three guidelines for cross-strait relations: one country, two systems; talks between the two sides; and creation of the three links (postal, transport, and trade). In response, Mainland Affairs Committee spokesman, Tsai Ing-wen outlined three types of respect required: respect our existence, respect the people's choice of government, and respect their choice of their future. After the December election, President Chen asserted that the election result had not changed his commitment to improving bilateral ties, but he added, "The [m]ainland authorities looked down on me and the new government before the elections, but I hope they can respect the choice of the Taiwan people after the elections." The remark of Lee Teng-hui was less conciliatory; he warned that the PRC's "ambition to swallow up Taiwan will surely grow day by day."

The central problem lies in the fact that no mutually acceptable formula for a long-term or interim political relationship has yet been found. The PRC insists that Taiwan must accept the one country, two systems formula, with the proviso that the system for Taiwan can allow greater self-governance than that applicable to Hong Kong or Macao. Taiwan authorities, however, have rejected that formula under any condition, and in this position they have the support of a strong majority of the Taiwan citizens. Polls in mid-2001 varied substantially in their results. Most indicated that approval of the one country, two systems concept had gained some ground, but the favorable vote ranged from 16 percent to nearly 30 percent, depending upon the poll. In contrast, between 70 percent and 80 percent supported the status quo, broadly defined. Thus, the central DPP thesis that the Taiwan people must be the ultimate arbiters of Taiwan's fate rests on solid political ground domestically.

Certain individuals have advocated the principle of federation or confederation as a means of building a political bridge, leaving the issue of sovereignty for the future. Such an idea was broached at the time of the last KMT party conference, but subsequently withdrawn before a vote was taken. Beijing has thus far made it clear that this approach is not acceptable. Thus, the political chasm between the two parties appears unbridgeable for the present, with both sides legitimately claiming that their respective policies have the firm support of their people.

At the same time, the risk of conflict, at least in the short run, seems slight. The fourth generation of China's leaders, scheduled to come to power shortly, are fundamentally technocrats not ideologues. Like the third generation, they are likely to concentrate on making China rich and strong, with domestic economic concerns foremost, and there are an ample number of problems to be resolved. Furthermore, the PRC has gone to great pains to improve its relations with all of its neighbors and with considerable success—Japan and India being partial exceptions. To undertake a conflict with Taiwan or to engage in ominous threats would endanger China's relations throughout East Asia and more especially with the United States. The costs—or risks—are too great. Furthermore, China is not prepared militarily for any major assault at this point.

The more distant future is perhaps less predictable. On occasion, Chinese leaders have asserted that China cannot wait indefinitely for reunification, and should the nationalist tides become both powerful and militant, a hazardous course might be undertaken. It should be remembered that there are many forms of pressure short of an invasion of Taiwan that can be applied, ranging from incidents with respect to Quemoy and Matsu or the strait, including blockades, to efforts to strengthen prounification elements in Taiwan by diverse means. In any case, the future of cross-strait relations will depend heavily both upon domestic developments in the two societies and upon trends with respect to the international environment.

Against this background, what are the options for—and the likely policies of—the United States? Few international problems create a greater dilemma for Washington. The United States has had a history of involvement in the Taiwan issue for over 50 years, with continuing differences within U.S. society over the appropriate policies to be pursued.

The Korean War caused the first reversal in U.S. policy, with the shift from abandoning the nationalists on Taiwan to a decision to patrol the strait and assist Taiwan as a part of the on-going conflict with China.

Another equally dramatic shift was initiated at the beginning of the 1970s when mutual concern about the Soviet Union brought Washington and Beijing into rapprochement, and step by step led to diplomatic relations and a severance of official ties with the Republic of China. Yet, there were strong elements of ambivalence on the part of the United States from the 1972 Shanghai Communiqué to the events of 1979. In the former, the United States acknowledged the Chinese position relating to Taiwan but did not necessarily accept it. The Taiwan Relations Act of 1979 that accompanied formal U.S. recognition of the PRC stipulated that the United States would continue to furnish military supplies to Taiwan pending a peaceful settlement of the dispute.

In the 1982 communiqué, the Reagan administration stated that it would reduce arms sales as events warranted. Sales, however, continued. Subsequently, Clinton, as a presidential candidate, charged that the previous administration had coddled dictators, with the reference in part to China. But as president, Clinton, like his predecessors, came to recognize the importance of a positive relationship with China. Indeed, he seemed to go further toward recognizing the PRC position with his "three no's" statement in Shanghai in 1998: no independent Taiwan; no two Chinas or one Taiwan, one China; and no membership for Taiwan in any organization for which statehood is required. Yet Clinton continued arms sales to Taiwan and accepted visits of officials on both sides. The effort was to balance Taiwan's desires and congressional sentiment with China's deep resentment of military sales, keeping those sales within moderate bounds. Moreover, Taiwan was not included in the Theater Missile Defense (TMD) and National Missile Defense (NMD) programs. Yet the House of Representatives was prepared to go much further with respect to military support for Taiwan, passing by an overwhelming majority an enhanced Taiwan security act in 1999.

China, meanwhile, continued to assert that Taiwan constituted the most important issue between the PRC and the United States and denounced U.S. policies toward Taiwan, insisting that they represented interference in China's internal affairs and an evidence of American hegemonism.

Candidate George W. Bush, like candidate Clinton before him, made a remark about China during the campaign that might be construed as negative, asserting that China should be regarded as a strategic competitor rather than a strategic partner as had been asserted by certain Clinton administration officials. Yet, as president, Bush soon moved toward the centrist position of his predecessors, and this position was strongly enhanced by the September 11, 2001, terrorist attacks and their aftermath. America now wanted to build the strongest coalition possible to support its Afghanistan campaign and, beyond this, a general assault against the terrorist threat globally. China, although cautious with respect to American military activities in central Asia, had a strong interest in opposing terrorists since they were associated with separatism in Beijing's view and had special relevance to Xinjiang. The United States also supported China's entry into the World Trade Organization, it having been accepted by Beijing that Taiwan's entry would follow immediately, under the proper designation. On the broader economic front, despite problems with the U.S. economy, U.S. investment and trade with China continued to be relatively strong. Thus, U.S.-PRC relations seemed to reach another high point. Indeed, certain Taiwan personalities voiced concern that U.S. support might dwindle.

However, the Bush administration continued to pursue past policies. Military assistance to Taiwan was forthcoming, albeit not of such advanced weapons as the Aegis-equipped submarines that Taiwan desired. It was also stipulated that instead of a yearly review and decision, weaponry would be provided on an as-needed basis. Transit visits for Taiwan officials were allowed as in the past. Most importantly, Washington now underlined the thesis that any resolution of the Taiwan problem should have the support of the Taiwan citizenry. And although the Bush administration continued to warn against any use of force, a policy of conscious ambiguity was maintained as to a possible U.S. response should force be used.

Meanwhile, U.S. relations with the PRC remain relatively good despite the policy differences that exist. China's protests against the Bush administration's announcement that it was withdrawing from the ABM Treaty were relatively moderate, similar to those of Russia. And while developments are being watched closely with respect to Afghanistan and, most particularly, with regard to U.S. military forces in Uzbekistan and elsewhere in central Asia, China has evidenced no great alarm, at least so far.

What lies ahead? As noted, China is likely to concentrate upon economic development and, in terms of its military policies, as rapid a military modernization as possible. For these purposes, it needs a low level of tension globally and especially in East and South Asia. Thus, like the United States, China is deeply troubled by the threatening crisis between India and Pakistan.

With respect to Taiwan, China is likely to encourage maximum cross-strait economic intercourse and widening contacts between both the general citizenry and select elements of the elite. Yet there is no visible sign that it is prepared to compromise on the key issue, that of Taiwan authorities accepting one China, with Taiwan a part of China and a separate system for Taiwan being advanced, enabling extensive self-governance, except in the area of foreign policy. Equally, there are no current signs that such a formula will be acceptable to the government—or the people—of Taiwan. Some officials have spoken of the need for China to become a democracy prior to reunification, others have insisted that in the past century Taiwan has developed its own culture, one underwriting a separate existence. Whatever the assertions, the status quo is currently the choice of a strong majority, as has been indicated.

In the face of these facts, what are the alternatives for the United States? One school of thought is that the United States should abandon its ambiguity and assert clearly that it will defend Taiwan if it is attacked, assuming that it does not declare independence. It is difficult, however, to see the advantage of such a policy, especially since it would deeply antagonize China and might embolden the more extreme independence elements on Taiwan.

Another view is that the United States should do all that it can to encourage both parties to accept the thesis of one China, not further defined, thereby enabling the opening of an official dialogue. Subsequently, the formula of a commonwealth or confederation might be advanced, with the issue of sovereignty postponed until later, as previously noted. Even if no agreement on this formula is possible—and at present, China would not accept it—the dialogue between the two parties could be continued until some workable, mutually acceptable position was reached.

In reality, there is no U.S. policy without its problems and uncertainties. For decades, the United States has been seeking to advance simultaneously along two somewhat incongruous paths. On the one hand, it has sought to improve its relations with the PRC by combining a policy of concert of powers with that of a balance of power. It has worked with China along with other nations on a widening range of issues including Korea, containment of weapons of mass destruction, and antiterrorism. At the same time, it has preserved its alliances in East Asia, believing that such a course is necessary to ensure peace and stability. Furthermore, in this troubled age, it is seeking to find ways of combining elements of unilateralism with multilateralism, conscious of the fact that given the current international institutional restraints, a prompt, effective, multilateral response to a grave threat is often not possible, but that such action as is taken must have multilateral support if it is to be truly effective.

Meanwhile, the United States has accepted Taiwan as a de facto separate political entity, seeking to uphold the principles of democracy and a market economy. The image of Taiwan is good in the United States, albeit Taiwan's issues are not of deep concern for most Americans. Nevertheless, policies perceived to be those of abandonment would provoke an instant sharply negative response at many levels. The repeated assertion that any declaration of independence by Taiwan would not be recognized or supported and that any use of force by China would be regarded with the utmost gravity is likely to remain U.S. policy. Furthermore, the thesis that any resolution must have the support of the Taiwan people is strongly in accord with American principles and not likely to be altered.

Thus, neither a major softening nor a substantial hardening of the present U.S. position on the Taiwan issue appears feasible or desirable at this time. However, the volatility of conditions dictates that the China-Taiwan relationship and the policies of others, including the United States, with respect to this matter should be frequently reviewed within the United States and with other countries as well. Moreover, on-going track II dialogues involving representatives from both China and Taiwan, such as those sponsored by the National Committee on American Foreign Policy, should be encouraged.

An additional possibility that should be given serious consideration is the creation of a standing committee in the United States that would be composed of both nongovernmental experts and government officials meeting at frequent intervals, with reports prepared indicating current developments that affect U.S. policies, and when appropriate, suggesting modifications. Two such committees under the aegis of the State Department, one relating to East Asia as a whole, the other to China specifically, existed between 1965 and 1980 and proved to be very useful.

In sum, the United States cannot avoid involvement in the Taiwan issue, given history and the contemporary scene. But its involvement should be such that it encourages by every means possible a peaceful resolution of the dispute and that this resolution has the concurrence of other Asia-Pacific nations, as well as both China and Taiwan.

CHAPTER 2

United States Policy toward Taiwan

Richard C. Bush

The remarks made by Secretary of State George Shultz in Shanghai in February 1987 constitute the best simple statement of U.S. policy toward Taiwan. Secretary Shultz's statement is as relevant today as it was when he made it. Commenting on the opening of economic and other cross-strait exchanges, he said:

> We support a continuing evolutionary process toward a peaceful resolution of the Taiwan issue. The pace, however, will be determined by the Chinese on either side of the Taiwan Strait, free of outside pressure. For our part, we have welcomed developments, including indirect trade and increasing human interchange, which have contributed to a relaxation of tensions in the Taiwan Strait. Our steadfast policy seeks to foster an environment within which such developments can continue to take place.

The United States fosters a positive environment in a number of general and specific ways. It does so generally through

- a robust set of bilateral alliances in East Asia;
- the forward deployment of naval and air force units—about 100,000 in number—in the East Asian region to deter aggression and foster stability;
- the aggressive pursuit of global economic liberalization, which fosters interdependence among the countries of the Pacific Rim and gives all a stake in peace and stability;
- the support of engagement of the People's Republic of China (PRC) in order to integrate Beijing and its rule-based regimes into the international system, to pre-

serve international peace and security, and to work closely with the PRC to resolve regional conflicts where we have common or parallel interests; and
- a strategic vision that affirms that the best way to achieve our national interests is to be actively involved in the affairs of East Asia on the side of peace, prosperity, and humane government.

With respect to the issue of the Taiwan Strait in particular, the U.S. context-creating approach is manifested by

- the clear and consistent reaffirmations of the one China policy as defined by the three communiqués that not only remain the cornerstone of Taiwan-PRC-U.S. relations but also have fostered peace and stability and facilitated the remarkable evolution that Taiwan has undergone;
- an insistence, expressed by President Carter at the time of normalization and most recently by President Clinton to Jiang Zemin in Auckland in September (1999), that the issue of the Taiwan Strait be resolved peacefully;
- the continued arms sales to Taiwan pursuant to the Taiwan Relations Act to ensure that the island's armed forces have a sufficient self-defense capability;
- the confidence that the two sides have the creativity to resolve this issue through cross-strait dialogue without U.S. government mediation (we have no substantive proposals of our own);
- a refusal to pressure either side to accept any arrangements that it does not believe are in its interests (and I don't believe that U.S. statements about "interim agreements" constituted pressure in any way);
- an understanding that any arrangements between Beijing and Taipei should be made on a mutually acceptable basis and not be imposed on one side by the other;
- an understanding that because Taiwan is a democracy, any arrangements between the two sides will ultimately have to be acceptable to the Taiwan public; and
- a willingness to support any outcome voluntarily agreed to by both sides of the Taiwan Strait.

The question of U.S. mediation or of assuming any other direct role in resolving this dispute needs to be elaborated. Whereas the United States has played a central role in trying to end conflicts in the Middle East, Northern Ireland, and Cyprus, in this case our interests in peace and stability will be best served by not taking a seat at the table. Indeed, it has been a tenet of U.S. policy since 1982 that we would not seek to mediate this dispute. Why is this the case?

First, the United States has acquired some experience in mediating disputes between these two actors. In the late 1940s, in a vain attempt to head off civil war in China, General George Marshall undertook to effect peace between the Communist and Nationalist parties. That effort failed because neither side possessed the political will to coexist with the other and because each side believed that Marshall was siding with the other. Of course, circumstances today are very different, but the Marshall mission remains a useful historical lesson on the dangers of good but naive intentions.

Second, the test of any negotiated settlement is the commitment of the parties directly concerned to abide by it. That commitment is likely to be higher for a settlement that the parties themselves have negotiated and less in a case in which a mediator is involved and can be blamed for the compliance failures of the other. To be concrete, any arrangements achieved as a result of negotiations between Beijing and Taipei alone are more likely to endure than those facilitated by an American go-between.

Some people on Taiwan think that the United States would secretly like to see the island reunified with the mainland more or less on Beijing's terms, certainly not on Taiwan's terms. And there are, I am sure, some people on the mainland who believe that the United States covertly would like to see Taiwan's permanent separation—even de jure independence—in order to preserve its strategic position in the Pacific. In fact, neither is an objective of the United States. Surprising as it may seem, the government of the United States takes no view on the substance of the ultimate outcome of the Taiwan Strait issue. What the United States cares about—its true interest—is process and context. For the United States, what is important is how decisions are made, not what those decisions are. That statement, in effect, is a summary of the U.S. approach to the Taiwan Strait issue.

CROSS-STRAIT RELATIONS OTHER THAN POLITICAL RELATIONS

In turning to cross-strait relations other than politics, it is important to remember that cooperation is quite strong in those kinds of relationships. At the time Secretary Shultz made his remarks, cross-strait exchanges were only beginning. Thirteen years later, they are extensive. More than 30,000 Taiwan firms have contracted to invest approximately $40 billion in the PRC, producing a gradual shift from small, single-proprietor enterprises to larger enterprises and joint ventures. Connections have even been established between state enterprises in the areas of oil and coal. The Tong Yi Company, for example, already has 70 factories on the mainland.

More than 200,000 Taiwan business people now live and work in the PRC where they have established more than 50 associations to promote their interests. Such firms employ approximately three million mainland workers, about 3 percent of the urban workforce. Thus, Taiwan helps Beijing realize its primary objective: preserving social stability. To the extent that the living quarters of mainland employees is different from the site of the factory, which is often the case, firms from Taiwan are probably improving the standard of living in poor parts of China.

Nowhere is cross-strait economic integration more complex and more vital than in the information technology sector. Firms from Taiwan and their mainland partners have moved beyond producing low-value products on which they concentrated less than a decade ago. As Taiwan's powerhouse computer companies move production of their low-end items offshore in order to stay competitive, they select the PRC as their overseas destination of choice. Firms from Taiwan are now producing 29 percent of their total global output, or U.S. $10 billion annually, on the mainland. A key incentive is not only cheap workers but also high-quality engineers. This investment is reshaping the composition of cross-strait trade to the point that Taiwan exports of IT products now account for perhaps 40 percent of all exports to the PRC.

Business is only one dimension of cross-strait interactions. Also significant are human contacts, scholarly and artistic exchanges, renewed religious ties, and Taiwan's role as a model for political development on the mainland. In all of these areas, including business, there are problems and ambiguities. Some in Taiwan ask, for example, whether mainland firms will use cooperation with Taiwan's partners to become competitors. Despite such questions, these ties are not trivial, for they are based on common interests and a shared cultural heritage. They remind people on both sides that they have a stake in cooperation, that there are tangible reasons to avoid conflict, and that the common ground they share can serve as the foundation on which other forms of cooperation, including political cooperation, can be built.

Three other developments during the last 13 years have had an impact on the Taiwan Strait issue. These developments are the cross-strait dialogue itself, Taiwan's democratization, and the PRC's military modernization.

THE CROSS-STRAIT DIALOGUE

First, it is worthwhile to reemphasize the importance of dialogue. Dialogue fosters an atmosphere in which tensions are reduced, misperceptions can be clarified, and common ground can be explored. One of the most salutary developments in East Asia during the early 1990s was the beginning of a dialogue between Taiwan's Straits Exchange Foundation (SEF) and the mainland's Association for Relations across the Taiwan Strait. Cancellation of the dialogue in July 1995 aggravated the tensions of the time, for it closed off a channel of communication. Then, last year, with the encouragement of the United States, the two sides resumed the dialogue through the visit of Dr. Ku Chen-fu, chairman of SEF, to Shanghai and Beijing in October.

It is clear that cross-strait dialogue becomes more difficult when one side or each side mistrusts the intentions of the other. For example, I think that people on Taiwan do not completely appreciate the impact that President Lee's special state-to-state formula has had on mainland views of his objectives. Whether intended or not (and I understand that there was an element of misinterpretation), his statement and the statements of others suggested that the authorities on Taiwan were no longer committed to the unification of China.

The result was increased tensions and instability. Although I can understand this phenomenon, I also think that to the extent that mistrust is the result of misperception or misunderstanding, then some sort of dialogue is the best way to eliminate misperceptions. Moreover, to the extent that cross-strait dialogue results in modest agreements, if the mainland decides not to implement them because it is unhappy with actions or statements made by Taiwan, it would reduce Taiwan's confidence in such agreements, particularly major and fundamental agreements.

TAIWAN'S DEMOCRATIZATION

I believe that Taiwan's democratization has profoundly transformed the Taiwan Strait issue. Taiwan's willingness to move forward on cross-strait relations is no longer merely a function of the views of Taiwan's top leader; it is also a function of the views of the public at large, the press, members of the legislature, and the leadership of opposition parties. Of course, political leaders have the responsibility to shape public opinion if they believe it is in the collective interest to do so. In the case of Taiwan, however, the people of the island will have to be convinced that any arrangements reached in cross-strait dialogue are in their fundamental interests. And to the extent that the people of Taiwan interpret the actions of the mainland as hostile or bullying, it becomes that much harder for the authorities to get support for cross-strait initiatives.

Beijing has taken a number of actions that have alienated the public in Taiwan and made the resolution of differences more difficult. These actions include continued insistence on the one-country, two-systems formula, even when it is clear that there is little support for it on the island; the missile buildup; blocking Taiwan's efforts to participate in the international community; emphasis on timetables; and vitriolic criticisms of Lee Teng-hui. Also, I think that major exercises conducted by the People's Liberation Army right before the election will have negative consequences for Taiwan's views of the mainland (to say nothing of U.S. views of the PRC). If cross-strait agreements are concluded sometime in the future, some of their elements will have to be implemented through the Legislative Yuan, where the public's views have a significant impact.

PRC MILITARY MODERNIZATION

I think military modernization is producing serious consequences, including the diminution of Taiwan's sense of security and openness to negotiations. Whatever the reason for the PRC's decision to build new weapons systems, they may actually reduce the mainland's overall security by fostering tension, anxiety, political instability, or an arms buildup in the region. This consequence would exemplify the notion of a strategic dilemma: Beijing cannot expect to pursue its defense policy in a vacuum. Its decisions to pursue military modernization will generate responses from other actors, including members of the U.S. Congress. In effect, we seem to be seeing the beginning of an arms race.

Moreover, PRC military modernization has already had an impact on cross-strait relations. The mainland's effort to build its military capabilities, particularly short-range ballistic missiles, has had a dual effect. On the one hand, it probably has reduced the chances that someone on Taiwan may declare de jure independence. But it has also reduced the probability that the authorities and the people on Taiwan will want to negotiate significant political agreements with the mainland. This dispute is not going to be resolved because each side has acquired more arms. It will be resolved by building mutual confidence that can be the foundation of a political settlement.

The complaints made by the mainland that the United States bears some responsibility for the lack of progress in cross-strait relations should not be taken seriously. I can find no evidence to support the hypothesis that U.S. arms sales reduce Taiwan's incentive to negotiate. Indeed, it is my personal view that Taipei is more likely to engage the mainland when it has a certain sense of security, which U.S. weapons help provide. I think PRC policies and behavior in and of themselves have a greater impact on Taiwan's desire to devise a creative solution to cross-strait differences than do arms sales.

RECENT DEVELOPMENTS

Lee Teng-hui's July 9, 1999, statement that cross-strait relations constitute a special state-to-state relationship sparked increased tensions between the two sides of the strait. Not only did Beijing unleash an intense propaganda barrage, but it also increased air activity over the Taiwan Strait, creating the risk of accident or miscalculation that, in turn, might have led to some sort of an escalation.

In response, the Bush administration sent me to Taiwan and Stanley Roth and Ken Lieberthal to Beijing, carrying messages appropriate to our interlocutors. Although I cannot go into detail about my discussions, I did make a departure statement that deliberately addressed the main issues.

First, I said that I had developed a better understanding of Taipei's views on cross-strait relations. That was not just empty talk. Before I left, I learned more than we had known about Taipei's increasingly negative view of the negotiating game that it was playing and the perceived fear that Beijing was backing it into a corner. I think this factor has not been given sufficient attention in the analyses that purport to explain why President Lee said what he did. One can make a case that President Lee's statement reflected the realization that political talks were inevitable and that it was necessary to create a conceptual foundation for those talks. One can make the case that what he said was consistent with Taiwan's long-standing position.

Second, I said that Taipei had a better understanding of Washington's views. I did not go to Taiwan only to listen. I went there to convey our views and concerns about the situation.

Third, I reaffirmed that all the elements of the administration's policy toward Taiwan remain in place.

Fourth, I stressed the abiding U.S. interest in the peaceful resolution of the cross-strait issue and said that the administration had a simple approach to this very complicated issue: it maintains that steps that promote a reduction of tensions, cross-strait dialogue, and peace and stability in the region are good. Conversely, steps that result in increased tensions, a freezing of dialogue, and regional instability and conflict are not good. Obviously, progress must occur on a mutually acceptable basis, but each side must have some measure of confidence in the intentions of the other. These statements are somewhat allusive, but I think the message is clear.

Fifth, I emphasized the one China principle as the cornerstone of U.S. policy. This comment was designed to speak to the impression—or misperception—that Taiwan had abandoned its commitment to the unification of China. In addition, I noted that defining the one-China principle specifically and realizing it concretely are steps best left to the two sides of the strait to work out on a mutually acceptable basis.

ELECTIONS

I returned to Taiwan recently on a routine visit, but I had the opportunity to meet with each of the major presidential candidates. Before leaving, I made a statement describing the approach that the United States was taking to the election. I said that the United States does not favor one candidate over another or one party over another. We vigorously support the transformation of Taiwan into a democratic system, and we're pleased that the people of Taiwan now have the ability to choose their leaders. The United States will work with whoever they choose to be their next president and vice president.

The United States will focus on the policies that the new president pursues and determine whether they promote the fundamental interests of peace and stability in the Taiwan Strait that are so important to the United States. If the new Taiwan administration's policies converge with our own interests, then there will be no problem. If they do not, then we will discuss the differences in a spirit of friendship.

My personal view about the election is that even if Soong Chu-yu or Lien Chan is elected, neither will be able to depart from the islandwide consensus in two important respects. The first element of that consensus is that the governing authorities on the island possess sovereignty within the context of one China. A corollary of that point is that Taiwan deserves a greater international role within the context of one China. None of the major candidates sees the one country, two systems formula as a basis for resolving the Taiwan Strait issue. The second element of that consensus is that the mainland should find some way to give credible assurances that force will not be used to resolve this dispute.

CONCLUSION

Because it cannot ignore its neighborhood and must acknowledge that its surroundings are not completely quiet and stable—that is, that the PRC is there and won't go away—Taiwan recognizes that the mainland represents an opportunity in economic terms. It is my impression that most elements of the political spectrum on the island understand that Taiwan cannot close itself off from its neighborhood. The challenge is for both sides to work out how to be good neighbors. In the meantime, Taiwan need not act in a way that excites the worst fears and misperceptions of the other side because that may increase tensions across the strait. Instead, it should strive for the best and work to bring it about. With creativity, prudence, and political will, Taiwan can help foster a more peaceful neighborhood, assuming that the other side is equally creative and forthcoming.

The second observation is that realistically the mainland must accept the reality of Taiwan's democracy. The public in Taiwan has become an actor in cross-strait relations. Its attitudes are shaped by mainland behavior. Also, on key issues such as sovereignty, Taiwan's role in the international arena, and the use of force, there has emerged a broad public consensus on the island. This consensus is not inconsistent with the principle that Taiwan is a part of China broadly defined. It is not inconsistent with the goal of the unification of China broadly defined. The public in Taiwan does not appreciate steps taken by the mainland that it perceives as threatening. I hope that as the leadership change enters into effect on Taiwan, the mainland will analyze both the fears and the deeply held beliefs of the public on Taiwan and will examine what steps are necessary to expand cooperation beyond the economic and social realms. A creative and responsive approach to the Taiwan Strait issue can give leaders the foundation on which to mobilize public support for a durable framework for peace and cooperation.

As we look to the future, the United States will continue in a steady way to build an environment in which positive developments can occur. For neither side will we be a problem, and for neither side will we be the solution.

UPDATE: To provide a sense of the direction of U.S. policy toward Taiwan in the fall of 2001, we include the following adaptation of an extract of a speech Dr. Bush was to make at a late-September conference.

Let me speak more directly to U.S. policy toward and U.S. relations with Taiwan. In our system, any change of administration brings a healthy infusion of new energetic people and new ideas. Our political transitions bring some changes in the substance, emphasis, and tone of U.S. policy, but they also maintain useful points of continuity.

What follows, then, are what I see as the main elements of the Bush administration's policy toward Taiwan, as they have emerged over the last eight months.

First and foremost, there is the fundamental emphasis on peace and an unconditional insistence that the Taiwan Strait issue should be resolved peacefully. This is a long-standing principle of U.S. policy, going back more than 40 years. It was enshrined in the Taiwan Relations Act and reaffirmed by every administration since then, and certainly by the Bush administration.

In light of the priority we place on the peaceful resolution of differences, changes in PRC behavior over the past few years have called into question Beijing's stated commitment to a peaceful resolution of the Taiwan Strait issue. These changes include Beijing's acquisition of more advanced military capabilities; its deployment of those capabilities in Taiwan's vicinity; and a negative shift in its statements about the circumstances under which it would use force.

Consequently, in order to guard against miscalculation by the PRC leadership and PRC military, it has become necessary to re-emphasize the concern that the United States feels about Taiwan's security and remind Beijing that the United States clearly has the capacity to come to the assistance of Taiwan should it be threatened by the mainland. President Bush has committed the U.S. government to helping Taiwan defend itself.

In addition, and pursuant to the Taiwan Relations Act, the United States will continue to provide arms sales to Taiwan based on its needs in light of the current situation. For example, the administration in April made some decisions on the weapons systems that Taiwan would need to ensure a sufficient ability to defend itself. We reject the idea that our arms sales make a peaceful resolution more difficult. Indeed, the United States believes that our arms sales give Taiwan a greater sense of security and the confidence to enter into a dialogue with Beijing, something that President Chen has said publicly.

A second element of the Bush administration's policy is that the United States will continue to follow a one China policy, as defined by the three U.S.-PRC communiqués and the Taiwan Relations Act. We will conduct our relations with Taiwan on an unofficial basis through the American Institute in Taiwan and the Taipei Economic and Cultural Representative Office. But within those parameters we intend to have a rich substantive relationship with Taiwan, seeking cooperation on a wide array of issues on which we have common and parallel interests.

The third element is the important and inescapable fact that Taiwan is a democracy. Given America's values, that is significant for its own sake. It also means that the United States will treat Taiwan and its leaders with the respect and dignity that is worthy of a fellow democracy. This was most evident in our reception of President Chen during the transits he made a few months ago.

Democracy is important in another way. The Bush administration believes that any agreement regarding the Taiwan Strait issue, in addition to being reached peacefully, has to be acceptable to the people on Taiwan. This should be self-evident. Indeed, it is inevitable that Taiwan's people, through their democratic institutions, will have a say in any cross-strait arrangements that are reached peacefully by their government.

On cross-strait relations, and this is my fourth point, the Bush administration believes that how the Taiwan Strait issue is resolved is up to the two parties concerned. That is, our one China policy in no way dictates for Taipei or Beijing how cross strait differences should be resolved substantively. Similarly, the United States favors and encourages dialogue, but has no intention of serving as a mediator in this dispute or of pressuring Taiwan to negotiate.

And fifth, the United States believes that Taiwan can contribute to international organizations and should benefit from international organizations. Obviously, this is a sensitive issue, since the PRC already occupies China's seat in most organizations and opposes Taiwan's participation wherever possible. And because these are multilateral institutions and often operate by consensus, there are limits to what any one country, even the United States, can do. But the administration does support Taiwan's membership in organizations like the World Trade Organization, and we worked hard to bring that about. We support Taiwan's participation in international organizations like the World Health Organization. In no way is this position inconsistent with our one-China policy. We believe the international community loses if Taiwan is excluded.

Of course, the United States-Taiwan relationship is one side of a triangle, and I wish to address briefly U.S. relations with the PRC and cross-strait relations.

Let me be clear. The United States seeks to have a positive and constructive relationship with the PRC. Our economic relationship with the PRC will benefit companies and consumers in both China and America. In the wake of the attacks on the United States on September 11, the United States and the PRC seek to work closely together to fight the scourge of terrorism. In addition, we have common or parallel interests regarding a number of regional hot spots, such as the Korean peninsula, and on a variety of transnational issues, such as drug trafficking. On the other hand, there are issues on which we disagree, such as human rights, Taiwan, and missile defense. Consequently, the Bush administration is pursuing engagement with China that seeks to maximize the areas of cooperation, address areas of difference frankly but respectfully through dialogue, and encourage China's adherence to international norms as it becomes more a part of the international community. We hope that such an approach will move China in the right direction, but we cannot be sure. The United States is not naive. We will follow China's actions carefully. And we will remain strong.

Returning to cross-strait relations, we now face a mixed situation. Tensions are down from 18 months ago. Economic interaction has intensified, which creates the possibility that shared interests will reduce the possibility of conflict. Joint accession to the WTO [World Trade Organization] will only intensify that interaction. And positive economic interchange can have a good impact on other dimensions, as well.

On the other hand, there has been no progress toward addressing key cross-strait political issues. Dialogue has been suspended for over two years. The absence of dialogue could still lead to some kind of conflict as the result of accident or miscalculation. A resumed dialogue could reduce misunderstanding and misperception, resolve practical problems, and create positive momentum toward an enduring peace. This is the lesson of 1992–93 and 1998.

Now the reasons that dialogue is still suspended are complex, and I don't want to bore you with a discussion of them. Speaking for myself only, I would make the following observations:

- First, it does not seem constructive for one side to set preconditions for a resumption of dialogue that the other side even suspects would be tantamount to conceding a fundamental issue before discussion begins.
- Second, it does not seem helpful (or logical) for Beijing to say that "anything can be discussed" once the one China principle is accepted, but rule out in advance discussion of approaches other than one country, two systems.

- Third, it seems to me that the broadening and deepening of economic ties should not be subject to political preconditions.
- Fourth, it doesn't seem terribly constructive for the PRC to discriminate against Taiwan companies (or U.S. companies for that matter), because of the political views of the executives of those companies.

Chapter 3

Some Thoughts on Cross-Strait Relations

Alan D. Romberg

INTRODUCTION

Objectively speaking, cross-strait relations are far less tense in spring 2002 than they were two years ago, when Chen Shui-bian was elected by Taiwan's voters as president of the Republic of China. And they are less tense than they were during most of the five years before that, when Chen's predecessor, Lee Teng-hui, sought to push the envelope on Taiwan's sovereign, independent status. Despite occasional lapses, both Beijing and Taipei have clearly decided to cool the rhetoric, even as they maintain principle and harbor concerns about the other side's intentions.

It is apparent that Chen's May 2000 inaugural pledge not to pursue independence or other steps so greatly feared by the People's Republic of China (PRC) leadership in the run-up to the election has had an important role to play in this. So, too, have decisions in Beijing about the importance of constructive relations with the United States. That said, many on the mainland perceive a disturbing pattern of incremental steps toward separate status—or even independence—and continue to warn of the dangers of taking this too far.

For its part, the Taipei leadership argues that its policies fit within the parameters of what Beijing labels as acceptable localism and should not be viewed as creeping independence or a direct challenge to the PRC over the question of one China. Still, Chen Shui-bian and virtually all other major political leaders in Taiwan take the position that the Republic of China is a sovereign, independent country that, while constitutionally encompassing all of the mainland, has operational jurisdiction limited to Taiwan, the Penghus, and the offshore islands, and that it has no formal links to the PRC. There are differences among Taiwan's political leaders about how to describe this, for example, whether to endorse one China, respective interpretations as an enduring position coming out of the 1992 Straits Exchange Foundation–Association for Relations across the Taiwan Strait (SEF-ARATS) negotiations. But since Beijing has—for now, anyway—rejected the second half of that formulation (i.e., respective interpretations), the debate in Taiwan has largely centered around other questions.

Both sides of the strait are currently focused on creating stronger economic relations: Taiwan out of economic necessity as well as a desire to defuse the issue domestically, Beijing both to reap the economic rewards of greater cross-strait trade and investment and to create a more favorable climate for political negotiations later on. Nonetheless, the ways in which both sides currently address economic issues are conditioned by the current political stalemate, and we can expect further tugging and hauling about the ground rules for future dealings, including political conditions one side or the other may seek to impose, as well as with respect to potential qualitative and quantitative limits.

THE VIEW OF CHEN SHUI-BIAN FROM BEIJING

The atmosphere prevailing in Beijing on the eve of the March 18, 2000, Taiwan presidential election was highly charged. Specific warnings were issued about the consequences of a victory by Chen Shui-bian, the candidate of the traditionally proindependence Democratic Progressive Party (DPP). Nonetheless, the PRC took Chen's inaugural commitment to the Five No's[1] as an indication that their worst fears would not be realized, at least in the near term. Still, the PRC suspected Chen's ultimate intentions, and although stresses eased as Beijing came to see him as a pragmatist rather than an ideologue, fear remained that the new Taiwan leader might take the island in unhelpful directions if it seemed to be in his political interests to do so.

Indeed, mainland observers became increasingly discontented over time as Chen appeared to them to be more concerned with catering to U.S. insistence that there be no big, destabilizing steps rather than with actually moving forward toward some sort of mutually acceptable cross-strait political framework. This was reinforced in their minds by Chen's reserved position on heading the National Unification Council (or even giving it a serious role); his refusal to state he was Chinese; his tentative endorsement of one China, respective interpretations, but then his pullback from that position; and by various steps now labeled *de-Sinicization*, such as the changing of the logo for the Government Information Office (GIO) to remove the map of China and advocacy of a new romanized system.

The concern was also underscored by what has been characterized as a rectification of names campaign. This refers to Taipei's decision to put "issued in Taiwan" on Republic of China (ROC) passports, proposals to change the title of its overseas offices to Taiwan Representative Office from Taipei Economic and Cultural Representative Office, and the GIO's recent revelation that, rather than "Republic of China," it is following the practice of the Presidential Office and is using "Taiwan" as much as possible "to describe the country's name" in order to show that the island "is standing up for itself."[2] Success of current efforts to lay a legal foundation for a future referendum on Taiwan's name and status would also cause strong reverberations in Beijing, even though no referendum is currently anticipated.[3]

Moreover, Beijing's concern has been heightened by what it perceives as U.S. complicity in all of this. It sees this reflected in a major arms sales package approved in April 2001, President Bush's statement shortly thereafter about doing "whatever it took" to help Taiwan defend itself, more liberal ground rules adopted for Chen when transiting the United States in May, and, most recently, the President's twice-repeated public reaffirmation—when in Beijing in February 2002—of fidelity to the Taiwan Relations Act (TRA), whereas he only directly vowed allegiance to the three U.S.-PRC joint communiqués in private. Most recently, Beijing was upset by the issuance of a visa to Taiwan's defense minister to pay a private visit to a February conference in Florida where he met on the margins with two senior U.S. national security officials also in attendance. All of this led to a notably sharp protest from Vice Minister Li Zhaoxing to Ambassador Clark Randt on March 16, 2002,[4] and the cancellation of an April 2002 U.S. Navy port call in Hong Kong as well as of anticipated People's Liberation Army (PLA) Navy calls at U.S. ports later in the year.[5]

All that said, there is no sign that this will have any immediate impact on efforts to strengthen day-to-day cross-strait relations, as discussed in the following sections.

SHIFTING PRC TACTICS

Recognizing that it had to cope with an administration in Taipei that had a history and approach to relations with the mainland sharply different from that of its Kuomintang (KMT) predecessors, Beijing began in the immediate aftermath of Chen's election to search for ways to generate greater support in Taiwan for the one-China principle. One of the first efforts, in late summer 2000, involved Vice Premier Qian Qichen issuing what came to be called the "three new sentences." The key feature was to change Beijing's standard statement that "Taiwan is part of China" into "Taiwan and the mainland are both parts of China." This paralleled a formulation in Taiwan's own National Unification Guidelines.

Some opposition (KMT and People's First Party [PFP]) politicians suggested that Taipei pursue the new formula to see if there was something meaningful in it. But, attended in Qian's version by provisions that there is only one China and that the territory and sovereignty of that China are indivisible, and especially given the disparity between the PRC's internal and external formulations (*ney way yeou bye*),[6] Chen declined. Moreover, to the criticism of his opponents, Chen increasingly came to identify the PRC's one-China principle with Beijing's position on one country, two systems, and he argued that accepting one China would thus be tantamount to surrendering ROC sovereignty.

Not to be discouraged, however, the PRC government work report approved by the National People's Congress in mid-March 2002, included the three new sentences. According to the Foreign Ministry, this fully demonstrated the mainland's "kindness, sincerity and tolerance towards solving the Taiwan question and realizing the reunification of the motherland as early as possible."[7]

Beginning in late summer 2001, having (unsurprisingly) failed to obtain Chen Shui-bian's agreement to the one-China principle, the PRC decided to pursue the potentially more fruitful opportunities presented by the recommendations of Taiwan's Economic Development and Advisory Council (EDAC) for liberalizing rules governing cross-strait trade and investment. This did not mean that PRC insistence on the one-China principle as the basis for political discussion had been abandoned, but rather that it would be de-emphasized for now in favor of an area that held out greater promise. Moreover, it fit with Beijing's view that the PRC could generate pressure on Chen from the Taiwan business community to drop his insistence that the three links (discussed below) had to be established through official channels only.

The PRC made yet another show of tactical flexibility when the DPP made major gains—and the KMT faltered—in the December 2001 Legislative Yuan elections. Beijing openly adopted as a formal policy what had been its informal approach for years: to allow individual DPP members to come to the mainland—in an "appropriate capacity" (i.e., not a party role)—as long as they were not "independence" advocates.[8] Beijing even went so far as to opine that the vast majority of DPP members were not independence advocates, but that only a very small handful of such diehard elements existed. The DPP, itself, however, was still considered unacceptable because it had not formally repealed an independence provision of the party charter, even though the party had adopted later resolutions that it insists have superseded and nullified that provision.

These various moves, while positive, should not be over-read.[9] They did not alter Beijing's fundamental requirement that Taipei accept the one-China principle before dialogue can be resumed or the PRC's adherence to one country, two systems as the best—sometimes called the only—formulation for unification.

PROMOTING ECONOMIC TIES

Over the past several years, even before the most recent shift of emphasis, cross-strait economic relations have bourgeoned as the authorities on both sides have eased the way through relaxation of restrictions. As suggested above, this trend has been strengthened in the last few months, as the PRC has emphasized that "cross-strait economic and trade exchanges should not be disturbed by political differences"[10] at the same time Chen Shui-bian has been advocating "more economics, less politics."[11]

According to Taiwan's Board of Foreign Trade, two-way trade amounted to almost $30 billion in 2001, accounting for 13 percent of Taiwan's total foreign trade, up almost two percentage points from the previous year. Exports from Taiwan also rose two points to almost 20 percent of the island's total outward shipments, and imports from the mainland climbed over one point to 5.5 percent of Taiwan's global total.[12]

It is also noteworthy that this substantial interdependence is very much a two-way street. Over 11 percent of the mainland's imported goods and services in 2001 came from Taiwan, second only to Japan's 17 percent or more of the PRC market.[13]

In addition, according to data from Taiwan's Ministry of Economic Affairs, the PRC remains Taiwan's favorite investment destination by a wide margin.[14] Almost three-quarters of Taiwan firms investing abroad in 2001 had operations in the mainland (versus 16.5 percent invested in second place, the United States). Moreover, of those companies planning to invest outside Taiwan in 2002, over 77 percent planned to do so on the mainland.[15]

Driving many firms to move in that direction are surging Taiwan labor costs, the rising value of the New Taiwan dollar, relatively strict environmental regulations in Taiwan, and scarce land on the island. Other attractions are the huge untapped market in the mainland and presumed further opportunities that will arise out of the PRC's accession to the World Trade Organization (WTO).

But there are some signs that, viewed overall, the rush to invest abroad, including specifically in the mainland, may be abating. A Taipei Computer Association and *Digital Weekly* magazine survey, for example, showed that those businesses planning to invest on the mainland in the coming year dropped from about 85 percent of all those surveyed at the end of 2000 to slightly over two-thirds of firms surveyed in late 2001 to early 2002.[16]

According to the latter poll, reasons for less emphasis on mainland investment included a greater sense of political and economic stabilization on the island, including less concern about the Taipei government's performance.[17]

High-tech investment in the mainland remains controversial in Taiwan. In spring 2002 there was a heated debate on the island over the question of allowing at least some 8-inch computer chip wafer fabrication facilities (fabs) to move to the mainland. Manufacturers argued vigorously that competitiveness factors required such a move. Others, however, expressed concern about both the political/security implications and the economic impact on Taiwan's high-tech sector. The solution that emerged was to allow three plants for 8-inch wafer fabrication to be established on the mainland before 2005, all to fall under rules set up under the rubric of the government's active opening, effective management approach to economic relations with the mainland. This will allow control of the value and sophistication of the technology transfers across the strait and will limit operations to firms that have made "considerable investment" in 12-inch fabs on Taiwan and then only after those firms have been fully operational for six months.[18]

Regulations on a wide variety of less-controversial product lines were progressively eased in anticipation of opportunities created by parallel accession to the WTO by Taiwan and the PRC. It was announced in mid-February 2002, for example, that Taiwan trading companies would henceforth be able to deal directly with mainland counterparts, import bans were lifted on some 2,000 PRC farm and industrial products, and Taiwan and PRC banks could now engage in direct remittances (though not in either New Taiwan [NT] dollars or Renminbi [RMB]).[19] Steps were set in motion on both sides of the strait to allow the other's bank branches to open. In late March, Taiwan's cabinet decided to loosen constraints on inbound investment from the mainland.[20]

Beijing has argued, supported by many Taiwan businesses, that until the three links are established, however, the cost of doing business with the mainland will remain unnecessarily high. Those three links, which were initially raised over 20 years ago[21] and later incorporated by PRC President Jiang Zemin into his 1995 Eight-Point proposal[22] include provisions for direct mail services, transportation, and trade.

Though at one point there was an impression that Beijing required Taipei's formal acceptance of one China as a precondition for establishing those links, it was made clear some time ago that, because these are not political connections, the links must merely be carried out as domestic relations[23] *under* (read: *in a manner consistent with*) the one-China principle. While all the practical implications of this have not made been clear, one example cited has been that, as with Taiwan–Hong Kong ocean links, ships coming into harbor would not fly national flags. Moreover, Beijing says that, since officially sponsored dialogue cannot resume until Taipei accepts the one-China principle, arrangements for the three links would have to be worked out through private firms or industry associations, not SEF and ARATS,[24] much less governmental agencies.

In his January 24, 2002, speech inviting DPP members to visit China, Qian Qichen also proposed holding discussions on establishing economic cooperation mechanisms. It is not clear, however, how that would work if official or quasi-official talks are precluded. In this regard, though some believe their common WTO membership could facilitate such discussions, this remains problematic from the PRC perspective.[25]

Despite business community pressure in Taiwan to go along with the PRC approach to private negotiations on the three links, there has been resistance in Taipei. In part, this has been directed at the content (especially air links, which have been seen as having national security implications), but it has also been importantly related to the PRC-proposed unofficial mechanism for setting the links up. Taipei insists that many of the changes in regulations and procedures cannot avoid government scrutiny or even direct negotiation. Nonetheless, since the EDAC recommendations were issued (and Chen Shui-bian called for their prompt implementation), and since both Taipei and Beijing have joined the WTO, a certain level of flexibility has been introduced into Taipei's thinking. How this will ultimately play out in practice is yet to be seen, but the interests of both sides would seem to be leading toward some sort of accommodation.[26]

WRESTLING WITH ONE CHINA

Meanwhile, at the same time it stresses its commitment to peaceful reunification, Beijing, as noted, continues to insist that there can be no return to dialogue until Taipei accepts the one-China principle. This was recently reiterated both by Premier Zhu Rongji in his work report to the Fifth Session of the Ninth National People's Congress[27] and by President Jiang Zemin in his meeting with "native Taiwanese deputies" to the Congress.[28] Though not reported on these occasions, the PRC call usually includes a requirement that Taipei endorse the 1992 Consensus. [29]

Taipei, for its part, continues to insist that it will accept no preconditions for returning to dialogue, but that, at the table, it is willing to talk about both one China and the 1992 Consensus. In addressing this subject recently, Taiwan Premier Yu Shyi-kun did not rule out agreement on the one-China principle, but he said that any assessment of it depends on how one China is defined.[30]

PRC observers claim to be encouraged by public opinion polls in Taiwan that show support for a one country, two systems formula rising to as high as 30 percent or more. But not only do other polls show such support hovering at much lower levels,[31] there is no likelihood that respondents answering positively on such polls would support a system that places them under the sovereign control of the PRC or, indeed, any central government that resides in Beijing. It is possible some have in mind divided or shared sovereignty.[32] It is more likely, however, that few have given any serious thought at all to such nuanced approaches to sovereignty but are merely expressing a willingness to contemplate some one-China umbrella arrangement in which Taiwan and the mainland coexist harmoniously side-by-side, neither subordinate to the other, domestically or internationally.

Contributing to this conclusion are not only the widely varying poll results on this subject, but also the fact that after many years of cultural and social assimilation, there has been a recent resurgence of ethnic divides within Taiwan (*waishengren* versus *benshengren*). Some observers attribute this to the reemergence of a Taiwanese sense of grievance over political inequality as compared with mainlanders. Whether or not this troubling trend, stirred up in the hothouse of Taiwan politics, will abate over time, it shows that feelings about ethnicity are still sensitive, and they likely will have a real and perhaps increasing impact on cross-strait relations for some time to come.[33]

Other developments continue to feed the PRC's concern about continuing incremental movement toward Taiwan independence. Emphasis on Taiwan local language, history, and culture, even the recent move to treat the Republic of Mongolia (as the does the PRC, it should be noted) as a foreign country[34]—all this has been interpreted as part of a large and growing body of evidence of creeping de-Sinicization.

Some Taiwanese, including Vice President Annette Lu, now openly advocate that the United States abandon the Shanghai Communiqué and the other two joint communiqués with the PRC and base American policy totally on the TRA.[35] Beijing has expressed concern, but as a practical matter, this extremist position will not prosper.

There are two principles at work here. The first is Beijing's one-China principle, including that one China exists today, that it encompasses Taiwan as well as the mainland, and that territory and sovereignty are indivisible. The other is Taipei's insistence that the Republic of China is a sovereign, independent state today and that it will accept no arrangement that either puts Taiwan under mainland sovereignty now or that mandates Taiwan will necessarily come under Beijing's sovereign rule in the future (however autonomous it may be). As they stand, those positions are irreconcilable. Thus, both sides are wise to focus for now on economic relations while they work to reduce tensions.[36]

If one could be assured there were no possibility of a crisis, living contentedly for the indefinite future with the status quo would not be a bad outcome for everyone. No one would be totally happy, and there would still be some jockeying and even tension from time to time. Movement connected with the leadership transition in the PRC and in the Taiwan political world (including 2004 presidential elections) would have to take cognizance of the potential risks of careless handling. Nonetheless, if there were some reliable assurances that neither side would adopt steps that provoked crisis, the resultant predictability would be welcomed.

But we cannot have any such assurance under current circumstances. Not only are further, provocative steps by one side or the other not precluded, but we have seen the kind of tensions that can be generated through unanticipated events such as the EP-3 (a reconnaissance plane) incident of April 2001. An incident growing out of an exchange of demonstration military moves by the two sides of the strait, for example, could escalate very quickly, notwithstanding the fervent hope of all to avoid conflict.

Maybe muddling through is the best one can hope for. But we need to face up to the fact that the current listen and watch approach of Beijing and the apparently self-satisfied approach of Taipei are inadequate to the real stakes. Far more flexible thinking is called for.

PRC colleagues say that there is no flexibility on the issue of sovereignty. They rule out, for example, any consideration of confederation or commonwealth, since that would involve first recognizing Taiwan has independent sovereignty, in violation of Qian Qichen's dictum that sovereignty is indivisible.[37] Although understandable from a current PRC perspective, this thinking will not lead to a mutually acceptable solution. Even if a KMT or PFP candidate were to win in 2004—Beijing's fervent wish, its denials notwithstanding—no such person would retreat beyond one China, respective interpretations, and the content of any Taiwan amplification of respective interpretations could well be even more problematic for Beijing in two years than it would be today.

Moreover, placing high odds on Chen's defeat is premature at best. His positive rating in public opinion polls has now moved above 60 percent from under 40 percent a year ago.[38] In part, this reflects his more deft handling of economic and political affairs. But in part it reflects the increasingly outspoken sense of Taiwanese identity mentioned above, which does not necessarily preclude a one-China approach but that will not sit still for subordination of Taiwan to the mainland. Although the overall electoral balance between so-called pan-blue and pan-green factions has not changed greatly, these tendencies cannot be ignored.

Thus, unless PRC thinking about the definition of one China is expanded, its approach to dialogue broadened, and its consideration of Taiwan's international space and security requirements more responsive, the prospect is for continuing political deadlock.

From Taiwan's side, as well, more creative and flexible thinking is needed if there is to be progress. Chen Shui-bian's insistence that the one-China principle is equivalent to one country, two systems is unjustified and unhelpful. So, too, is the government's rigid position that only formal, government-to-government negotiations can be used to arrange the three links. Instead of focusing its energies on replacing "Republic of China" with "Taiwan" in every possible way, even where it has no practical utility, Taipei would do well to think hard about whether there is not a concept of one China—however different from the PRC's current concept, especially regarding one country, two systems—that the people of Taiwan can live with. As candidate George W. Bush said, "I would hope Taiwan would also hear the call that a one China policy is important for the peaceful resolution of the dispute between China and Taiwan... [and] has allowed... Taiwan to develop into a market-oriented economy and flourishing democracy."[39]

PLAYING WELL TOGETHER

In the meantime, both sides need to adopt positions that reinforce stability rather than merely score points off their counterparts across the strait.

Despite the current efforts on both sides to avoid confrontation, the fact is that the military dimension of the cross-strait face-off continues to grow. The U.S. National Intelligence Officer for strategic and nuclear programs, Robert Walpole, recently testified at a Senate hearing that the number of PRC short-range ballistic missiles deployed opposite Taiwan is expected to grow to several hundred by 2005. He judged that the growing arsenal of such missiles provides the mainland a survivable and effective conventional strike force with expanded coverage.[40] Moreover, Beijing is actively pursuing acquisition of advanced airplanes, ships, missiles, and other weapons systems obviously designed to counter presumed American involvement in a Taiwan contingency.

And on the other side of the strait, Taiwan continues to strengthen its defensive forces in order to counter growing PRC strength. Moreover, there is active discussion among some strategic thinkers in Taiwan about the need to develop offensive strike capabilities as part of a credible deterrent, rather than simply preparing to defeat attacking missiles and invasion forces. If it were to become doctrine that the best defense is a good offense, this would have important implications for the cross-strait military dynamic as well as for U.S. arms sales and other military-related decisions.

Before Lee Teng-hui's trip to Cornell in June 1995, there were signs that the PRC could accommodate a larger international role for Taiwan, as long as it did not challenge Beijing on the question of sovereignty. That tolerance was subsequently put in cold storage and has remained there ever since. Beijing had no choice about Taiwan joining WTO, although it continues to try to rewrite history by identifying Taiwan's status as "a separate customs territory of China." (This irksome habit does nothing but annoy people in Taiwan; it certainly does not encourage Taipei to think about cooperative approaches.)

The PRC continues to block Taiwan's participation in every conceivable international organization, made up of sovereign states or not, official or not. A reported recent example was seen when a privately organized—and properly visaed—group of Taiwan doctors, dentists, pharmacists, medical technicians, nurses, and medical students traveled to Lesotho to provide free medical services but was denied entry at PRC insistence.[41]

PRC colleagues broadly hint that, if Taipei accepted the one-China principle, they have developed an extensive list of proposals that would provide Taiwan entrée to a wide range of international activities. One has to assume that this has been conveyed to Chen's government, at least indirectly. But unless Beijing gives Taipei the political space to deal on the basis laid out earlier (i.e., without requiring acceptance of the sovereign authority of a central government in Beijing), it will not be enough to break the impasse.

Some authorities and experts in the mainland think that allowing people in Taiwan to be "masters of their own house" on a day-to-day basis should be good enough to attract them to a one-China deal meeting Beijing's current definition. It would not.

THE AMERICAN CONNECTION

This is not a chapter about American policy. But it is appropriate to at least note that Americans understand they have a role to play here and to say a word or two about how they view that role.

Though some Americans doubtless are concerned about the growing dependence of Taiwan on the cross-strait economic relationship—and would be opposed to any move toward reunification—it has not been American policy for over 30 years to try to determine the substance of relations between Taiwan and the mainland. Instead, the U.S. focus has been on the need that any resolution of questions between them be peaceful. This position is not comfortable for Beijing, with its view of the Taiwan question as strictly an internal affair. But it reflects the reality that the United States has a strategic national interest in the maintenance of peace and stability in East Asia.[42]

The policy problem for Washington is to square that strategic national interest with another: to maintain strong, positive, and productive relations with the PRC. Meeting the challenge of balancing these two critical considerations has not always proven easy over the three decades since the Nixon/Kissinger opening, and the effort to do so has not always been managed well. But it is no less a requirement today than it has ever been.

The advent of the Bush administration has raised particular questions in PRC minds about the steadfastness of this approach. Many believe that there has now been a U.S. tilt in the direction of not only ensuring Taiwan's security but of giving it a degree of dignity in political relations that both transcends anything seen since normalization in 1979 and that verges on active support for separate status.

There is no question that this administration, either on its own initiative or in acquiescing to Taipei's importuning, has added frills, at least, to the political side of the equation as noted earlier in this chapter. But, to this point, anyway, the fundamentals of the one-China policy remain intact, as President Bush reaffirmed in Beijing in February 2002.

CONCLUSION

The fact that both sides of the strait are now competing to demonstrate their good intentions and reasonableness rather than their toughness is a positive development. If they are to reach a state of reliable stability, they need to take this a significant step further, to find ways to demilitarize the cross-strait issue. But this will not happen until they find a mutually acceptable political framework, not to finally resolve the issue, but at least to keep it within bounds. Until then, there is a real, even if small, danger of a tragic war.

Under current circumstances, the two sides are talking past each other. To recall, Beijing insists on acceptance of one China before resuming dialogue; Taipei insists on resuming dialogue before discussing one China. There is no intersection between these two approaches.

Beijing bridled at the personal view expressed by American Institute on Taiwan (AIT) chairman, Richard Bush, when he was in Taiwan in early 2002, criticizing the PRC requirement that Taipei accept one China before dialogue could resume. It is doubtful that he was acting under instructions or that his statement reflected a considered U.S. policy decision to start taking positions on the substance of cross-strait dialogue. But Dr. Bush was voicing what most

Americans feel, that it is unreasonable to ask either side to make fundamental concessions before sitting down at the table.

As a practical matter, I do not expect Beijing to back off of its insistence on Taipei's acceptance of one China before the Wang-Koo dialogue can resume. Nor, however, do I expect that Taiwan will back off of its refusal to do that. In this situation, both sides need to find a way to bypass this roadblock and to conduct an authoritative but low-key conversation in which they can explore the entire range of key issues to lay a predictable and mutually acceptable foundation for moving forward.

As noted earlier, PRC colleagues say that they have many ideas that Taiwan will find pleasing once they return to the table under the one-China principle. One presumes these address not only Taiwan's international space but also security. Taiwan colleagues say that there are prospects for accepting the one-China principle (albeit in some variant of one China, respective interpretations). They can only do so, however, if they have some confidence about the implications.

Both will have to live with the inherent contradictions between the PRC assertion that Beijing represents Taiwan in the international community and Taipei's refusal to accept this. With good will and imagination, however, this is manageable.

Whether Taipei could also directly endorse the so-called 1992 Consensus is another difficult question, but one that is perhaps not impossible to work out. Indeed, if the two sides can agree on a formula about one China, the central element of 1992 will have been addressed.

None of this will happen, however, without talking about it, whoever is in charge in Taiwan.

One of my Taiwan-specialist PRC interlocutors asked me the following: If two families live next door to each other, the child of one family is acting badly, and the neighbor encourages that bad behavior, what is one to think of the motives of that neighbor? My response was that it is very unhelpful to think of the PRC as a parent and Taiwan as its child. And the PRC needs to stop demanding, like a parent, that Taiwan accept its terms "because I said so."[43]

As to the neighbor, the United States, it seems to me that there need not—and should not—be interference in an amicable process to resolve differences between the two parties next door. But if there is danger of chaos and mayhem in the neighborhood, that neighbor may well feel compelled to step in to avert an emergency caused either by violent behavior, on one side, or moves to burn the house down, on the other.

That said, to stick with my colleague's metaphor, what is really needed is to recognize that all members of the first family are adults, and what is required is adult family dialogue, where problems can be identified and talked through—and solutions worked out—with respect for all parties' dignity and interests. That is not impossible in this situation, it is just very difficult.

NOTES

1. In his inaugural address on May 20, 2000, Chen included the following pledge: "[A]s long as the CCP [Chinese Communist Party] regime has no intention to use military force against Taiwan, I pledge that during my term in office, I will not declare independence, I will not change the national title, I will not push forth the inclusion of the so-called 'state-to-state' description in the Constitution, and I will not promote a referendum to change the status quo in regard to the question of independence or unification. Furthermore, there is no question of abolishing the Guidelines for National Unification and the National Unification Council." Available from the World Wide Web: http://www.president.gov.tw/2_special/index_e.html.

2. Maubo Chang, "GIO Promoting Use of 'Taiwan': Official," *CNA*, 18 March, 2002. There is a certain irony here, inasmuch as Taipei has resorted to various stratagems to be able to refer to itself as the Republic of China abroad, an identification no longer allowed by countries that "de-recognized" it and normalized relations with Beijing.

3. State Council Taiwan Affairs Office Deputy Director Wang Zaixi addressed this issue in late March in an interview with a Taiwan newspaper: "If the Taiwan authorities act willfully on this [the Referendum Act], it will certainly produce serious consequences and cause tension in the cross-strait relations." (Wang Ming-yi, "Wang Zaixi, Deputy Director of State Council's Taiwan Affairs Office: Democratic Progressive Party Is Not a Monolithic Bloc," *Taipei Chung Kuo Shih Pao*, 29 March 2002.) Thus far, however, the DPP and the Taipei Cabinet have been quite reserved about acting on that proposal. (Cf. Stephanie Low, "DPP cautious on referendum law," *Taipei Times*, 1 March 2002.)

4. Cf. "China Summons US Ambassador to Make Representations," *People's Daily*. Available from the World Wide Web: http://english.peopledaily.com.cn/200203/17/eng20020317_92254.shtml.

5. "Foreign Ministry Spokesman Answers Journalists' Questions at News Conference on 21 March 2002," Beijing Ministry of Foreign Affairs. Available from the World Wide Web: http://www.fmprc.gov.cn.

6. Qian's formulation suggested internal cross-strait dealings would be on an equal basis, a long-standing PRC position. But to the external world, the PRC firmly insists on another long-standing position, its role as the sole legal representative of all the Chinese people, including in Taiwan, and it has fought hard to deny Taiwan any international standing or participation, even where statehood is not an issue.

7. "Phrases on One China Principle in Gov't Report Significant: Spokesman," *People's Daily*. Available from the World Wide Web: http://english.peopledaily.com.cn/200203/28/print20020328_92977.html.

8. This was first made public in Vice Premier Qian Qichen's January 24, 2002, speech commemorating Jiang Zemin's January 30, 1995, Eight Point Proposal. Due to some confusion regarding what stance DPP members were supposed to take on one China in order to be welcomed, Beijing clarified it was not demanding that such DPP visitors take an oath endorsing the one-China principle. (Cf. "Wang Zaixi Reiterates Motherland's Welcome for DPP Members at Large to Visit Mainland," *Beijing Zhongguo Xinwen She*, March, 2002.)

9. A point which, interestingly, some in China felt it necessary to underscore. Cf. Xin Yue, "Taiwan Authorities Should No Longer Be 'Confused,'" *Beijing Renmin Ribao*, 19 February 2002, overseas edition.

10. Huang Shaohua, "China is Marching toward Reunification with Firm and Confident Pace," *Beijing Zhongguo Xin Wen She*, 14 March 2002.

11. Sofia Wu, "President Calls for Normalization of Cross-Strait Ties," *CNA*, 26 February, 2002.

12. These relative percentages hide, however, an absolute drop in the value of trade by 7.4 percent. See David Hsu, "Taiwan's Trade with Mainland China in 2001 Down," *CNA*, 28 February, 2002.

13. "Taiwan exports to China up, investment down," *Asia Pulse/CNA*, in *AsiaTimes* online at http://www.atimes.com, 6 March, 2002, and Xinhua news agency report of 29 March, 2002.

14. Total PRC-approved Taiwan investment since the late 1980s is now estimated in the range of $60 billion. See Benjamin Kang Lim, "Taiwan and China Launch Flurry Of Contacts," Reuters, 3 March, 2002. About half of this amount has already been expended (Xinhua report, 29 March, 2002).

15. "Mainland Most Popular for Taiwan's Overseas Investment," *Asia Pulse/CNA*, in *AsiaTimes* online at http://www.atimes.com, 13 March, 2002.

16. "Mainland Investment Fever Dwindling: Poll," *CNA*, 4 March, 2002.

17. Ibid.

18. Victor Lai, "Taiwan Allows Conditional Transfer of 8-Inch Wafer Fabs: Premier," *CNA*, 29 March, 2002.

19. "Taiwan Relaxes Ban on Direct Trading with China," Associated Press, in *South China Morning Post*, 16 February, 2002. Available from the World Wide Web: SCMP.com.

20. "Taiwan's Cabinet Decides to Ease Half-Century Ban on Chinese Investments," *Hong Kong AFP*, 27 March, 2002.

21. In the January 1, 1979, National People's Congress Standing Committee "Message to Compatriots in Taiwan" reported by Xinhua on 31 December, 1978.

22. Jiang's speech, "Continue to Promote the Reunification of the Motherland," was delivered on January 30, 1995, and reported that day by Xinhua.

23. According to the Taiwan Affairs Office's Wang Zaixi, the PRC want the routes labeled as "special domestic routes," but Taiwan insists they be called "special international routes." Said Wang, "This would be difficult to achieve. Problems can be overcome only if we make the definition fuzzy." (Wang Ming-yi, "Wang Zaixi...Is Not a Monolithic Bloc," op cit.)

24. Taiwan's Straits Exchange Foundation (SEF) and the PRC's Association for Relations Across the Taiwan Strait (ARATS) were established in late 1991 and early 1992 as quasi-official bodies to handle cross-strait ties in current circumstances.

25. Whereas Taipei would like to use WTO channels, Beijing says it is inappropriate, not only because these would be official, but also because their dealings are domestic and should be worked out directly between them, not under the umbrella of an international trade organization.

26. On March 19, 2002, Taiwan Premier Yu Shyi-kun vowed to set up the Three Links as soon as possible, "as long as national security and economic development can be ensured." (Flor Wang, "'Three Links' The Sooner the Better: Premier," *CNA*, 19 March, 2002.)

27. Reported by Xinhua, 5 March, 2002.

28. Reported by Xinhua, 8 March, 2002.

29. This refers to an arrangement reached between Taiwan and the Mainland in late 1992 in which each endorsed a version of one China as a basis for dialogue in spring 1993 between SEF Chairman Koo Chen-fu and ARATS Chairman Wang Dao-han. Since then, however, a disagreement has arisen over what the nature of the consensus was, whether it is still valid, and even whether there ever was a consensus. Chen Shui-bian has refused to endorse it up to now.

30. "Assessment of 'One China' Depends on Definition: Premier," from *Taipei Times*, 6 March, 2002, as carried by *Taiwan Headlines*, 6 March, 2002. Available from the World Wide Web: http://www.taiwanheadlines.gov.tw/.

31. For example, a recent Mainland Affairs Council survey showed only 9.2 percent support, 69.2 percent opposition, and the remainder indifferent. (Fang Wen-hung, "9.2 Percent of Taiwanese Support 'One Country/Two systems': Poll," *CNA*, at *Taiwan Headlines*, 22 February, 2002. Available from the World Wide Web: http://www.taiwanheadlines.gov.tw/.)

32. As noted, the three new sentences would rule out divided sovereignty. But at various times in the past, officials and other important personages on both sides have raised the concept of shared sovereignty. Cf. Ralph N. Clough, *Cooperation or Conflict in the Taiwan Strait?* (Lanham: Roman and Littlefield, 1998), p. 98.

33. There are numerous articles on this question of ethnic divisions. One of the more accessible discussions appeared in the *Singapore Straits Times* on 17 February, 2002: "Goh Sui Noi," ("Taiwan's Great Divide"). Available from the World Wide Web: http://taiwansecurity.org/News/2002/ST-021702.htm.

34. But the Constitution is not changed, which nominally includes Mongolia within the Republic of China.

35. "Taiwan's Lu urges U.S. to Dump 3 U.S.-China Communiques," *Kyodo*, 29 March, 2002. See also Flor Wang, "Think Tank Asks Bush to Abandon Shanghai Communique," *CNA*, 27 February, 2002.

36. Moreover, even if they agreed on some broad political principles today, it is generally acknowledged that there is no realistic prospect of (re)unification for decades to come. (In the PRC, standard practice is to refer to *reunification*, highlighting Beijing's position that Taiwan has historically been part of China and is not unified with the motherland today only because of historical circumstances. In Taiwan, there is a growing tendency to highlight not only that Taiwan has never been part of the PRC, but that, in many people's minds, its status as part of China is questionable. In this view, any future link-up would simply be *unification*. This usage was even common under the KMT (e.g., the National Unification Council.)

37. See the argument made, for example, in Liao Yi, "Instituting 'One Country, Two Systems' Is Most Beneficial—Interviewing Guo Zhenyuan, Researcher of China International Affairs Institute," Beijing Xinhua Hong Kong Service, 27 March, 2002.

38. "Approval Rating for Taiwan's President Hits an 18-Month High after Cabinet Reshuffle," Associated Press, reported in *The China Post*, 1 March, 2002, online edition, http://www.chinapost.com.

39. GOP debate in Los Angeles, March 2, 2000. Available from the World Wide Web: http://issues2000.org/Celeb/George_W_Bush_China.htm

40. James Kuo and Fang Wen-hung, "Mainland China to Continue to Deploy Missiles Opposite Taiwan: CIA," *CNA*, 11 March, 2002.

41. Sofia Wu, "Beijing Blocks Entry of Taiwan Medical Volunteers to Lesotho," *CNA*, 4 March, 2002.

42. This position, initially adopted when Taiwan was still under a strict authoritarian regime, has been strongly reinforced with the emergence of full-blown democracy on the island.

43. This translates in realpolitik terms as "because I have the PLA to back me up."

CHAPTER 4

Cross-Strait Relations at a Crossroad: Impasse or Breakthrough?

Ying-jeou Ma

BACKGROUND

Taiwan's Change of Government in May 2000

Taiwan's second popular presidential election took place on March 18, 2000. Chen Shui-bian, candidate of the opposition Democratic Progressive party (DPP), won the presidency with 39 percent of the votes cast, followed by People's First party (PFP) candidate James Chu-yu Soong with 36 percent, and Kuomintang (Nationalist party; RMT) candidate Lian Chan with 24 percent.[1] Chen, 50, and his running mate, Annette Hsiu-lien Lu, 56, were inaugurated on May 20, 2000, as the 10th president and vice president of the Republic of China (ROC). President Chen appointed Tang Fei, 68, former minister of defense, as premier. Tang resigned on October 3, 2000, after holding office for only 137 days for reasons of poor health as well as disagreement with the DPP leadership on the continued construction of the Fourth Nuclear Power Plant.[2] Chang Chun-hsiung, 63, then secretary general of the Presidential Office, succeeded him. Of the 34 cabinet posts, only a few are filled by card-carrying DPP members; the rest are DPP-supporting independents, scholars, and some former RMT officials who have joined the new cabinet as individuals. One independent cabinet member worth noting is, of course, Tsai Ying-wen, chairwoman of the Mainland Affairs Council (MAC), which is in charge of formulating and executing Taiwan's policy toward the People's Republic of China (PRC) on the Chinese mainland. Tsai was formerly a professor of international trade law at National Chengchi University, was associated with a confidential think-tank group, and was appointed by former President Lee Teng-hui to the Presidential Office to be in charge of research on Taiwan's sovereignty and international status. The former president's statement in a German radio interview characterizing cross-strait relations as "a special state-to-state relationship," the so-called two-state theory, on July 9, 1999, was reported to be Tsai's brainchild.[3]

Until the presidential election of March 18, 2000, the Kuomintang had dominated Taiwan's political scene since 1949, when it lost the civil war to the forces of the Chinese Communist Party (CCP) and retreated from the Chinese mainland. The election not only changed the political landscape in Taiwan but fundamentally altered the traditional RMT-CCP confrontation that had existed across the Taiwan Strait for the last half-century. Taiwan's peaceful change of government made it a full-fledged democracy. Yet it also injected new variables into the already troubled cross-strait relationship. Its profound implications remain to be seen. The election was understandably selected by the international media as one of the top 20 news events of the world in 2000.[4]

President Chen's Strength and Weakness Regarding Cross-Strait Relations

President Chen Shui-bian has been a supporter, but not a fundamentalist one, of Taiwan independence (TI). Born in southern Taiwan's Tainan County in September 1950 to a poor family, he graduated from the Law Department of National Taiwan University, the best in the country, in 1974.[5] He practiced maritime law for seven years and gained a national reputation as the defense attorney during the Formosa Incident. He entered politics in 1981 and won a seat in the Taipei City Council in December; achieving a high number of votes. He did well as an opposition councilor but failed in his bid to win the Tainan County magistrate election in December 1985. Soon after the election, his wife was hit by a small truck while the couple was walking in a thanksgiving parade with his supporters. She was paralyzed from the waist down. Later, while his wife was a candidate in the legislative election and in December 1986 won a seat in the Legislative Yuan (national parliament), he was jailed for eight months for libel. Once out of jail, Chen Shui-bian first worked as a legislative assistant to his wife and then, in 1989, was elected as a legislator. His performance in the Legislative Yuan again won him national popularity. During his second term, he ran for and won with 43.6 percent of the vote the Taipei mayor's office in 1994, defeating both the KMT and New Party (NP) candidates, who were victims of the KMT's split. Chen did fairly well as mayor but lost his office in 1998 to a KMT candidate.[6] Extremely disappointed, he did a thorough soul-searching and was able to make a political comeback by taking advantage once more of the KMT's serious infighting.

He became the first non-KMT president of the ROC in May 2000. During his presidential campaign, he continued to support the TI's "one China, one Taiwan" official line but vowed neither to change the status quo nor to declare the birth of an independent Taiwan if he was elected president. He emphasized that he would follow a "new middle road" and make peace with the PRC.[7] On the one China principle, he said that one China could be a topic for future negotiations with the PRC but not a precondition for such negotiations.[8]

Being a TI supporter obviously put President Chen in a difficult position in handling cross-strait relations. Although the CCP leaders have little trust in their KMT counterparts, they at least have something in common—namely, the shared memory of the past and the ultimate, long-term goal of China's reunification. The DPP, having been established for only 14 years and having had no mainland experience at all, is an entirely different political party. Its party charter's insistence on TI is in opposition to the PRC's one China principle and totally unacceptable to the PRC. It would be difficult, if not impossible, for President Chen to establish mutual trust with the PRC leadership if the party charter remains unchanged. On the other hand, fully aware of his liabilities, President Chen boldly modified his pro-TI position early in his presidential campaign to pacify the PRC, the United States, and the international community in general. Furthermore, citing previously anti-Communist U.S. President Richard Nixon's dramatic opening to Communist China in 1971, President Chen and his DPP staff maintained that he is in a better position than a KMT president to strike a deal with the PRC. This view is not entirely far-fetched because Chen, as a clever politician, does have flexibility. When he was a legislator in the early 1990s, he proposed that Taiwan and the PRC adopt the one nation, two states formula to solve their differences.[9] This was an adaptation of the so-called German formula, namely, "one Germany, two states" (*Eine Deutschland, zwei Staaten*), clearly a far cry from TI in the sense that Taiwan is still part of the larger Chinese nation. In the following analysis, we will see more of his flexibility in handling cross-strait relations.

The PRC reacted cautiously to the victory of its least-favorite candidate in Taiwan's presidential election. Only a few days before the March 18, 2000, election, PRC Premier Zhu Rongji blasted TI supporters in Taiwan.[10] The move proved counterproductive, similar to the effects of the menacing missile test that the PRC conducted off Taiwan's coast exactly four years before, in March 1996, when Lee Teng-hui was running for re-election as president. At that time Lee won a landslide victory with 54 percent of the votes cast. The missile test gave President Lee the opportune moment to appeal to his countrymen for more support. And he got it. This time Chen won the election unexpectedly, again with unsolicited help from the PRC. Ever since Chen's victory, the PRC has taken a "listen to what he says and watch what he does" attitude,[11] similar to its stance toward former President Lee during the period 1996–2000. Meanwhile, Beijing continues to advocate its fundamentalist policies of one China, two systems or simply the one-China principle, without elaborating on specific responses to events taking place in Taiwan.

PRESIDENT CHEN'S APPROACH TO CROSS-STRAIT RELATIONS

The New Middle Road and the Five No's: Conditional Departure from TI

Chen's unexpected election victory shocked many people in Taiwan. Keenly aware of his minority position, he maintained an extremely low profile after the election and before the inauguration. He visited many RMT elders, sought their advice, mended fences, and generated a lot of goodwill. His appointment of Tang Fei, a popular defense minister in the previous KMT cabinet, as premier obviously was motivated by Tang's background in four distinct areas. He is a former four-star air force general and chief of the general staff, a long-time and loyal KMT member, a mainlander, and a Chinese unification supporter. Thus Chen tried to win the support of more than 60 percent of the voters who did not vote for him during the election. Chen then declared that he was building an "upright and all-people's government."[12] He also repeated his campaign promise that he would not declare Taiwan an independent state and would set up a cross-party group led by Dr. Yuan T. Lee, president of Academia Sinica and one of the 1986 Nobel laureates in chemistry, to deal with cross-strait relations. A week before his inauguration, Chen announced that the part of his inaugural address dealing with cross-strait relations would "satisfy the Americans, please the international community, and not provoke China."[13] On the eve of Chen's inauguration on May 20, 2000, the opinion polls conducted by the media showed that around 70 percent of the people polled approved of his performance.[14] The rating went up to 79 percent a month after his inauguration.[15] That gave him further confidence about building an "upright and all-people's government."

President Chen's inaugural address of May 20, 2000, did contain important statements that diluted his TI coloration. He stated the following:

> As long as the CCP regime has no intention to use military force against Taiwan, I pledge that during my term in office, I will not declare independence, I will not change the national title, I will not push for the inclusion of the so-called state-to-state description in the Constitution, and I will not promote a referendum to change the status quo in regard to the question of independence or unification. Furthermore, there is no question of abolishing the Guidelines for National Unification and the National Unification Council.[16]

What he promised not to do, in essence, is what the Constitution of the Republic of China, which he vowed to uphold at his swearing in ceremony, would not allow him to do anyway. His promises also duplicated the KMT's party line of past years. Chen, however, was not merely stating what was obvious to every constitutional lawyer and making a virtue out of necessity. What is significant about the Five No's is not what and how the statement was made, but who made it. President Chen was a former (or is a current) TI supporter who had frequently criticized the one-China Constitution, which was adopted in 1947 by the National Assembly on the Chinese mainland and represented at the time all of the approximately 500 million Chinese people (including those of Taiwan). Once he had vowed to propose a new constitution. The Five No's statement shows how much President Chen has modified his position on the core value of his political beliefs. This is a significant move that indicates he has come a long way. Making such a move may incur high political costs for him. Yet all his promises hinge on the PRC's willingness not to use force against Taiwan, and these promises are good only as long as President Chen is in office. However, as conditional as such promises may seem, the Five No's statement received popular approval at home and abroad as a mature, responsible policy capable of at least stabilizing cross-strait relations when Chen established his new administration after his inauguration. The PRC reacted calmly and simply to President Chen's inauguration by reiterating the one-China principle. Obviously, Beijing thought it needed more time to get the measure of this new leader of Taiwan and did not find it appropriate to respond right away.

The 1992 Consensus: Did It Really Exist?

The euphoria generated by the inaugural address faded as the new DPP government, first led by Tang Fei and then by Chang Chun-hsiung, began to face tough challenges from the Legislative Yuan: of 220 seats, 114 (more than half) belong to the KMT and only 67 (less than one-third) are held by DPP members or firm supporters. The health of Premier Tang, who had a major chest operation just before the inauguration, and the teamwork of the new cabinet, whose many new hands are not familiar with the running of a government, became issues. On June 20, when President Chen held a one-month-in-office press conference, he referred, among other things, to the October 1992 meeting between the Strait Exchange Foundation (SEF), representing Taiwan, and the Association for Relations Across the Taiwan Strait (ARATS), representing the mainland, as a meeting in which the only consensus on the one-China question was no consensus at all or an agreement to disagree at the most.[17] Seven days later, on June 27, President Chen stated to a group of visiting American scholars from the Asia Foundation, including China specialist Harry Harding, that he accepted the one-China, with different interpretations by each side consensus reached by the two sides in Hong Kong in 1992. The statement was included in the press release issued by the Presidential Office on June 27, 2000, and was widely reported by the media.[18] Barely 24 hours later, Chairwoman Tsai Ying-wen of the MAC hastily called a press conference to clarify that what the president meant was no different from what he said on June 20—namely, that no consensus had been reached in 1992 on the one-China principle.[19] A few days later, Tsai went further and said that the consensus was not one China with different interpretations by each side, but rather "[each side] differently interprets one China."[20] This game of words added a new strain of confusion to the already cloudy cross-strait relationship.

From then on, the 1992 Consensus seemed to become a nightmare to the DPP government, which tried desperately to deny its existence. In fact, many who were directly involved in preparing and conducting the November 1992 negotiations in Hong Kong that led to the consensus—including Chairman Koo Cheng-fu of the SEF; Chin Chin-yi, former vice chairman and secretary general of the SEF; Dr. Kao Kung-lian, vice chairman of MAC; and the author, who was MAC's senior vice chairman and spokesman—remember clearly that such a consensus on the one-China principle was reached and that each side had agreed in correspondence that the meaning of one China, on which they disagreed, was to be interpreted orally by each side. Although no written agreement was signed, correspondence between SEF and ARATS following the November meeting attested to the existence of such a consensus.[21] The formulation "one China, different interpretations by each side" was actually coined by the media. Furthermore, it is obvious that, had no such consensus existed, the epoch-making Koo-Wang talks held five months later on April 29, 1993, in Singapore[22] and the four agreements signed then would not have been possible given the PRC's absolute insistence on recognizing the one-China principle.

What the DPP government came up with next on this thorny issue was even more amazing. On July 31, 2000, when President Chen called a press conference, he said that although there was no consensus on one China in 1992, there was a "1992 spirit," namely, "dialogue, exchange, and shelving disputes."[23] Such a formulation, obviously intended to downplay the issue and distract popular attention, had the effect of pouring fuel on the fire. Many people, including those in the media, began to question the credibility of the DPP government. They argued that, although the DPP government had every right not to agree to the one-China principle to which it has long been opposed, it should not deny the existence of a historical fact. By so doing the new administration made itself even less credible, not only to its counterpart on the Chinese mainland but to the general public in Taiwan. The issue remains a lively one in Taiwan today because all the opposition parties (the KMT, the PFP, and the NP) agree on the existence of such a consensus and have called on the new administration to recognize it. The new administration's failure to do so in effect continues the stalemate across the Taiwan Strait that has lingered for more than six years. High-ranking officials of the MAC keep saying that the resumption of talks between the two sides is not the only way to maintain peace in the Taiwan Strait and to promote cross-strait relations.[24] Under such circumstances, promoting the three mini-links is the only thing the DPP government can do on its own to show progress in cross-strait relations without touching on the one-China issue.

On the other hand, the PRC has insisted that recognizing the one-China principle is the precondition to resuming talks between the two sides or at least that the talks should be resumed under the one-China principle. Also, it has demanded that Taiwan go back to the 1992 Consensus as a first step. It should be kept in mind that what the PRC means by the 1992 Consensus is one China, not one China with different interpretations by each side. The PRC omitted the latter half of the 1992 Consensus as Taiwan understands it in the mid-1990s, when cross-strait relations became sore for fear that Taiwan would take advantage of the phrase "different interpretations by each side" to promote TI or similar policies. The emergence of the two-state theory in July 1999 gave credibility to Beijing's fear. As a result, PRC scholars, let alone the PRC government, are reluctant to mention the "different interpretations by each side" part of the 1992 Consensus. That could also explain why the DPP government does not want to go back to the 1992 Consensus, which is no different from the one-China principle as the PRC interprets it.

The Relevance of the Three Mini-Links

Shortly after the presidential inauguration, the MAC announced that it would permit the establishment of direct links between Kinmen (Qimoy) and Xiamen (Amoy) and between Matsu and Mawei.[25] Kinmen, belonging to Kinmen County, and Matsu, belonging to Lianjiang County, both of Fujian Province, are 67 nautical miles apart. They are the only major offshore islands close to the Chinese mainland that are still under the control of the ROC government. They became world renowned when they were bombarded by more than half a million shells fired by the PRC forces across the narrow strips of water during August and September of 1958.[26] The Kinmen/Matsu crisis involved not only Taiwan and the PRC but also the United States and the Soviet Union, because at that time Taiwan and the United States were bound by the Mutual Defense Treaty of 1954. Therefore, since 1958, these islands have been under heavy garrison. When martial law on Taiwan was lifted in July 1987, it remained in effect on the islands until the mid-1990s. In April 2000, the Statute for the Reconstruction of Offshore Islands came into existence.[27] This statute permits direct links between Kinmen and Matsu, on the one hand, and the Chinese mainland, on the other. That means that the current prohibition on direct links with the mainland is inapplicable to Kinmen, Matsu, and Penghu (the Pescadores, located in the Taiwan Strait between central Taiwan and the Chinese mainland).

The above statute was passed after the presidential election on March 18, 2000, but before the inauguration on May 20. The previous KMT cabinet had also approved the plan to proceed with establishing the three mini-links but did not have enough time to implement it. The DPP cabinet followed the policy, and the MAC used this move to show progress in cross-strait relations under the DPP government, apparently hoping that, if everything went right, regular links would follow. In their view, the PRC may be reluctant to oppose a move that it demanded approximately 10 years ago under the slogan "The two gates [men] open to each other and the two horses [ma] go together first." They believe that the PRC will at least passively agree to cooperate on the three mini-links, and, if everything goes well, the PRC might agree to enlarge the scope to three regular links. By then, in their opinion, it may not be necessary to solve the tough one-China issue. That, of course, by and large, is wishful thinking on the part of the DPP government.

Residents of Kinmen and Matsu have long wanted such links, as do residents along the coast of the Chinese mainland opposite these islands. Some of them are former residents of Kinmen and Matsu who have been unable to go home in the last 50 years. Many more want to do business with the two islands, whose residents have a much higher standard of living and greater purchasing power. After all, the two islands are geographically close to the mainland and far away from Taiwan. The fact that they have been attached to Taiwan politically, economically, and militarily is simply due to the 50-year-old civil war between Taiwan and the Chinese mainland. Tension began to ease when the PRC stopped shelling the islands on January 1, 1979, and issued its "Letter to the Taiwan Compatriots" on the occasion of the formal establishment of diplomatic relations between Beijing and Washington.[28] Illegal trade and travel have been rampant since then and so are fishery disputes between fishermen from the two sides. Local military and police authorities have had to arrest mainland fishermen, who use dynamite in fishing, for violating Taiwan's fishing laws and to disperse mainland fishing boats operating too close to the coasts of Kinmen and Matsu. Policing these infractions is troublesome, and many mainland fishermen end up serving their sentences in Keelung Prison, more than 100 nautical miles away in northern Taiwan. The need for emergency assistance and disaster relief could also make possible cooperation between these islands and the Chinese mainland.

The three mini-links were formally launched on January 1, 2001.[29] County magistrates of Kinmen and Lianjiang went to Xiamen and Mawei, respectively, to meet their counterparts. Despite the fact that they were warmly received, the PRC's central and local authorities were deliberately cool to the idea for fear that Taiwan would use this move to evade the one-China issue. At the moment, this initiative has had the effect of legalizing some of the erstwhile illegal smuggling, which the PRC called a small amount of trade. But aside from the visits by Kinmen and Lianjiang county magistrates on the first day, as of March 4, 2001, only one passenger-carrying ship has been permitted to operate between the two sides because Taiwan and mainland residents are not permitted to use these two islands as transit points to and from the Chinese mainland.[30] In addition, both the mainland and Taiwan require that for entry to and exit from Kinmen or Matsu, residents travel as a group. No one may travel individually. It will take some time before trade and tourism can reach normal levels. The opening of the three mini-links did give residents high hopes for the future, yet what followed did not fulfill their expectations. Furthermore, to enforce the ban on people and goods in transit, much tighter security measures were imposed, making the movement of people and goods between Taiwan and the two offshore islands even less convenient than before. In any case, given the PRC's inaction, the significance of the three mini-links on cross-strait relations is largely symbolic now.

On the other hand, Tsao Er-chung, a KMT legislator, and Chen Cheng-ching, Lianjiang County Council speaker, went to Fuzhou, the capital of Fujian Province, on January 28, 2001, and signed an agreement with a mainland organization called the Fuzhou Mawei Cultural and Economic Cooperation Center aimed at promoting interchange between Matsu and the Fujian coast.[31] The MAC initially said that, without authorization from the MAC, this agreement had no legal effect. On January 30, Tsao met with MAC Chairwoman Tsai Ying-wen and reached a consensus that the agreement is between nongovernmental entities of the two sides and will be treated as such.[32] The agreement shows the eagerness of Matsu residents for improving Matsu's economic conditions by conducting more trade and other contacts with the geographically close Fujian coast. It also demonstrates the PRC's strategy of differentiation in dealing with the central and local governments of Taiwan. In any case, so far the three mini-links have not worked well. It remains to be seen whether traffic will pick up in the next two or three months. If not, then the policy can be deemed a failure.

The Cross-Party Group and Its Policy Advice

Officially, President Chen's purpose in setting up a cross-party group was to provide consultations on cross-strait relations. Unofficially, it is intended to bypass the National Unification Council (NUC). The NUC is a consultative task force that was set up in 1990 to provide advice to former President Lee Teng-hui. It is composed of representatives from the Presidential Office (such as the secretary general to the president), Executive Yuan (cabinet, the premier, the chairman of the MAC), the chairman of the SEE, the president of the Legislative Yuan, mayors and city council speakers of Taipei and Kaohsiung cities, leaders of political parties, and opinion leaders at home and abroad. The NUC has a research arm composed of front-line officials (such as the deputy secretary general of the Presidential Office, the vice chairman, and spokesman of MAC), scholars, and specialists. Originally, it met once every season. President Lee gave important policy speeches at the opening session. During the last five years, the frequency of the meetings has decreased to once a year at most, obviously reflecting the stalemate in cross-strait relations.

The DPP has always boycotted the NUC. It refuses to participate for fear that its presence will be interpreted as endorsing the unification of China, thereby seriously weakening its supreme policy on TI. The DPP once suggested that President Lee change the title of the council or set up a separate committee on national development to make the party's participation easier. Huang Hsin-chieh, the exchairman of the DPP, was about to join the council a few years ago, but backed out at the eleventh hour under great pressure from his own party.

When Chen Shui-bian became president, he promised not to abolish the NUC or to repeal the National Unification Guidelines (the fifth "no") in his inaugural address. Yet it is obvious that the governing idea is to freeze its operation and leave it frozen indefinitely. On the other hand, he does need a consultative body to advise him on mainland affairs, hence the establishment of the Cross-Party Group, which was slated to be composed of representatives from each political party and nonparty independents. But the KMT and the PFP have decided to abstain, claiming that Chen should restore the operation of the NUC. Hao Lung-bin, a legislator and the NP's chairman (and minister of environmental protection since March 7, 2001), joined the group when it was formed, but quit in protest a few months later. Although some members of the group are KMT members who participate as individuals or independents, the original idea of making the group a forum in which all the political parties could reach consensus on mainland policy did not come to fruition.

The group did manage to hold a dozen or so meetings in order to integrate wide-ranging views on issues such as one China, the 1992 Consensus, the three links issue, and so on. The fact that Dr. Yuan T. Lee, chairman of the group and president of the Academia Sinica, called himself Chinese and said that the DPP government should go back to the 1992 Consensus raised the outside world's expectations of the group, although its spokesman quickly clarified that the statement was the personal view of Dr. Lee and did not represent the viewpoint of the group. Nevertheless, the final conclusion that was issued on November 26, 2000, clearly suggested, among other things, that President Chen respond to the PRC on the one-China question in accordance with the Constitution of the ROC.[33]

The group's conclusion, composed of three understandings and four suggestions, met with varied responses in Taiwan, some positive and some negative. The opposition parties again criticized the composition of the group as being unrepresentative. There are some who believe that the group has come a long way in integrating so many diverse opinions. They believe that the reference to the ROC Constitution was particularly timely and useful. But the PRC ridiculed the group's conclusions as "neither one thing nor the other," a Chinese idiom meaning something insolent.[34] Nevertheless, one should not lose sight of the group's major concern—namely, the one-China issue and the mechanism to integrate existing organizations such as the NUC. In fact, the author believes that the most important function of the group is to prepare an exit for President Chen to get out of the tangle associated with the one-China issue and the NUC. Whether President Chen should call a meeting of the NUC and chair the meeting himself or let members of the NUC freely elect a chairman is a question of great symbolic significance to Taiwan and to the PRC and has been discussed in the media in the last several months. In essence, although the group's representation became an issue when it was established, it has been able to come up with something not entirely useless and may yet serve as an exit for President Chen to solve his dilemma in dealing with the one-China issue. Of course, it all depends on how he reacts to the conclusions of the group.

President Chen's New "Integration" Initiative

Seemingly in response to the conclusions of the Cross-Party Group, President Chen did say something new in his Cross-Century Remarks on December 31, 2000. First, he referred to what he had said in his inaugural address: that leaders of the two sides should jointly handle the one-China issue under principles of democracy and equality. He then said,

> Actually, according to the Constitution of the Republic of China, "one China" should not be an issue. We hope the mainland can have [a] better understanding of the doubts in the minds of the people of Taiwan. If the mainland can neither respect nor understand the will of the 23 million people of Taiwan to make their own decision, this will lead to unnecessary differences between the two sides.

He continued,

> We would like to appeal to the government and leaders on the Chinese mainland to respect the existence and international dignity of the Republic of China; publicly renounce the use of force; and overcome the current dispute and deadlock through tolerance, foresight, and wisdom. The integration of our economies, trade, and culture can be a starting point for gradually building faith and confidence in each other. This, in turn, can be the basis for a new framework of permanent peace and political integration.[35]

Again, the reactions in Taiwan were varied. In the MAC's year-end press conference on January 19, 2001, Chairwoman Tsai Ying-wen gave the official interpretation of President Chen's political integration remarks by saying that "political integration" could mean "a direction, a process or an objective, and political integration does not necessarily exclude any of the three options Taiwan has, namely, unification, independence and status quo."[36] Obviously, she tried to tone down the impact and change the direction of the remarks, because in the ordinary meaning of the word *integration*, the only option that could most likely be excluded is independence.

The reactions of the political parties were poles apart and clear-cut. The TI fundamentalists were outraged. DPP legislators complained that President Chen went too far too fast before the PRC and the Opposition Alliance (that is, the three opposition parties) could release any kind of meaningful goodwill. Most of the members of the New Tide Faction of the DPP, the most powerful one, asked the president not to pursue the integration theory. On the other hand, the three opposition parties praised President Chen for this new statement. In addition, pro-unification fundamentalist groups applauded the remarks.

There are two new elements that are worth observing. First, this is the first time President Chen clearly admitted that the Constitution of the ROC contains the one-China principle and is a one-China constitution. In as much as this is self-evident, almost every constitutional scholar (except TI supporters) pointed out the truth of the statement in the past. Even Frank Hsieh, chairman of the DPP and a lawyer, said as much. Naturally, he was under heavy fire within his own party and was under great pressure to keep quiet. Now that President Chen has made the same statement, TI fundamentalists have criticized him too, but he seems able to withstand such pressure. After all, as president of the ROC, Chen is under a constitutional duty to do so. Second, this was the first time that President Chen stressed to such an extent the economic, cultural, and political integration that has occurred between the two sides of the Taiwan Strait.

The most significant meaning of political integration is that it points to a new thinking that not only discounts the separatist attitude that he promised in his inaugural address that he would not follow but explores the possibility of a permanent association with the PRC short of outright unification. If this interpretation is correct and President Chen has the courage to reach consensus with his own party comrades and the opposition parties and push it through, many of the problems the DPP government has encountered in Taiwan in handling cross-strait relations could be gradually ameliorated. But whether that would be readily acceptable to the PRC remains to be seen. In short, the new remarks not only have served to place TI farther away from where it used to be, but have moved it to a stage that could lead to a certain form of association with the Chinese mainland.

Of course, one has to keep in mind that this is only a statement, not a concrete policy or program. What President Chen will do to implement his statements remains to be seen. In this regard, his track record is unimpressive. In the past nine months, policies that had seemed to be magnificent went nowhere, either because they were not workable or because they met with strong opposition from his own party. On the other hand, the opposition parties welcomed such remarks because their voters could accept them. In fact, the ROC has been an independent sovereign state for 90 years. Currently not under the rule of any foreign nation, it has no need whatsoever to declare its independence a second time. No country in the world has done or would do that. Therefore, the independence option is not needed; the only options Taiwan has are to maintain the status quo or to be reunited with the Chinese mainland. Here the integration concept could possibly take care of both. This is why the opposition parties welcome, whereas the DPP opposes, such a move.

FROM EUPHORIA TO DISILLUSIONMENT: CROSS-STRAIT RELATIONS DURING THE LAST NINE MONTHS

To get an insight into the DPP government's performance on cross-strait relations, one should not overlook the new administration's overall performance and its impact on relations across the strait. First, a look at Taiwan's stock market is instructive because, to a great extent, it reflects the country's economic health and its people's confidence in their government. On March 17, 2000, the day before the election, the Taiwan stock index was 8,763. After the election, on April 5, it went up to 10,186. By the time President Chen was inaugurated on May 20, it dropped to 9,162. The index continued to go down rather quickly to 7,961 on July 26, 6,432 on September 29, and 5,404 on October 20. It reached the lowest point of 4,614 on December 27. During the month of January 2001, there was some good news: the index bounced back to 5,847 on the January 18, the last trading day before the Chinese New Year holiday. It went down and up again and stood at 5,610 on March 13, 2001. The market, in effect, has dropped more than 4,000 points on average, or 47.7 percent overall, for most of the period over the last nine months. The total market value of stocks decreased more than New Taiwan (NT) $4 trillion (or U.S. $125 billion).

If chain reactions such as losses of business are included, the amount could be as high as NT $10 trillion (or U.S. $312 billion).[37] During the year 2000, approximately 4,995 companies closed their factories, an increase of 25 percent over the previous year, according to the Ministry of Economic Affairs. The unemployment rate rose to 3.35 percent, the highest in 15 years.[38] The number of companies moving to the Chinese mainland increased substantially. Large domestic investments—those over NT $200 million (U.S. $6.2 million)—dropped 50 percent from NT $137.9 billion (U.S. $4.3 billion) in January 2000 to NT $68.1 billion (U.S. $2.1 billion) in January 2001.[39] As of February 21, 2001, the trade surplus stood at NT $347 million, down 72.5 percent from the same period last year.

Meanwhile, in January 2001, President Chen's approval rate in the opinion polls dropped sharply to around 38 percent, compared with 82 percent when he had been one month in office, and the disapproval rate went up from approximately 10 percent to a record 48 percent.[40] His approval rate dropped further at the end of February 2001 to 34 percent, an all-time low, and the disapproval rate went up to 53 percent, an all-time high, according to the TVBS Poll Center.[41] Meanwhile, Premier Chang's rating in the same poll was 28 percent (approval) and 59 percent (disapproval)—also a record for an incumbent premier. In brief, the DPP government is by far the most unpopular government in the history of the post-1949 ROC.

The downturn began in July, when the people of Taiwan saw a live scene on TV in which the DPP government took no action to rescue four workers who were trapped in a flood in southern Taiwan. They waited for hours before they were swept away. This was followed by the resignation of Premier Tang Fei in early October because of disagreements with the DPP leadership over the Fourth Nuclear Power Plant. Tang was in office for only 137 days, the shortest-lived premiership in the ROC's history since 1949. It also signified the end of President Chen's all-people's government. The situation worsened after new Premier Chang Chun-hsiung made the abrupt decision on October 27, 2000, to discontinue the construction of the Fourth Nuclear Power Plant. This decision was made without consulting in advance with the Legislative Yuan, to which the Executive Yuan is responsible, according to the ROC Constitution, and which a few years before had passed a resolution with a two-thirds majority demanding the construction of the plant by the Executive Yuan (the cabinet). Meanwhile, Vice President Lu Hsiu-lien became involved in disseminating an unconfirmed story about a rumored love affair between President Chen and his female aide. The outspoken vice president decided to sue for libel Taiwan's premier political news magazine, *The Journalist*, which had printed the story. In mid-January, the serious oil spill from a Greek oil tanker off the coast of Pintung County demonstrated the ineptitude of the Environmental Protection Administration in conducting rescue and clean-up operations. Of all those events, the discontinuation of the building of the Fourth Nuclear Power Plant is no doubt the most important, because the project is one-third completed. To discontinue the construction would not only waste the investment that has already been made but would also involve the payment of hundreds of billions of New Taiwan dollars in damages to local and foreign contractors and costs in restoring the construction site. Meanwhile, the about-face has shaken the confidence of foreign investors, who found the DPP government to be not only antinuclear but also antibusiness. Nevertheless, an antinuclear policy has been the sacred campaign platform of all DPP candidates in every election. President Chen's platform was no exception. The party decided not to budge an inch.

In November 2000, Premier Chang brought the issue to the Judicial Yuan to seek the interpretation of the Council of Grand Justices to vindicate its position on the constitutionality of the decision to discontinue the construction of the plant. The council's interpretation (number 520), released on January 15, 2001, did not use the word violation, as in "violation of the Constitution," to describe the decision, but the *ratio decedendi* clearly opined to that effect. The interpretation stated that the decision was procedurally flawed, and the Judicial Yuan asked the Executive Yuan to report to the Legislative Yuan the reasons for its decision. On January 30, the Legislative Yuan called a provisional meeting to hear Premier Chang's report and decided by a vote of 134 to 70 to demand that the Executive Yuan (cabinet) resume construction right away.

The DPP caucus in the Legislative Yuan, the DPP headquarters, the Executive Yuan, and the Presidential Office initially intended to fight the issue to the last member. Yet public opinion began to support the resumption of construction and called for an end to interparty struggles. President Chen decided to change his mind in early February amid strong objections to and criticism from the DPP headquarters and the Legislative Yuan caucus regarding continuation of the construction. Premier Chang officially announced the continuation of construction of the Fourth Nuclear Power Plant on February 16, 2001, on the one hand, but hinted that he favored a plebiscite on this issue to be held together with the year-end Legislative Yuan election, on the other hand. The plebiscite issue exploded in the Legislative Yuan in late February when it was back in session. Many opposition legislators criticized the premier both for his previous decision, which they judged to be wrong, and for his latest error of judgment.

Meanwhile, antinuclear groups in Taiwan organized a demonstration on February 24 to protest the cabinet's about-face on the Fourth Nuclear Power Plant. They demanded a plebiscite. They planned to assemble 100,000–200,000 people, but, according to the police, only 8,800 turned out on that day. The crowd included DPP leaders and one cabinet member. The Taipei media expressed their amazement at the need for a ruling party to take a public policy issue onto the streets.

If the situation is looked at as a whole, the Fourth Nuclear Power Plant issue has paralyzed Taiwan's politics and, to some extent, its economy for more than four months. The plunge in the stock market, the depressed economy, the business community's disillusionment, and the general public's widespread loss of confidence have not seemed to teach the DPP government any lessons. Another round of political struggle is quietly ready to begin. *The China Times*, a major newspaper in Taiwan, commented in its editorial, "[f]rom October 4, 2000, to February 17, 2001, the 137 days of Premier Chang just seemed to have vanished; nothing seemed to have happened. Everything is back to square one."[42] When it became apparent that the restoration of the plant would occur, the stock market, quite interestingly, began to go up a bit. It is clear that the message was delivered to President Chen and his staff.

The economic downturn, mounting unemployment and crime rates, and political instability have combined to make Taiwan's outlook appear dismal at the beginning of the new century. In the area of cross-strait relations, the business community has long expected the DPP government to take bolder action vis-à-vis the Chinese mainland and to improve the economic situation in Taiwan. Again, the DPP government has not moved fast enough to sustain the confidence of the business community. There have been enough domestic troubles to make them rather cautious and even conservative. Other than the three mini-links, the DPP government has taken little action to date.

Questionable Assumptions and Unenthusiastic Action

President Chen and his staff believe that as long as he promises not to declare Taiwan's independence, the PRC will have little reason to use force against Taiwan. In their opinion, there is no need to respond too soon or to make too many concessions too fast, particularly on issues such as the 1992 Consensus and the one-China principle, in general. They have concluded that the United States, generally pleased with President Chen's performance so far; will not exert pressure on Taiwan, especially at a time when the new American president needs some time to develop an understanding of the intricacies of China policy. They also believe that the resumption of the Koo-Wang talks is not indispensable to maintaining good cross-strait relations. Permitting the three mini-links could have the same result. Vice President Lu said that the Koo-Wang talks are like "walking through the back door."[43] The government prefers to negotiate the establishment of the three links after the two sides become members of the WTO. They are convinced that the immediate priority is to continue pleasing the United States and the international community by not provoking the PRC. President Chen said in December 2000 that there should be no problem on cross-strait relations in the following year. Consequently, there is no need to make any concession on the issue of one China. In mid-February, the president said that his "lawyerly character" has given him the necessary pragmatism to handle cross-strait relations. He emphasized that the table is set and the tea is ready. He again invited leaders of the PRC to resume talks with Taiwan.

The above is based on a collection of policy statements made over the last nine months by leaders and officials of the DPP government. Ever since May 20, 2000, the DPP government—including the Presidential Office, the Executive Yuan, and the MAC—has not made public a single comprehensive policy paper that explains clearly and thoroughly its approach to cross-strait relations. The media, academia, and the opposition parties have had to make guesses about what the DPP government wants to do next.

Obviously, some of its assumptions are flawed. First, responding to the one-China principle does not mean making concessions to the PRC, but merely acknowledges an obligation derived from the Constitution. All four former presidents of the ROC in the past 50 years adhered to that principle and did not surrender to the PRC. As president of the ROC, Chen should have understood the history and reasoning very well. By evading that duty he is apparently neglecting his mandate. On the other hand, according to the 1992 Consensus, Taiwan is entitled to a different interpretation of the term *one China*, and the only interpretation of one China permitted by the Constitution is the ROC. This interpretation is obviously not acceptable to the PRC, but neither is the PRC's official interpretation of one China acceptable to Taiwan. Both of them have to settle their differences according to the 1992 Consensus. That is precisely the usefulness of the 1992 Consensus—agree to disagree.

Second, the resumption of cross-strait talks is possible only when the one-China issue is resolved, shelved, or at least managed. Meanwhile, the resumption of talks would facilitate the establishment of the three links wanted so eagerly by Taiwan's business community. Consequently, the current inaction on the part of the DPP government is not in the interest of Taiwan. In effect, the status quo—namely, the official go slow policy—is most unfavorable to Taiwan's interest in the sense that the PRC could get the capital and talent it wants from Taiwan without giving anything in return. Instead, Taiwan sits there, unable to do anything about the westward flow of capital and talent. Even President Yuan T. Lee said that time is not on Taiwan's side.

Third, the entry of Taiwan and the PRC into the WTO and the negotiations on the three links are not necessarily connected. The PRC's admission has been stalled because negotiations with the European Union have not resolved differences. Even if both sides enter the WTO this year, there is no guarantee that cross-strait negotiations would automatically take place right away. The PRC could still insist that the one-China issue be resolved first. Therefore, the issue cannot be evaded. Taiwan has to find a way to handle it when it joins the WTO before the end of this year, as is generally expected. It seems pointless for the two sides to wait until they have entered the WTO to begin negotiations. If they do, it would only cause further delays in improving cross-strait relations.

Fourth, going back to the 1992 Consensus or beginning to negotiate the three links issue does not mean any concession to the PRC. As pointed out earlier, the ROC Constitution is a one-China constitution. Furthermore, Taiwan business people want to trade with and invest directly in the Chinese mainland. It is in the interest of Taiwan to expand economic relations with the mainland and to inject some orderliness into the status quo. The process would involve expansion, not concessions.

Fifth, whether there will be problems in cross-strait relations in the coming year is anybody's guess. But one should keep in mind that the 16th Congress of the Chinese Communist Party will take place in October 2002. President Jiang Zemin's potential competitors could criticize his performance on two fronts: U.S.-PRC relations and cross-strait relations. It is only natural for him to take a strong and inflexible stance as the date approaches for the congress to convene. On the other hand, the next presidential election in Taiwan will be held in March 2004, and the election campaign will begin no later than the fall of 2003, if not earlier. The candidates will not want to look weak in their advocacy of policy toward the PRC. Consequently, the years 2002 and 2003 will not be suitable for such ice-breaking talks by senior officials on either side. The year 2001 is the only year that offers an opportunity to the two sides of the Taiwan Strait to resolve their differences with minimal influence from domestic factors. Given that mutual trust has not been established, there is much confidence building still to be done. It is imperative for the two sides to make meaningful efforts to break the stalemate this year. Inaction in improving cross-strait relations could cost Taiwan dearly in lost opportunities.

The DPP Government's New Three No's in Policy Formulation: No Consistency, No Coherence, and No Vision

The general impression of the DPP government's mainland policy and its implementation is that it is rife with inconsistency and incoherence. The flip-flop on the 1992 Consensus in June 2000, as stated above, is only one example of policy inconsistency; there have been many more. The discrepancies in the president's and the vice president's remarks on cross-strait relations, between those of the president and the MAC, between those of the vice president and the MAC chairwoman, the DPP chairman and secretary general, and DPP headquarters and its Legislative Yuan caucus appear so frequently in the media that few people really understand the thrust of the DPP government's mainland policy. In addition, the MAC, the cabinet agency in charge of the formulation of mainland policy, has not published a single policy paper that clearly outlines the DPP government's goals, strategy, and implementation timetable. It is generally recognized that this can be attributed to the DPP's ideology-oriented decision-making process. President Chen told a foreign journalist that he is an "ethnic Chinese,"[44] giving the impression that he is a resident of Chinese descent in a foreign country. Premier Chang did no better when he was asked whether he was Chinese. He said, "something similar to that."[45] The result of such kinds of decision making oriented in ideology is a lack of vision and direction and much distortion. In other words, as long as there is no immediate threat across the Taiwan Straits and the United States is pleased, the DPP government is reluctant to take any action to improve cross-strait relations, let alone touch the issue of one China.

The Inability To Make Proper Responses

In the past nine months the PRC has generally adopted a listen to what he says and watch what he does attitude, but it has occasionally modified certain policies regarding Taiwan. For instance, the PRC's Vice Premier Qian Qichen said during an interview with *The Washington Post* in early January 2001 that there is only one China, China is composed of the mainland and Taiwan, and China's sovereignty and territory cannot be divided.[46] He also said that the one-China, two-systems formula still leaves some room for discussion. This is obviously intended to dispel doubts that one China means only the PRC and that one country, two systems is a one-size-fits-all formula for Hong Kong and Taiwan. Part of the new wording on one China is almost identical to that in the National Unification Guidelines.[47] Many people believe that PRC Vice Premier Qian quietly accepted the National Unification Guidelines' definition of one China. Meanwhile, there seems to be a certain flexibility in the stringent one-country, two-systems formula. In addition, the PRC has also quietly changed its policy regarding the visits of Taiwan's local government officials in their official capacity. In the past, officials from Taiwan who were visiting the Chinese mainland were invariably addressed as "Mr./Ms. So-and-So," not by their official titles. They were referred to not as officials but as "well-known personalities from Taiwan." Now they are addressed by their official titles. When Bai Hsiung-hsiung, deputy mayor of Taipei, visited Shanghai in September of last year and in February of this year, he was invariably addressed as deputy mayor. Feng Guoqin, Shanghai's deputy mayor, who visited Taipei in early January 2001, had no difficulty in addressing the author as Mayor Ma. This is a far cry from the situation that existed barely one year ago.

Unfortunately, the DPP government did not grasp the opportunity to respond properly. It could have said in public that Taiwan welcomes such statements and made corresponding suggestions for improving cross-strait relations. On the other hand, the MAC could also have taken advantage of the PRC's new attitude to make new regulations governing the exchange of local government officials across the Taiwan Strait. For instance, DPP Chairman Frank Hsieh, currently the mayor of Kaohsiung City, was invited by the mayor of Xiamen (Amoy) to visit that city, but his application, submitted to the MAC in July 2000, is still pending in the MAC. It was reported that President Chen had received a confidential intelligence report that Mr. Hsieh's itinerary in the Chinese mainland included several improper activities that could fall into the PRC's united-front trap. One can only come to the conclusion that the DPP government is only interested in pleasing the Americans but not interested in improving cross-strait relations. All indications are that such a policy cannot last for long.

On the other hand, it is not fair to blame the DPP government alone for its inability to make proper responses. The PRC should be blamed as well because it, too, has failed to respond properly on at least three occasions: President Chen's inaugural address, the inauguration of the three mini-links, and President Chen's Cross-Century Remarks. Had the leaders of the PRC said in public that they considered these statements or actions positive and they were willing to pursue them further, President Chen would have been encouraged to continue along the same lines. Precisely because of inaction on the part of the PRC, the only advice President Chen received from his mainland affairs advisers was not to proceed further and to take a wait-and-see attitude. Such an unfortunate retrogression is clearly due to unfamiliarity and a lack of mutual trust, which will take both time and additional exchanges to develop. The key is for each side to give the other the benefit of the doubt and to respond positively whenever an opportunity arises.

BREAKING THE IMPASSE AND MAKING A BREAKTHROUGH: A CONSCIENTIOUS PROPOSAL TO THE DPP GOVERNMENT

Going Back to the 1992 Consensus

The DPP's Taiwan Independence Party charter makes accepting the one-China principle extremely difficult. But unless such a principle is accepted, there is no possibility that the two sides will resume the talks between SEF and ARATS that have been interrupted since 1995. The DPP government is feeling pressure to take action. In fact, it could not be otherwise for the ruling party of the ROC. Even President Chen and Chairman Frank Hsieh of the DPP agree that the ROC Constitution is a one-China constitution, whether they like it or not. The DPP fears that once Taiwan accepts the one-China principle, it will fall into the hands of the PRC. Consequently, the party refuses to budge. If pressure were insurmountable, then party leaders would delay the decision as long as possible. In fact, all these problems are fraught with difficulty, but were thoroughly discussed nine years ago in the NUC Research Group and in the MAC. The conclusion was a middle-ground solution, namely, the 1992 Consensus—one China with different interpretations by each side. This formula balances the constitutional requirement of one China and the cross-strait reality of two political entities. It is flexible enough to give both sides room to maneuver but not too flexible to deviate from the one-China principle. If President Chen accepts the 1992 Consensus, he would not compromise the ROC's sovereignty and dignity because the consensus not only conforms to the ROC Constitution but would also improve cross-strait relations because he would be honoring a commitment Taiwan made nine years ago.

Restore the Operation of the NUC or Combine the Council with the Cross-Party Group

The existence of the NUC has vital symbolic meaning in the cross-strait context. The PRC has never liked it; its propaganda machine used to criticize it as the National Nonunification Council. The NUC nevertheless conveys a clear sense that Taiwan has not abandoned the goal of China's reunification and plans to pursue that goal, although current differences in ways of life of the two sides now make it difficult if not impossible to set a timetable for China's eventual reunification. This is the only nexus that could hold the two sides together politically. The absence of such a nexus would make peace and stability across the Taiwan Strait even more remote. Therefore, President Chen should consider acting as the NUC's chairman or combine the NUC and the Cross-Party Group and act as the head of the new organization. He could expand the composition of these organizations to include TI supporters if they are willing to join. If the operation of the NUC is restored, or if the NUC and the Cross-Party Group are combined and President Chen acts as its head, the message being sent would be loud and clear enough to neutralize the opposition parties in Taiwan and reduce tension across the Taiwan Strait. Moreover, the chances of resuming the Koo-Wang talks would be much greater, if not virtually certain.

Resume the Long-Interrupted Talks between SEF and ARATS

If the steps above are implemented, there should be much less difficulty in resuming the talks between SEF and ARATS. The first step is to re-extend the invitation by SEF to Mr. Wang Daohan, president of ARATS, to visit Taiwan. The visit was originally scheduled in 1999, after the SEF's Koo Chengfu visited the mainland in late 1998, but was canceled when the special state-to-state-relationship theory emerged. If Wang accepts the invitation, it will mean that the PRC is ready to talk to Taiwan.

Prepare for Negotiations on the Three Links Together with Questions Relating to Security Guarantees and International Space

If Wang Daohan is willing to visit Taiwan, then Taiwan should begin to prepare for complicated negotiations on the establishment of the three links under the WTO framework. Taiwan should also include in the agenda questions of security guarantees in the Taiwan Strait and Taiwan's international space. The negotiations would take at least two years because they involve the conclusion of at least five agreements on air transport, ocean transport, postal links, trade, and investment guarantees, among other potential agreements. These agreements would be entered into by two political entities on an equal footing and not by sovereign nations. According to Taiwan's Statute Governing Relations between the People of the Taiwan Area and the People of the Mainland Area (the so-called Mainland Relations Act), these agreements have to be approved by the Legislative Yuan to become legally binding in Taiwan. Subjects such as air transport and trade are too important to be left to negotiations between airlines or trading companies. After all, there is an authority in charge and a complete set of laws and regulations in effect on either side of the Taiwan Strait. Agreements negotiated between companies must be approved by appropriate ministries or bureaus, anyway. Allowing government agencies to negotiate and conclude agreements would make things much easier. Once the negotiations begin, cross-strait relations will be back on track, or at least back to the 1993 level when the first Koo-Wang talk took place.

The issues of security guarantees and international space are too important to be left out of cross-strait negotiations, but they will have to be negotiated separately. They are not only the Taiwan people's focus of concern but also represent the most sensitive taboo for the PRC. Nevertheless, the PRC has indicated many times that as long as the one-China principle is accepted, anything can be negotiated. Meanwhile, international space has been a flash point between the two sides for many years. A certain broad consensus is needed to prevent it, at least, from getting out of control. In any case, the inclusion of these two issues would not mean that they are readily solvable at the moment, but would show the sincerity of both sides to face the issues squarely.

PROSPECTS FOR THE FUTURE

The past nine months have attested to the continuance of the cross-strait stalemate that began in 1995. Both sides have maintained a wait-and-see attitude toward each other. Although the chances of confrontation have decreased, there have been few signs of improvement. The interrupted Koo-Wang talks and other consultations between SEF and ARATS have not resumed. Meanwhile, Taiwan's trade with and direct investment in the Chinese mainland have continued to increase rapidly, ignoring the go-slow policy of the ROC government. For instance, two-way trade jumped 21 percent from U.S. $25.9 billion in 1999 to U.S. $31.3 billion in 2000, with a surplus of almost U.S. $20 million in Taiwan's favor.[48] Investment stood at U.S. $48 billion, with more than 40,000 Taiwanese companies investing in the Chinese mainland.[49] Even the high-tech industry in the Hsinchu Science-Based Industrial Park, Taiwan's Silicon Valley, located 78 kilometers southwest of Taipei, showed increasing interest in investing in the Chinese mainland. In economic affairs, Taiwan's competitive edge vis-à-vis the Chinese mainland is facing a serious challenge.

On the other hand, the rise of the DPP to ruling party status changed the political landscape of Taiwan but did not enhance the quality of politics or government efficiency. The past nine months also saw the difficulties and frustrations of a minority president fighting on three fronts: the opposition parties (KMT, PFP, and NP), his own party (DPP headquarters and the Legislative Yuan caucus), and the other side of the Taiwan Strait (the PRC). President Chen did well in his inaugural address by announcing the Five No's. But what followed was less than satisfactory. Many factors contributed to the inconsistency and incoherence of President Chen's approach to cross-strait relations during this period, the most important being the ideology underlying the DPP's party charter, namely, TI. The flip-flop on the 1992 Consensus is a typical example, which is why the PRC still considers President Chen to be a soft TI supporter.

A consensus is quietly building among many knowledgeable people in Taiwan—officials, academicians, and business people alike—that time is not on

Taiwan's side and that maintaining the status quo is not in Taiwan's interest. The DPP government's grand strategy, designed not to provoke the PRC, is appropriate, but hardly sufficient to break the stalemate across the Taiwan Strait and steer the course of events in Taiwan's favor. Something positive has to be done and done properly in a timely and consistent manner to change the atmosphere so that a benign rather than a vicious cycle can emerge in cross-strait relations.

Despite all these difficulties, President Chen's New Year's message could fundamentally change the course of the DPP government's approach to cross-strait relations, if he is able to push it through. His blueprint for the future of Taiwan and the PRC is a "political structure based on eternal peace and political integration." This formula is broad enough to cover almost all possible scenarios, including those of the opposition parties but not that of the TI fundamentalists, for the ultimate future of Taiwan and the PRC. It could mean federation, confederation, a commonwealth of states, or even a European Union–type of association. As a matter of fact, the second phase of cross-strait relations under the National Unification Guidelines, which the three opposition parties support, can be called the integration phase, in which the two sides will establish official relations, initiate the three links, and begin regular exchange visits between high-ranking officials. To make the new concept workable, however, President Chen must first develop a comprehensive and coherent policy and strategy and speak and act consistently in the future. Second, he has to coordinate DPP officials in the Executive Yuan, party officials in the DPP headquarters, and officials in the DPP caucus in the Legislative Yuan to make sure that they all agree with him on this concept. Third, he has to bring the opposition parties into the consensus-building process in future dealings with the PRC. Fourth, he has to propose the initiative in a more concrete form at a proper time to engage the PRC. All these efforts will be difficult to accomplish but are worth trying. After all, whether President Chen handled cross-strait relations well will be one of the most important criteria in assessing the success or failure of his presidency.

If President Chen is able to do so, it could also usher in a new strategic scenario affecting regional stability in East Asia. In the international arena, cross-strait political integration could mean a regional role for Taiwan, disassociated from right-wing Japanese forces, in building a contained China united front and in avoiding an arms race with the PRC. Taiwan could then play a role in fostering Sino-Japanese detente and promoting the growth of a stability-oriented East Asian regionalism.[50] On the cross-strait front, political integration could mean the process of building a loosely associated new entity composed of Taiwan, the PRC, Hong Kong, and Macao based on economic, cultural, and other kinds of integration. This would mean the demise of the active nation-building efforts some have vigorously pursued in the past in Taiwan. On the other hand, for Taiwan and the PRC, this new form of association could deliver both independence and reunification at the same time. Of course, the new arrangement would involve a decision that not only President Chen would make, but one that would pose a common challenge to all the people of Taiwan and the Chinese mainland.

The stability of cross-strait relations in the next three years depends a lot on how President Chen handles it. As the past has shown, his personal character shapes his leadership style, which in turn determines his policy orientation. In this regard, let us not forget that President Chen is a supporter of TI, but is not a fundamentalist. He is a pragmatist, not an ideologue. One should not overestimate his political beliefs nor underestimate his flexibility in handling cross-strait relations. His inaction at the moment could mean that he is waiting for the opportune time to make necessary adjustments, just as he did in the controversy over the continued construction of the Fourth Nuclear Power Plant a while ago.

NOTES

1. "Zhongtong daxuan chenshuibian dangxu an, zhengquan biantian, guomindang xiaye" ("Chen Shui-bian Elected, Administration Changed Hands, KMT Lost Power"), *Lianhe Bao* (*United Daily News*), 19 March, 2000, p. 1; "Decision in Taiwan: Taiwan Nationalist Ousted After Half-Century Reign," *The New York Times*, 19 March, 2000, p. A1.

2. "Tangfei qingci duowei shouzhang gandao kexi, Linjunyi buyuan huiying" ("Tang Fei Resigns; Many Cabinet Members Express Regret; Lin Junyi Declines Comment"), *Taiwan Ribao* (*Taiwan Daily News*), 4 October, 2000, p. 2.

3. "Tsai Ying-wen: liangguolun zhongyao muliao" ("Tsai Ying-wen: The Key Staff Member for the State-to-State Theory"), *Lianhe Bao* (*United Daily News*), 12 April, 2000, p. 3.

4. "Meilianshe qian ershida xinwen paihangbang chulu, Taiwan bangshangyouming" ("Taiwan Is on the List of AP Top Twenty News Items"), *Central News Agency*, 26 December, 2000.

5. President Chen's Profile. Available from The Office of the President of the Republic of China World Wide Web site: http://www.oop.gov.tw/1_president/index.html.

6. "Ma yingjiou, Xie changting dangxuan" ("Ma Ying-jeou and Hsieh Chang-ting Elected"), *Zhongyang Ribao* (*Central Daily News*), 6 December, 1998, p. 1; "Nationalists Oust Taipei Mayor in Vote Watched by China," *The New York Times*, 6 December, 1998, p. A6.

7. "Chenshuibian: quanming zhengfu tixian xinzhongjian luxian" ("Chen Shuibian Says All People's Government Embodies New Middle Road"), *Zhongguo Shibao* (*China Times*), 19 January, 2000, p. 4.

8. "Chenshuibian: Tiangan tanpan yizhong shi yiti fei qianti" ("Chen Sbui-bian Says in Cross-Strait Negotiation, One China Is a Topic Rather Than a Precondition"), *Zhongyang Ribao* (*Central Daily News*), 21 March, 2000, p. 3.

9. *Lifayuan gongbao* (*Legislative Yuan Bulletin*), vol. 80, issue 24, no. 2448, 22 March, 1991, pp. 201–204.

10. "Weilal liangan guanxi ren manbu jingji" ("Still a Bumpy Road Ahead for Future Cross-Strait Relations"), *Zhongguo Shibao* (*China Times*), 14 March, 2000, p. 1.

11. "Dui Taiwan xin lingdaoren yi tingqiyan guanqixing" ("Taiwan's New Leader, PRC Should Listen to What He Says and Watch What He Does"), *Wenhuibao*, 19 March, 2000, p. A3.

12. Shui-bian Chen, victory speech after the presidential election, March 18, 2000. Available from the World Wide Web: http://www.oop.gov.tw/1_president/index_e.html.

13. "Chenshuibian: wuerling hou liangan guanxi ke youxiao gaishan" ("Chen Shui-bain Says Cross-Strait Relations Can Be Improved Markedly After May 20"), *Lianhe Bao* (*United Daily News*), 17 May, 2000, p. 1.

14. "Zuixin mindiao xianshi Chenshuibian biaoxian liuchengwu minzhong manyi" ("The Latest Poll Shows 65% Approval Rate for Chen Shui-bian"), a survey conducted in May 2000. Available from the *China Times* World Wide Web site: http://www.chinatimes.com.tw/report/abian2000/89508p50.htm.

15. "Jiouzhi manyue jizhehui hou, chen zongtong shengwang shangsheng dao qichengjiou" (Poll Shows President Chen's Approval Rate Rises to 79% after His One-Month-in-Office Press Conference), *Lianhe Bao* (*United Daily News*), 22 June, 2000, p. 2.

16. Shui-bian Chen, Inaugural Speech, May 20, 2000. Available from the World Wide Web: http://www.mac.gov.tw/english/Mac Policy/cb0520e.htm.

17. Presidential Press Conference, June 20, 2000. Available from The Office of the President of the Republic of China World Wide Web site: http://www.oop.gov.tw/1_president/index.html.

18. Chen zongtong jieshou yige zhongguo gezi biaoshu? Minjindan liwei chijing, zaiyedang kending" ("President Chen to Accept 'One China with Different Interpretations?' DPP Law Makers Stunned While Opposition Parties Applauded"), *Ziyou Shibao* (*The Liberty Times*), 29 June, 2000, p. 2.

19. Mainland Affairs Council's Press Conference, June 28, 2000. Available from the MAC World Wide Web site: http://www.mac.gov.tw/cnews/cnews89062803.htm.

20. "Tsai Ying-wen: jiouer nian liangan huitan gongshi, wofang renzhi shi gezi biaoshu yige zhongguo" ("Tsai Ying-wen Says the Consensus Reached by the Two Sides in 1992 Was 'Each Side Differently Interprets One China'"), *Gongshang Shibao*, 7 July, 2000, p. 11.

21. "92 gongshi, haijihui wenj ian mingzheng" ("92 Consensus: One SEF Document Clearly Proves It"), *Zhongyang Ribao* (*Central Daily News*), 25 October, 2000, p. 4.

22. "Guwang huitan yibo sanzhe, qioutang cuoshang juechu fengsheng" ("Koo-Wang Talks Encounter a Variety of Barriers, Chiou-Tang Meeting Rises from Death"), *Ziyou Shibao* (*The Liberty Times*), 29 April, 1993, p. 2.

23. Presidential Press Conference, July 31, 2000. Available from The Office of the President of the Republic of China World Wide Web site: http://www.oop.gov.tw/1_president/index.html.

24. "Tsai Ying-wen: weijian zugo minzhong zhichi yizhongyuanze" ("Tsai Ying-wen Says Not Enough Support for One China"), *Zhongyang Ribao* (*Central Daily News*), 21 October, 2000, p. 2.

25. "Tsai Ying-wen: jinma xlaosantong xiwang niandiqian shishi" ("Tsai Ying-wen Says Kinmen and Matsu Hope for Mini-Three Links to Be Implemented Before Year End"), *Lianhe Bao* (*United Daily News*), 5 June, 2000, p. 1.

26. *China Yearbook, 1958–59* (Taipei, China Publishing Co., 1959), pp. 2–3.

27. "Liangan xlaosantongyingxiangpingguji guihua fangxiang" ("The Impact of Evaluation and Direction Setting on the Mini-Three Links Between the Two Sides"),

2 October, 2000. Availabe from the MAC World Wide Web site: http://www.mac.gov.tw/economy/emlOO2.htm.

28. *Zohongguo Shibao* (*China Times*), 2 January, 1979, p. 1.

29. "Liangan xiaosantong jinma in zhengshi qihang" ("The Mini-Three Links Kicks Off Today at Kinmen and Matsu"), *Lianhe Bao* (*United Daily News*), 2 January, 2001, p. 1.

30. Available from the MAC World Wide Web site: http://www.mac.gov.tw.

31. "Matsu mindai mifu Fuzhou xieshang, Luweihui chen wei shouquan, wu falu xiaoli" ("Matsu's Elected Representative Sneaked to Fuzhou to Negotiate. The Mainland Affairs Council Said the Agreement Had No Authorization, Hence No Legal Force"), *Lianhe Bao* (*United Daily News*), 29 January, 2001, p. 1.

32. "Matsu Mawei jiaoliu xieyi shu minjian gotong" ("Accord Between Matsu and Mawei Is Private-Sector Communication"), *Zhongguo Shibao* (*China Times*), 30 January, 2001, p. 4.

33. "Kuadangpai xiaozu jianyi Chen zhongtong yixian hujying duian yizhong zhuzhang" ("Cross-Party Group Suggests that President Chen Respond to the PRC's 'One-China' Stance in Accordance with the Constitution"), *Zohongguo Shibao* (*China Times*), 27 November, 2000, p. 1.

34. "Dui kuadangpai xiaozu sanrenzhi sijianyi Beijing pingwei wenzi youxi, luweihui yihan" ("MAC Regrets Beijing Considers the Cross-Party Group's Three Understandings and Four Suggestions a Game of Words"), *Zhongguo Shibao* (*China Times*), 1 December, 2000, p. 1.

35. Available from The Office of the President of the Republic of China World Wide Web site: http://www.oop.gov.tw/1_news/index_e.html.

36. "Tonghelun Tsai Ying-wen zhi yu zongtong wu qijian" ("Tsai Ying-wen Says She and the President Have No Different Views on the Integration Theory"), *Lianhe Bao* (*United Daily News*), 20 January, 2001, p. 4.

37. "Chi-yuan Lin, Hesi juice cuowu, Renmin sunshi canzilong" ("The Wrong Decision Making on the Fourth Nudear Plant Cost Heavily"), 8 January, 2001, National Policy Foundation Commentary. Available from the World Wide Web: http://www.npf.org.tw/Publication/FM/090/C/FM-C-090-004 .htm.

38. "Unemployment rate in January 2001." Available from the Directorate-General of Budget, Accounting and Statistics World Wide Web site: http://www.dgbasey.gov.tw/.

39. "Shangyue zhongda touzi jiao qunien tongqi shuaitui 50%" ("Large Domestic Investment Cases in January Dropped 50% Compared to Last Year") *Lianhe Wanbao* (*United Evening News*), 21 February, 2001, p. 7.

40. A survey conducted by *China Times* on December 28, 2000. Available from the World Wide Web: http://news.sina.com.tw/sinaNews/chinatimes/CFOCUS/2000/1231/2509263.html.

41. A survey conducted by TVBS Poll Center, 26–27 February, 2001. Available from the World Wide Web: http://www.tvbs.com.tw.

42. Editorial, "Jinian pingkong xiaoshi de 137 tian" ("In Memory of the 137 Days that Vanished Without Reasons"), *Zhongguo Shibao* (*China Times*), 21 February, 2001, p. 2.

43. "Luxiulian: liangan buxu guwan hui zou houmen" ("Lu Hsiu-lien: No Need for Koo-Wang Talks to Walk Through the Back Door"). *Zhongguo Shibao* (*China Times*), 6 December, 2000, p. 2.

44. "Chen zongtong: woshi taiwanren, ye yi zuo huaren weirong" ("President Chen Says 'I Am Taiwanese and Proud to Be Ethnic Chinese As Well"), *Lianhe Bao* (*United Daily News*) 18 October, 2000, p. 2.

45. "Zhangkui: zhongguo liangzi fanzhengzhihua, bugan suibianyong" ("Premier Chang Says the Word 'China' Has Been Over Politicized and He Will Not Use It Lightly"), *Zhongguo Shibao* (*China Times*), 21 October, 2000, p. 2.

46. "Beijing Signals New Flexibility on Taiwan; Comments Appear Aimed at Bush," *The Washington Post*, 5 January, 2001, p. Al.

47. National Unification Guidelines, adopted by the National Unification Council at its third meeting on February 23, 1991, and by the Executive Yuan Counci1 at its meeting on March 14, 1991.

48. *Cross-Strait Economic Statistics Monthly* 88 (1999); *Cross-Strait Economic Statistics Monthly* 100 (2000). Available from the Mainland Affairs Council World Wide Web site: http://www.mac.gov.tw.

49. Ibid.

50. "Yun-han Chu, Xinshiji de liangan guanxi luchu yixian shuguang" ("A New Ray of Hope Shed on the Cross-Strait Relations in the New Century"), *Zhongguo Shibao* (*China Times*), 8 January, 2001, p. 2.

Chapter 5

The DPP's Position on Cross-Strait Relations

Wilson Tien

Thank you for the kind introduction. Ladies and [g]entlemen, I am very honored to have the opportunity to talk about the Democratic Progressive Party's cross-strait policy today.

The Democratic Progressive Party (DPP) candidate Chen Shui-bian won the presidential elections on March 18 of last year, resulting in the first peaceful transfer of power in Taiwan. Almost a year has passed since the DPP became the ruling party, yet many people feel that they still do not understand the DPP, especially the DPP's cross-strait policy. Before the DPP became the governing party, many people feared the DPP's more "extreme" or "adventuresome" cross-strait policy might bring about conflict in the Taiwan Strait, thus dragging the U[nited] S[tates] into an unwanted war.

Many people are relieved over President Chen Shui-bian's performance on cross-strait relations since taking office; many applaud his performance and believe his policies are flexible. Some people, however, remain highly skeptical about the DPP's cross-strait policy. For example, some believe that the fundamentalists within the DPP have pressured the president, preventing him from being more flexible on cross-strait issues. While such views are basically groundless, they represent a deep-rooted uneasiness toward the DPP. My job is to explain the DPP position on cross-strait relations and, hopefully, relieve some of this uneasiness.

Let us begin from the DPP's fundamentalist position on Taiwan's sovereignty.

Speech delivered by Wilson Tien on April 20, 2001, to St. John's University, the Dr. Sunyat-Sen Monthly Lecture Series.

The official position of the Democratic Progressive Party is that Taiwan is a sovereign and independent country. According to Taiwan's Constitution, the official name is The Republic of China. The DPP has formally adopted this position in the Resolution Regarding Taiwan's Future passed by the DPP's National Party Congress in 1999.

These statements probably need further elaboration.

First, what does it mean to say, "Taiwan is a sovereign and independent country"?

Taiwan possesses all of the elements of a sovereign state: a legitimate government, population, and a well-defined territory. The fact is that the People's Republic of China [PRC], while claiming sovereignty over Taiwan, has never ruled Taiwan since the PRC's establishment in 1949. Thus, Taiwan is in fact a sovereign country from our perspective.

Yet why is a sovereign country both excluded from international organizations such as the UN and incapable of establishing formal diplomatic relations with the majority of the countries in the world?

The reason is quite simple. It is not a question of whether or not Taiwan is a sovereign state. The reason is that China suppresses Taiwan's international space, a political reality that has nothing to do with whether or not Taiwan is a country.

Try to imagine one scenario. The Chinese leaders wake up one morning and have suddenly changed their attitude regarding Taiwan's international status. They decide not to sabotage Taiwan's efforts to join the UN and not to use their Security Council veto to deny Taiwan['s] UN membership bid. Furthermore, they do not break diplomatic relations with countries that establish official diplomatic relations with Taiwan. Under this scenario, the international community would embrace Taiwan immediately. No one would be surprised if Taiwan became a member of the UN and formed diplomatic relations with the majority of the countries in the world.

Unfortunately, this scenario remains imaginary and no one knows whether or not it will ever occur. Thus, the core problem is not whether Taiwan is a sovereign nation; rather, it is how Taiwan might find a formula of peaceful coexistence with China.

Moreover, when the DPP recognized that Taiwan is already a sovereign and independent country, it also indicated that Taiwan would not declare independence. There is no need to declare independence if Taiwan has been, and is now, in fact, independent. This is where we stand. We believe that Taiwan is a sovereign state and a declaration of independence is not necessary.

Some people were worried that once the DPP came into power, it might declare independence, leading to immediate conflict across the strait and forcing U[nited] S[tates] involvement. There is no such possibility given the DPP's fundamental policies outlined above. In fact, after the inauguration of President Chen Shui-bian in May of last year, no one has expressed concerns over the Chen administration's cross-strait policy. President Chen's actions have matched the DPP's fundamental principles. There is no difference between what the DPP stands for and what the administration has done so far.

With regard to the official name, "The Republic of China," those familiar with the history of the DPP all know that DPP politicians have complex feelings about the name "The Republic of China." The main reason is that we believe that the name Republic of China cannot appropriately represent Taiwan. In fact, the official name of the country is not of vital importance to us, as long as it properly represents Taiwan and does not confuse international society. The name "Republic of China" often does, in fact, confuse the international community into thinking of Taiwan as China. It is thus not a suitable name for Taiwan. Because of that, the DPP platform calls for "the establishment of a sovereign and independent Republic of Taiwan" by a referendum.

But we also try to understand the reality we are facing right now. If Taiwan changed its official name from the Republic of China to the Republic of Taiwan or something else, then it would be too sensitive an act. It could be interpreted by China as a refusal of any possibility of unification and a highly provocative act. Once Taiwan touches that sensitive "one China" nerve, there is a likelihood of a conflict in the strait. Thus, although the DPP has problems with the name the Republic of China, it is willing to accept the name and will not seek to change it in the foreseeable future.

Perhaps some people think that the DPP's position is extreme in this insistence on a sovereign Taiwan. How does it plan to face China's "one-China" principle? Is a conflict inevitable in the Taiwan Strait?

Before answering these questions, we need to explain how the DPP views Taiwan's relations with China.

First, we understand that Taiwan's geographical position cannot be moved around.

Perhaps some people think it is funny when I mention this fact; no tectonic plate can be moved freely. Indeed, it is extremely meaningful to recognize this fact when formulating our China policy.

If there were quite a distance between Taiwan and China, Taiwan would have more freedom and space. The reality, however, leaves Taiwan relatively fewer choices given its physical proximity to China.

Second, we recognize that China is a unified and powerful neighbor.

China's size is approximately 300 times that of Taiwan, and its population is about 60 times that of Taiwan. If China is not unified or is a comparatively weak country, then Taiwan would probably have more options.

Third, perhaps due to strategic reasons, history, or nationalism, China strongly advocates the unification of Taiwan and China. If Taiwan defies its wishes, China will use force to attack Taiwan, forcing Taiwan to became a part of China.

For the above reasons, the DPP believes that, unless fundamental changes occurred in China, peaceful coexistence between Taiwan and China relies upon a paradigm acceptable to both parties. Otherwise, any unilateral, radical move on the part of Taiwan will actually create a difficult problem for Taiwan's future. Because, as I mentioned, Taiwan cannot be moved around, we must face our neighbors.

For example, if China does not change and Taiwan takes advantage of the inharmonious relationship between the U[nited] S[tates] and China and rejects any possibility of unification, China will harass Taiwan over the long run, and there will be no peace in the Taiwan Strait.

With a clear understanding of the scenario I just described, the DPP is willing to think about a political arrangement that can guarantee peaceful coexistence between Taiwan and China. Yet we also do understand that such a political arrangement requires negotiations and might well include some negotiations on sovereignty issues. That is to say, given the above-mentioned realities and recognitions, we believe that Taiwan might be able to set up a deal in which Taiwan sacrifices a part of its sovereignty in exchange for permanent peace across the strait, as long as the proposed political arrangement is reasonable, worthwhile, and acceptable to the Taiwanese people.

Fortunately, there are historical cases of using partial sovereignty in exchange for peace, such as the European Union, the Commonwealth, or a even confederate system. Those cases can serve as possible themes of political dialogue across the strait. On several occasions, President Chen Shui-bian has mentioned that "one China" can be an issue on the agenda for political negotiations across the strait. This is exactly what he meant when he said that.

Currently, the political arrangement proposed by China is limited to the one country, two systems model.

Chinese leaders have continuously guaranteed Taiwan its own army and its own leader and promised that everything will remain the same after Taiwan accepts the one country, two systems model. Such guarantees, however, only exist based on the goodwill of the Chinese leaders, without any third-party guarantors. We are quite reserved with regard to their guarantees. To Taiwan, "one country, two systems" means that Taiwan abandons all of its sovereignty in return for a peace without any guarantees, but only goodwill. Taiwan will never accept such an exchange, which is recognized only as a surrender.

Some people have made the following analogy: China is like a neighboring tiger and Taiwan is a rabbit that must face the tiger. The rabbit's goal is survival. The tiger then says to the rabbit do not fear, as long as you come to my house and live with me and accept my arrangement, I will give you sufficient freedom and I promise not to eat you. Should the rabbit trust the tiger's goodwill and jump into the tiger's place? Or should the rabbit look for ways to guarantee its survival while negotiating with the tiger? In that case, there is still an opportunity for the rabbit to live even if negotiation fails. If the rabbit believes in the tiger's friendly gesture and moves in with the tiger, and if and only if the tiger keeps its promises, then the rabbit will be safe. But if the tiger has second thoughts, then the rabbit has made the wrong choice; it has no way out but to die. This is why we are not interested in China's one country, two systems proposal. There is no sure guarantee but only goodwill in such a proposal.

The basic condition for any acceptable scenario for Taiwan seems to rest on Taiwan and China being on equal footing. Equality between the two sides as a basis offers some guarantees for Taiwan.

Our belief in the inevitability of a final political arrangement, coupled with our sensitivity regarding the two sides being equal, sparked an interest in the recent statements by the Chinese Vice Premier Qian Qichen.

Since last year, Mr. Qian Qichen stated that "[t]here is only one China, the mainland and Taiwan both belong to that one China; China's sovereignty and territory cannot be divided." After reiterating such remarks on numerous occasions, Qian's statements seemed to have gradually become the new basis for China's Taiwan policy. Or have they?

Many American experts on cross-strait relations and officials have expressed interest in the new three statements for the flexibility that has not been present previously. Therefore, they asked Taiwan to respond positively to Qian's remarks.

From the DPP's perspective, Qian's new three statements are more flexible than China's previously rigid position, but we all have some doubts.

1. In the White Paper titled *The Taiwan Question and the One China Principle*, published in the year 2000, before Taiwan's presidential elections, the one China principle is defined as "there is only one China in the world; Taiwan is part of China, the People's Republic of China is the only legitimate government of China." Mr. Qian Qichen's new statements seem to conflict with those of the White Paper, which makes us wonder which one actually represents the official position of China, Qian's version or the White Paper version.
2. The occasion's in which Qian Qichen proposed the new three statements have been meetings with Taiwanese visitors or the Taiwanese media. One wonders if this is propaganda exclusively for Taiwan or is it a formal position that can be announced to the international community?
3. How is possible to have a political arrangement based on undivided sovereignty while ensuring equal footing between the two?

Although we still have doubts about Qian's remarks, we believe this is at least a good beginning. It indicates that China gradually is coming to understand Taiwan's position. China has begun to pay attention to how Taiwan reacts to its words. This should be a good development for future interaction across the strait.

In the future, will peace exist in the Taiwan Strait, or is it already plagued by a possible conflict?

It seems that at least in the next few years there will be peace in the Taiwan Strait. First, China does not possess the necessary military capabilities to invade Taiwan. Second, China has set economic development as its priority. The resolution of the Taiwan problem will not be one of China's top priorities.

Other events on the timetable for China include the APEC meeting to be held in Shanghai in November, possible entry into the WTO this year, China's bid for the 2008 Olympic Games, and more importantly, China's political succession next year. The Chinese leadership will be preoccupied by these events, therefore maintaining cross-strait relations at a moderate level will be in their best interest.

Whether the U[nited] S[tates] adjusts its China policy will also be a major factor that greatly influences the stability of the Taiwan Strait.

What about the longer-term future? Will Taiwan and China find a mutually satisfactory political arrangement within the next 10–20 years? How might the relationship between Taiwan and China develop?

To answer these questions, I may need to further clarify the Democratic Progressive Party's view on Taiwan-China relations in the future.

If the Chinese economy moves forward, then the best scenario for Taiwan is that economic development brings about democratic reforms in China. Hopefully, the Chinese leadership will recognize that democracy is still the best system to deal with domestic political conflicts. And China is destined to have more and more conflicts as its economy continues to develop.

A more democratic and prosperous China will be more attractive to Taiwan. China will also have more confidence in itself, facilitating a different and more flexible paradigm of permanent peaceful coexistence across the strait. We believe that a more confident, prosperous, and democratic China will provide the best opportunity for cross-strait peace. A petty China that lacks confidence and that believes in the active development of military strength to survive will probably destroy any opportunity of cross-strait peace.

Ultimately, the direction of China's development is not for us to decide. In the past 10 years, China's military budget has increased by at least 15 percent every year. China's strategy in the Asia Pacific region seems to be focused on eliminating the U.S. influence. This development concerns us.

We hope that with China's economic development, there will be a reduction in China's interest in using military power to obtain leadership in Asia. If China can learn to use influence, rather than military might, to affect neighboring countries, then this will be the best result for Taiwan, other Asian neighbors, and even the U[nited] S[tates].

If, however, China's development is to change the status quo in Asia, setting the goal of purging U.S. influence, then Taiwan's active pursuit of a settlement with China through a final political arrangement will not correspond with U.S. interests. Taiwan's own interests will also be harmed. This is why we are extremely cautious about any settlement with China, as we do not know where China is headed at this point.

Some people naively thought the Democratic Progressive Party should be happy to see an inevitable conflict between the U[nited] S[tates] and China. This is actually a very serious misunderstanding.

We do not wish for a conflict between the U[nited] S[tates] and China. The Taiwan Strait is where conflict would most likely occur in the Asia Pacific region. If a conflict arises between the U[nited] S[tates] and China, Taiwan may become the battleground for such a conflict. This would not be in Taiwan's interest. Therefore, it is in our interest to avoid the occurrence of conflicts between the U[nited] S[tates] and China.

With regard to this, there is not much Taiwan can do. The wisdom of the Chinese leadership may be the main focus. Under such uncertain situations and premises, the Democratic Progressive Party can only choose to carefully respond. Our basic approach on cross-strait issues will be pragmatic and flexible, while ensuring that Taiwan's interests are not sacrificed.

Thank you very much.

CHAPTER 6

Taiwan's New Policy toward Mainland China

Julian Jengliang Kuo

The Democratic Progressive Party's (DPP's) rise to power has changed the political landscape in which Taiwan's policy toward China is carried out. The DPP has long challenged the one-China principle in two senses. First, because it came into existence long after the conclusion of the Chinese Civil War fought by the Chinese Communist Party (CCP) and the Kuomintang (KMT), the DPP seeks to redefine Taiwan's political identity apart from that war. As it seeks to do so, it is experiencing difficulty in its relationships with the People's Republic of China (PRC) and the United States. Both tend to treat Taiwan as an unsolved problem of modern Chinese history. Second, based on a new conception of Taiwan's identity, the DPP is eager to break away from the orthodoxy of the 1972 Shanghai Communiqué in which the United States and the PRC stated that Taiwan is a part of China. The DPP is against one (political-legal) China in the present tense.

Owing to the DPP's long-held position on Taiwan's independence, its rise to power inevitably provoked suspicion and distrust on the part of the PRC. To avoid cross-strait confrontation, President Chen has tried every means possible to soften the DPP's position on independence since his presidential victory. He has also sought to build mutual trust that could facilitate cross-strait reconciliation. The PRC, however, has remained rigid in its interpretation of the one-China orthodoxy and has failed to adjust itself to Taiwan's new political situation.

PRESIDENT CHEN'S ADJUSTMENTS

In his inauguration speech President Chen asserted that if the PRC refrained from using force, he would not declare Taiwan's independence, would not change the title of the Republic of China (ROC), would not inscribe the special state-to-state theory in the Constitution, and would not authorize a plebiscite to change the status quo of the ROC during his term. Also, on the presumption that the PRC would not use force, he declared that the National Unification Commission and the National Unification Guidelines would not be abolished.

President Chen sought to appeal to the value of international peace by shifting the DPP's position on independence onto the conditional plane of "no force, no independence." In this light Taiwan's de jure independence would be limited to a defensive response if the PRC resorted to the use of force against Taiwan. It should also be noted that Chen's new thinking is not equivalent to proposing the abolition of Taiwan's independence without any condition. The claim to the right of independence is still regarded both as a countervalue and as a counterweight to the PRC's use of force, and it remains one of the alternatives that Taiwan may resort to in extraordinary situations.

President Chen has retained the idea of Taiwan's independence for two reasons. First, consonant with the values of democracy, it embodies the belief that the Taiwanese people are entitled to the right to self-determination. In short, Taiwan's future should be open-ended. It can be decided only by the Taiwanese people and cannot be determined without their consent. Second, the idea of Taiwan's independence is also viewed as the ultimate and the most effective counterweight to the PRC's use of force in cross-strait bargaining.

By insisting that Taiwan's future remain open and by asserting a status equal to that of the PRC, President Chen rejected the one-China principle as a precondition for resuming cross-strait talks. Instead, he views one China as an issue for further discussion, suggesting that so far there is no bilateral consensus on the meaning of one China.

Unfortunately, the PRC reacted against President Chen's idea of one China, treating it as an issue, and countered it by alleging that a "1992 (bilateral) consensus" (*jiuer gongshi*) had been reached on the one-China principle. The PRC contended that although Taiwan and it (the PRC) had expressed different interpretations of one China during the Hong Kong talks of 1992, both sides agreed on the central proposition that "there is only one China and Taiwan is a part of China."

The PRC's claim was immediately disputed by Taiwan's Mainland Affairs Council (MAC), which characterized it as an act of deliberate distortion. According to MAC, the 1992 Hong Kong talks resulted in no consensus, and so, it maintained, the dialogue could be described as agreeing to disagree (on the implications of one China).

The crossfire over the so-called 1992 Consensus has made it difficult for both sides to resume their talks. It should be noted, however, that the dispute is nothing new. It is only the continuation of a position taken in a MAC white paper issued in 1994 that moved away from the original definition of one China as a political and legal concept set forth in the National Unification

Guidelines of 1991. The trend toward greater de facto independence and a more assertive Taiwan began to appear irreversible, reaching its peak in July 1999, when President Lee first alluded to the cross-strait political situation as two equal states by proposing the special state-to-state theory. In short, in redefining one China, President Chen and the DPP are not newcomers but successors of President Lee and the KMT. Both have sought to move beyond the one-China myth and have refused to take one (political-legal) China as the only common ground for cross-strait consensus.

President Chen is strongly opposed to the PRC's internal-external (*neiwai yubie*) approach to the one-China principle because it enables the PRC to espouse a particular version of one China when the PRC deals with Taiwan and a different version when it deals with the international community. According to this argument, the PRC defines one China as a single common political entity (named China) and does not refer to the existing state of the PRC or to the ROC when dealing with Taiwan. When dealing with the international community, however, the PRC defines itself both as the sole legitimate government of China and one China, denying the political existence of the ROC. Many Taiwanese have criticized this internal-external approach, viewing it as a deliberate tactic used by the PRC to erase Taiwan's political existence. Chen's criticism of this approach is not confined to the DPP. Similar views are held by the mainstream KMT.

Unlike President Lee, who shied away from all kinds of political dialogue, President Chen is more active and open to discussing all issues that may lead to improving cross-strait relations. In showing its willingness to explore new possibilities of developing an effective cross-strait framework, MAC proposed a new concept of "the future one China" (*weilai yizhong*), pointing to the possibility of establishing special political relationships between the ROC on Taiwan and the PRC. As he sought to foster a good atmosphere for cross-strait dialogue, President Chen characterized the 1992 Hong Kong talks as "the spirit of 1992" (*jiuer jingshen*), affirming that dialogue, exchanges, and suspending disputes have been the three major positive elements of cross-strait relations since 1992. In making that assessment, he showed that he was interested in reviving a good atmosphere for mutual understanding and compromise.

Instead of trying to assert a simplistic dichotomy between independence and unification, the Chen administration has stated that it is necessary to develop a more effective cross-strait framework in the future. To do so, President Chen has recommended that both sides resume bilateral talks through formal channels as soon as possible. He also said that track II would be welcome if it helped to bring about the resumption of the official bilateral dialogue. The PRC, however, deliberately bypassed the Chen administration and began to develop an anti Chen united front stemming from the establishment of extensive contacts with Taiwan's elite, including leaders of opposition parties, prounification forces, business groups, and even some of the

DPP elite. It is not surprising that Beijing's intrusive maneuver has evoked criticism from President Chen and MAC.

DOMESTIC CONSTRAINTS FACING THE NEW ADMINISTRATION

The PRC's indifference to President Chen's expressions of goodwill has put Chen in an awkward position. The DPP's radical wing has criticized him for being too modest and has claimed that his inability to formulate a strategy coupled with the PRC's dismissive attitude constitutes proof that his decisions have been injudicious. Chen's concessions were said to be too many and too frequent. Singled out for sharp and sustained criticism was Chen's remark that he might consider accepting the premise of one China, different interpretations. Many of the DPP elite argue that Chen's hasty concessions have encouraged the PRC's hardliners to validate their high-profile approaches to Taiwan.

Faced with the PRC's attempts to bypass his administration and to shape a united front against him, Chen insisted that before any substantial progress could be sought on the three links and economic normalization, bilateral talks between SEF and ARATS would have to be resumed on the assumption that orderly cross-strait relations would be institutionalized as a result of fostering and concluding bilateral agreements. Chen's emphasis on government first, however, was challenged by the opposition parties. The People First Party (PFP), newly established by James Soong, for example, pushed for establishing a direct naval link between the Matsu pilgrimage and Fujian Province. When MAC insisted that the three links not be connected until bilateral talks had been resumed, it was confronted with strong pressures exerted by the PFP. The PRC joined in support of the PFP and the Matsu pilgrims against the Chen administration. Ironically, the PRC took a politics-first stance and refused to resume bilateral talks on the issue of the three links.

Moreover, right after Chen's presidential inauguration, the PRC issued invitations to Lian Chan (the KMT's chairman) and James Soong (the PFP's chairman) to visit the mainland, initiating the game of divide and conquer against President Chen and the DPP. The PRC also tacitly encouraged the KMT legislative caucus to set up in parliament a task force on cross-strait relations that could act as a countervailing force against President Chen in an attempt to upset the new administration and promote its own interests.

The PRC tried to play off the elite of the DPP against the Chen administration in other ways, as well. For example, during the turmoil of the Matsu pilgrimage debate, the mayor of Xiamen City unexpectedly invited the DPP's Frank Hsieh, the mayor of Kaohsiung City, to visit Xiamen. Mr. Hsieh's positive response caused another storm in Taiwan. Curiously enough, Hsieh has long been viewed as President Chen's major rival in the DPP. It required no great act of imagination to impute political calculation as Beijing's motive for inviting Hsieh.

The PRC's willingness to use Taiwan's domestic politics against President Chen revealed its interest in destabilizing Chen's leadership. But the PRC's maneuver is likely to end in failure, culminating in a vicious cycle of escalating confrontation across the strait similar to what happened during President Lee's second term when the PRC used similar tactics against him.

SEEKING NEW COMMON GROUND

Even before Chen's victory, the DPP expected that the cross-strait deadlock over the one-China principle would be more difficult to break during a Chen administration because of the PRC's long-term animosity toward the party and its distrust of the DPP's leaders. Early in Chen's presidential campaign, therefore, the DPP proposed that both sides bypass the unsolvable sovereignty debate and use the window of opportunity implicit in joining the World Trade Organization (WTO) to rebuild common ground. Chen suggested using WTO as a ready-made framework for pursuing cross-strait economic normalization, including making adjustments in go-slow policies, opening three links, and other matters. He maintained that by using the WTO to promote bilateral economic normalization, Taiwan and the PRC can delineate new common ground for fostering mutual interests across the strait. According to Chen, forging solid common interests similar to those that form the basis of the European Union can enable both sides to engender mutual trust and establish a feasible cross-strait framework in the future.

After Chen's inauguration, the DPP's new approach to cross-strait relations was best summarized by the former vice premier of the Executive Yuan, Mr. Yiu Xikun, in a speech he delivered on China policy on June 25, 2000. Arguing for a pragmatic and constructive approach to cross-strait relations, he said that "in the face of new circumstances, the new administration will look at cross-strait relations from an international perspective, will use an open mind to deal with cross-strait relations, and will work out new opportunities for cross-strait relations through economic cooperation."

He recommended that Taiwan adopt an open and flexible attitude, maintaining that "the new domestic consensus is...building up, including an emphasis on autonomous national development and the expectation of cross-strait peace. The new administration will not insist on any precondition for cross-strait dialogue, will not exclude any direction in cross-strait relations, will not reject any form of cross-strait exchanges, and will not be limited to any ideological framework. In short, the new administration will reserve room for cross-strait interactions."

Unfortunately, the DPP's new thinking has virtually been ignored by the PRC. The government of the PRC has said nothing about President Chen's suggestion of using the WTO as new common ground. Some PRC hardliners have asserted that Taiwan must join the WTO under the one-China principle, not only seeking to suffocate the DPP's new thinking but also evoking the origin of the controversy.

The PRC's dogmatic politics-first stance has upset many of the moderate DPP elite, subjecting them to attack by the DPP's radical wings. In fact, since President Chen's inauguration speech of May 20, 2000, quite a few of the party's elite have been nervous about his downplaying of the issue of Taiwan's sovereignty. They are angered by the PRC's dismissive reaction to Chen's moderate proposals and have become more and more eager to act as a force braking his compromises.

In sum, the PRC's relentless dogmatism about the one-China myth remains the most difficult barrier to normalizing cross-strait relations. It is regrettable that the PRC has fabricated a self-fulfilling prophecy that has forced President Chen and the DPP to fit into the proindependence mold shaped by the PRC from its gallery of stereotypical images. Before it could be consciously determined, the conclusion was foregone, for the PRC seeks only the answer it wants.

Chapter 7

The 1992 Consensus: A Review and Assessment of Consultations between the Association for Relations across the Taiwan Strait and the Straits Exchange Foundation

Xu Shiquan

On July 9, 1999, Lee Teng-hui announced his theory of two states, destroying the foundation for the dialogue and consultations authorized by the two sides, causing the planned visit to Taiwan in the fall of 1999 by Chairman Wang Daohan of the Association for Relations across the Taiwan Straits (ARATS) to be aborted, and once again—as occurred after Lee's 1995 visit to the United States—stalemating cross-strait relations. On March 18, 2000, candidate Chen Shui-bian of the Democratic Progressive party (DPP) was elected the new leader of the ruling regime in Taiwan. Because of the DPP's stance in favor of Taiwan independence and Chen's personal advocacy of Taiwan independence, not only did the political deadlock intensify, but a serious crisis developed in the relationship between the two sides. Despite this intensification, through its study and assessment of the environment around Taiwan and its ability, and its confidence in its ability, to control the overall situation regarding the Taiwan issue, China's mainland adopted a policy toward Taiwan's new leaders of "listening to their words and watching their deeds"; it warned the Taiwan independence forces against taking any extreme measures, thereby stabilizing the situation in the straits region and leaving both time and space for a reversal of the deadlock between the two sides. In adopting this policy, the mainland displayed and reinforced its consistent stance of trying its utmost to resolve the Taiwan issue peacefully. With the same objective in mind, this chapter explores possible avenues for breaking the current political deadlock between the two sides.

THE ONE-CHINA PRINCIPLE IS THE BASIS FOR BREAKING THE DEADLOCK

The one-China principle is the cornerstone of the Chinese government's policy toward Taiwan. It is only on the basis of the one-China principle that any breakthrough in the political deadlock between the two sides will be possible. Looking back at the history of cross-strait relations since 1949, we can clearly see that most of the time, despite a military confrontation and numerous serious clashes between the two sides, both sides have always maintained a one-China stance; the struggle revolved around the question of who represented China and was, in effect, the continuation of China's civil war. Taiwan did not enact a law stating that China's sovereignty and territorial integrity had been split, that Taiwan was no longer part of China, that there existed two Chinas. On this common political ground the mainland's ARATS and Taiwan's Straits Exchange Foundation (SEF) reached a consensus in 1992, whereby each side orally expressed the joint understanding that it adhered to the one-China principle. This swept away the major obstacles that had been encountered since both parties began contacts and discussions, allowed both sides to reach agreements quickly on the cross-strait use of notarized documents and on the tracing of and compensation for lost cross-strait registered mail, and paved the way for the historic talks in 1993 between Chairman Wang Daohan of ARATS and Chairman Koo Chen-fu of SEF.

Yet as Lee Teng-hui began to implement his secessionist line more openly, the regime in Taiwan gradually altered and deviated from the 1992 Consensus, unilaterally and simplistically referring to "one China, separately expressed," hoping thereby to compel the mainland to accept an open interpretation of one China and thus allowing Lee Teng-hui to play up legally and openly his separatist proposals as if both sides were two equal political entities, were engaged in a two-China phase, and subscribed to a two-state theory. Disregarding the facts, the new leaders of Taiwan's ruling regime publicly denied the 1992 Consensus, saying that what had been achieved in 1992 was "a consensus without consensus."[1] Although the 1992 Consensus between the two organizations was twisted and transformed by Lee Teng-hui and Taiwan's new authorities into a dispute between the two sides, the contribution made by the 1992 Consensus toward promoting the development of cross-strait relations is there for all to see. It did not come easily; it was a compromise acceptable to both sides within the framework of one China reached after ARATS, prompted by an earnest desire to solve the problem, negotiated with SEF and brought about concessions. As far as the stances on reunification and independence taken by the various parties in Taiwan were concerned, apart from the DPP the 1992 Consensus was acceptable to all the major political parties and to mainstream public opinion as the most realistic means to break the political deadlock between the two sides. The principal obstacle was erected by the Taiwan independence fundamentalists within the DPP. It should be remembered, however, that they cannot obstruct mainstream public opinion in Taiwan forever. Hence, through a review and an analysis of how both organizations reached a consensus in 1992, this chapter seeks to show the necessity of returning to this consensus and to explore the possibility that both sides will do so.

A REVIEW OF THE 1992 CONSULTATIONS BETWEEN THE TWO ORGANIZATIONS

The Taiwan Straits Exchange Foundation was established on November 21, 1992, and on March 9 of the following year it opened its doors and commenced operations. The Taiwan authorities established this nongovernment intermediary organization to deal with many problems that were associated with the proliferation of contacts between the two sides that began when family visits were permitted on November 2, 1987. Because the Taiwan authorities could not immediately abandon their three no's policy (no contacts, no talks, no compromises), they created this nongovernmental unit to resolve issues that they could not handle directly in their own name.[2] On December 16, 1991, the mainland established ARATS, whose mission was to promote ties between the two sides, develop cross-strait relations, and bring about the peaceful reunification of the motherland. ARATS regarded the resolution of concrete problems related to cross-strait ties to be "one of the important tasks it was authorized to engage in."[3]

The Beijing Talks

Acting out of their common purpose, the two organizations held their first functional talks in Beijing during the latter part of March 1992 and conducted working talks on two topics: the cross-strait use of notarized documents and the tracing of and compensation for lost cross-strait registered mail.

Once the two sides had begun contacts and discussions about issues that occurred in exchanges, they discovered that, although they were discussing functional questions, an important matter would have to be clarified before any issue could be resolved smoothly—that is, the acknowledgment that functional issues between the two sides were the domestic issues of one country. Hence the one-China principle was involved.

On April 4, 1991, then vice chairman and secretary general of SEF Chen Chang-wen headed the foundation's first delegation to visit the mainland. On April 29, during a meeting with Chen Chang-wen, deputy director of the State Council's Office of Taiwan Affairs, Tang Shubei, was authorized to list five principles that should be observed in the handling of concrete issues arising from contacts between the two sides. The second of these principles stated, "In dealing with affairs relating to contacts between the two sides, we should adhere to the one-China principle and oppose any form of 'two Chinas' or 'one China, one Taiwan' and oppose 'one country, two governments' and other similar proposals or behavior." From November 3 through November 7, Chen Chang-wen again led a delegation to Beijing and entered into procedural talks about cooperation in attacking crimes such as maritime smuggling and robbery in the Taiwan Straits. During the talks, Tang Shubei again expressed the hope that SEF would adopt an attitude of adhering to the one-China principle and would strive for a consensus. For the first time, both parties discussed adherence to the one-China principle during functional talks, but a consensus was not reached.[4]

On March 22, 1992, after the start of talks between the two organizations in Beijing, SEF and its supervisory body, the Taiwan Mainland Affairs Council (MAC), insisted that the one-China principle was "unrelated to technical issues" under discussion, such as the use of documents.[5]

Moreover, the Taiwan side began to insist on using terms such as "the authentication of documents," applying the procedure used between countries' diplomatic missions to deal with the use of the mainland's notarized documents in Taiwan. Regarding the tracing of and compensation for lost cross-strait registered mail, the wording initially used by SEF was "making arrangements for tracing and compensating for indirect registered mail between the two sides," applying the procedure used for mail between countries and insisting that the movement of cross-strait mail was indirect and that tracing and compensation should be handled by SEF and ARATS rather than directly by the postal authorities on both sides. Representing SEF, Shi Hwei-yow (at the time chief of the Legal Services Department of SEF) explained that the policy of the Taiwan authorities was one of "no official contacts" with the mainland and that "cross-straits developments had not yet reached the stage of direct postal links."[6] It is clear that SEF's actions and proposals were in violation of the one-China principle.

Tang Shubei, who was then executive vice chairman of ARATS, stated the mainland's position at a press conference on March 30 after the conclusion of the Beijing talks. He said,

> [t]he crux of the difference between the two sides lies in the way one China is presented. We feel that there are no problems with the usage of documents within a country, nor are there problems with tracing registered mail. At present, because the two sides have not been reunified, it is necessary to find some special solutions for business

matters involving the cross-strait use of documents and for initiating tracing and compensation for cross-strait registered mail. On this matter we are willing to work together positively with the appropriate parties from Taiwan. However, because at present the two sides have not been reunified, we must first make it clear that what we are discussing or resolving are matters within one country. As everyone knows, both the Nationalist party and the Communist party believe there is only one China; the documents that have been passed by the Taiwan side relating to reunification also acknowledge that there is only one China. Since there is a consensus on one China on both sides, why can't both parties resolve concrete working issues in accordance with this principle? The one-China question should not become a problem bedeviling the talks between the two sides.

He also pointed out,

we do not want to discuss political issues with the SEF; we just want to affirm one thing, namely, that there is only one China. As for the meaning of one China, we are not prepared nor do we plan to discuss that with the SEF. The two sides have not been reunified, but we are one country. We are unyielding on this principle. As for what form should be used to express this principle, we are willing to enter into discussions.[7]

Regarding the outcome of the Beijing talks, Ma Ying-jeou, then vice chairman of the Taiwan MAC, "felt extremely regretful" that the mainland insisted on the one-China principle and insisted that document use and matters regarding registered mail were Chinese domestic issues. And yet he reaffirmed that "our side has adhered all along to a 'one-China' policy," and he stated that "after these discussions, the views of the two sides began gradually to come closer, which is helpful to the resolution of the problem." Regarding next steps for the talks, he indicated that they would be in touch with ARATS after internal consultations.[8] For his part, Tang Shubei stated that the working talks "were productive and that both sides had achieved consensus in many areas. However, because time was relatively short, there were still some differences in the views of both sides on some questions, and this is natural. We look forward to conducting further talks at a time convenient to both sides."[9]

The Beijing talks between ARATS and SEF were the first formal talks held since the establishment of the two authorized nonofficial organizations. Although no agreement was reached, through direct face-to-face communications each side was better able to understand the other's position, and consensus was reached on some matters at a time when it was hard to resolve the differences. The essence of the differences lay in the issue of the one-China principle. Although the Taiwan side said that it adhered to a one-China policy, it emphasized the differences between the two sides about its meaning and proposed using a formula of "each speaking for itself" to explain the meaning of one China. The purpose of the Taiwan side in adopting such a stance was to highlight its sovereignty and jurisdictional authority and to seek the status of an equal political entity. The mainland side, on the other hand, insisted on the one-China principle and stated that the functional matters under discussion by the two sides were the internal affairs of one country, its purpose being the upholding of national sovereignty and territorial integrity. Yet, in light of the differences between the two sides on the meaning of one China, and particularly because those differences cannot be resolved quickly, in order to allow the talks to achieve progress, the mainland side proposed that, in as much as both sides were implementing a one-China policy, they could temporarily not discuss the meaning of one China. Because the Taiwan side insisted on "each speaking for itself," the mainland side made clear its unswerving position on adhering to the one-China principle but affirmed its willingness to discuss the form in which this principle should be expressed.

After the Beijing talks, ARATS summed up its position: the concrete issues in cross-strait ties are the internal affairs of China and should be resolved through discussions in accordance with the one-China principle; in functional talks, provided that the basic position of the one-China principle is stated, the political meaning of one China need not be discussed; the ways in which it could be expressed are open to full discussion, and ARATS is willing to listen to the opinions of SEF and all sectors in Taiwan. This consistent attitude was evident in all the efforts the association made to resolve this problem.[10]

The Beijing talks were not entirely successful, but based on the discussions between the two sides, ARATS revised its draft agreement and gave the text to SEF's representatives in the hope that the other side would submit written revisions or a proposed draft; it had a positive outlook for the achievement of a final agreement. On the other side, in light of the policy objectives it had for the talks between the organizations, the Taiwan authorities also hoped that the talks could continue and would show progress. As analyzed in an article in *Lianhebao*, to begin by resolving problems of unofficial exchanges was "the core of its [the Taiwan authorities'] mainland policy, hence the success or failure of SEF in its [Beijing] trip would also indirectly test whether or not this construct of a mainland policy was effective," and "[it] was more likely to shake the people's confidence in the 'government.'"[11] Therefore, "in keeping with the latest developments in the course of cross-straits negotiations," the Taiwan authorities decided to act through the National Unification Council (NUC) and "propose a policy interpretation of the concrete definition of 'one China' in a new and complete way and to use this as the basis for the arguments of the Taiwan representatives at the cross-strait negotiation table."[12] On August 1, 1992, the NUC adopted a conclusions document entitled On the Meaning of "One China." In that document the meaning of one China was expressed as follows:

> Both sides of the Taiwan Straits adhere to the principle of "one China," but the two sides attach different meanings to this. The Chinese Communist authorities regard "one China" to be "The People's Republic of China," and after unification, Taiwan would become a "Special Administrative Region" under its jurisdiction. Our side feels that "one China" should refer to the Republic of China, which was founded in 1912

and has continued to exist to the present; its sovereignty extends to the whole of China, but at present its governing power only extends to Taiwan, the Penghu Islands, Quemoy and Matsu. Taiwan is indeed part of China, but the mainland is also part of China.[13]

ARATS subsequently responded to the Taiwan NUC's resolution of August 1. A responsible member of ARATS told a reporter from the Xinhua News Agency,

> [w]ith regard to the meaning of "one China" in the talks between the SEF and our Association on an agreement over functional matters, relevant parties in Taiwan stated their "conclusions" on August 1 and confirmed that "both sides of the Taiwan Straits adhere to the principle of one China." Our Association feels that making this point clear has great significance for the cross-straits talks on functional affairs. It demonstrates that adherence to the one-China principle in talks on functional affairs has now become the consensus on both sides of the straits. Of course, our Association does not agree with the Taiwan side's understanding of the meaning of "one China." Our position of favoring "peaceful reunification and one country, two systems" and opposing "two Chinas," "one China, one Taiwan" and "two equal political entities" has been consistent.

But this spokesperson also reaffirmed that "in talks on functional affairs, provided that the basic attitude of supporting the one-China principle is stated, the meaning of one China need not be discussed."[14]

From the positions of the two sides described above, we can see that although there were significant differences between them on the meaning of one China, and although each had its own proposals on how to handle these differences, there was an important convergence and consensus on the essential question of adhering to the one-China principle. This laid the foundation for both sides to continue their talks and to reach some agreements. On September 17, 1992, Zou Zhekai, then vice chairman and secretary general of ARATS, and Secretary General Chen Jung-chie of SEF had a meeting in Xiamen and unofficially exchanged views on the matter of expressing the one-China principle. Zou Zhekai said to Chen Jung-chie and Shi Hwei-yow, who was also present,

> [t]he conclusion of the Taiwan side on the one-China principle shows that there is already a consensus on adhering to the one-China principle in discussions of functional matters between the two sides. However, we do not agree with the explanation of the meaning of one China by the relevant parties in Taiwan; nor can we discuss the meaning of one China with the SEF.

He suggested that SEF seriously consider directly using the wording "both sides of the Taiwan Straits adhere to the one-China principle."[15] Subsequently, both organizations agreed to conduct working talks in Hong Kong. SEF's lead negotiator would be Shi Hwei-yow and ARATS's would be Zhou

Ning, deputy director of its Consultation Division. The dates were set for October 28–29, 1992.

The Hong Kong Talks

The actual main subject of the talks was how to eliminate the differences over the one-China principle between the two sides in talks on functional affairs. Both sides had been authorized to discuss the issue.[16] It should be said that both parties displayed a certain degree of flexibility. SEF no longer flatly refused to discuss the one-China principle; ARATS agreed to discuss the wording with which SEF would clearly indicate its adherence to the one-China principle. After the talks began, Zhou Ning of ARATS presented five written formulas for expressing the statement that both sides of the straits adhered to the one-China principle:

1. Document usage across the straits is an internal affair of China.
2. Document usage across the straits is a Chinese affair.
3. Document usage across the straits is a Chinese affair. In light of the fact that different systems exist on both sides of the straits (or because the country is not yet completely reunified), there are unique aspects to these functional matters. These can be suitably resolved through consultations on an equal basis between ARATS, the Chinese Notaries Association, and SEF.
4. As both sides of the Taiwan Straits make efforts toward national unification, they shall adhere to the one-China principle and shall suitably resolve the cross-strait usage of notarized documents (or other functional matters).
5. Based on the consensus that both sides of the Taiwan Straits adhere to the one-China principle, the ARATS, the Chinese Notaries Association, and SEF shall, through consultations on an equal basis, suitably resolve the question of the cross-strait usage of notarized documents.

With formal authorization from the MAC, Shi Hwei-yow proposed five written formulas and three oral ones. The five written formulas he proposed are these:

1. Both sides shall proceed from the principle of one China, two equal political entities.
2. Both sides shall proceed from the principle of seeking a democratic, free, equally wealthy, and unified China; cross-strait affairs are the affairs of the people of China.
3. Given that both sides of the straits have been in a prolonged state of separation and in recognition of the fact that both are seeking to unify the country through their common efforts, they feel it necessary to resolve the verification of documents (or other matters under discussion) in a suitable way.
4. Both sides shall proceed from the principle of seeking a peacefully and democratically unified China.

5. Both sides shall proceed from the principle of seeking the peaceful and democratic unification of the two sides of the Taiwan Straits.[17]

No formula was agreed to after both sides proposed their five written formulas. Based on authorization from the MAC, SEF proposed three oral formulas:

1. Given that China is still in a temporary state of division, both sides are seeking to unify the country through their common efforts, and unofficial cross-strait contacts have been steadily increasing; in order to protect the interests of the people on both sides of the straits, the verification of documents should be suitably resolved.
2. The verification of documents on both sides of the Taiwan Straits is a matter between the Chinese people on both sides of the straits.
3. Although both sides seek to unify the country through their common efforts and adhere to the one-China principle, they acknowledge that they differ over the meaning of one China. In light of steadily increasing unofficial cross-strait contacts, however, and in order to protect the interests of the people on both sides of the straits, the verification of documents should be suitably resolved.[18]

In an exchange of views, although their positions had drawn closer, the two sides did not reach any agreement. At the request of SEF, ARATS agreed to extend the talks by a half day until October 30, but they were still unable to reach agreement. Yet ARATS gave a positive assessment of the Hong Kong talks by stating that "these working talks have not only made considerable progress on concrete business matters; they have also made progress on the expression of the one-China principle in talks between the two sides on functional affairs."[19] Hence, ARATS wrote twice (on October 29 and November 4) to SEF suggesting an assessment of the results of the talks, proposing further talks on related questions in Beijing or Taiwan, in Xiamen or Quemoy, and suggesting that responsible persons from the two organizations sign an agreement.[20] On November 1, a representative of SEF issued a written statement saying that regarding the expression of the one-China principle in talks between the two sides on functional affairs, "we suggest that within a mutually acceptable range, each side state its position orally." ARATS examined SEF's third oral formula and said that it expressed SEF's attitude of seeking unification and adhering to the one-China principle. Although it argued that "it is acknowledged that they differ" over the meaning of one China, ARATS proposed that "in discussions of routine affairs, as long as the position of adhering to the one-China principle is stated, the political meaning of one China [need] not be discussed." Therefore, it stated that it was considering whether a position of adhering to the one-China principle together with SEF, and using the method in which each would make its own oral statement, would be acceptable. ARATS hoped that SEF could confirm that this was the official view of the Taiwan side.[21]

On November 3, SEF wrote to ARATS, formally notifying it that it was "using the format of an oral statement to express" the one-China principle. That day the association's deputy secretary general, Sun Yafu, notified the foundation's secretary general, Chen Jung-chie, by telephone that the working talks between the two organizations conducted in Hong Kong on October 28–30 had been concluded. He suggested that further talks on related issues be held in Beijing or Taiwan, in Xiamen or Quemoy, and that responsible persons from the two organizations sign an agreement at one of those four sites. Sun Yafu also notified Chen Jung-chie by telephone that ARATS fully respected and accepted SEF's suggestion of expressing the one-China principle through oral statements. He proposed consultations over the specific contents of the oral statements.[22] On November 3, SEF issued a press release confirming that ARATS had indicated it respected and accepted "the suggestion previously made by our SEF that both sides each express the 'one-China' principle through an oral statement." It noted that "our foundation has already obtained the consent of our supervisory body that it is acceptable for each side to express itself through an oral statement. Regarding the specific content of the oral statements, our side will express itself on the basis of the 'National Unification Guidelines' and the National Unification Council's resolution of last August on the meaning of 'one China.'"[23]

The foundation's letter of November 3 to ARATS and Sun Yafu's phone call on the same day to Chen Jung-chie led to a "breakthrough development"[24] in the talks between the two organizations on document usage and the tracing of and compensation for lost registered mail. On November 16 and 30, ARATS wrote twice to SEF, giving a written statement of its position. In its letter of November 16, ARATS said,

> [d]uring these working talks, your representative suggested that in the context of mutual understanding, we use the format of having each of our organizations make an oral statement expressing the one-China principle and propose specific contents to be expressed (see the appendixes). This would include making clear that both sides of the Taiwan Straits adhere to the one-China principle, and this content has subsequently appeared in Taiwan publications.

The letter formally notified SEF that the key points of the association's oral statement would be that "both sides of the Taiwan Straits adhere to the one-China principle and are making efforts toward national reunification. However, the political meaning of 'one China' will not be involved in the discussions of functional affairs between the two sides." The content of the oral declaration contained in the letter to SEF was the third formula for oral declarations proposed by SEF in Hong Kong on the afternoon of October 30, that is, "As both sides seek to unify the country through their common efforts, although they both adhere to the one-China principle, [they acknowledge] that they differ over the meaning of one China."[25] On December 3, SEF replied to ARATS letters of November 16 and 30. The letter welcomed

ARATS's "willingness to show a positive attitude and sign an agreement, which would enable the problem to be fully resolved." It also reiterated SEF's stance on orally expressing the one-China principle that had been published in the press release of November 3, that is, it would be stated on the basis of the "August 1 resolution" of the "National Unification Council" and the "National Unification Guidelines."[26] ARATS suggested that the two organizations set a time to release the specific contents of their oral declarations simultaneously. Lee Ching-ping, then the foundation's deputy secretary general, said, "This will require further study."

From the description given of the talks between the two organizations, we can see that as a result of more than a year of efforts and engaging in the working talks in Hong Kong, both sides had finally overcome the principal obstacle that had emerged in discussions of routine affairs and were able to affirm through oral declarations that they adhered to the one-China principle and that differences over the political meaning of one China would not be raised in discussions of functional affairs. This was the true course of events surrounding the 1992 Consensus.

An Assessment of the 1992 Consensus

The 1992 Consensus was the result of serious consultations and mutual compromises between ARATS and SEF, both of which earnestly desired to resolve problems "in the context of mutual understanding" and for which both had received full authorization from their respective supervisory bodies. Any distortion and denial of the consensus would be a distortion and denial of the facts as well as an insult to the efforts made by both parties. Looking back at how the two organizations achieved a consensus, we can see that it did not come easily and should be cherished.

The matters discussed by the two organizations showed that adhering to the one-China principle was an unavoidable issue in the talks on functional affairs between the two sides. From the beginning, ARATS had put its finger on the crux of the problem, pointing out that the one-China principle could not be ignored either in promoting cross-strait exchanges or in dealing with specific problems that emerged while handling contacts and in talks on functional affairs. Provided that both sides came to an understanding and consensus on this matter, other problems could be resolved as they cropped up. For its part, SEF insisted that "talks between the two sides on functional affairs are unrelated to political topics" and emphasized that "it is acknowledged that they differ" over the political meaning of one China. Hence, during the Beijing talks, SEF had not yet been authorized to discuss its position on stating the one-China principle, and it therefore adopted a stance of avoidance or even rejection. Because of the stalemate over this fundamental question, when the two sides began to discuss specific matters such as document usage and the tracing of and compensation for lost registered mail, obvious divergences began to emerge in areas ranging from the choice of words to ways of handling issues.

Though it would appear that many of the differences described in the chart are technical in nature, if traced to their roots, they involve adherence to the one-China principle—that is, it must first be affirmed that the issues being discussed by the two organizations are internal affairs of China; otherwise, both sides will go off in different directions and an agreement will be hard to reach. The mainland cannot make the slightest concession in its position on upholding national sovereignty and territorial integrity. During the Hong Kong talks, SEF was authorized to discuss how to express the one-China principle, and it successively proposed eight such formulas, thereby displaying its spirit of mutual understanding. Out of an earnest desire to solve the problem, ARATS immediately gave a positive response and made matching concessions, agreeing that both sides could express the one-China principle through oral declarations and confirming the specific contents of the oral declarations through letters. Because the Hong Kong talks allowed both sides to achieve a consensus on adherence to the one-China principle and overcome the main obstacle in their talks on routine affairs, ARATS Executive Vice Chairman Tang Shubei and SEF Vice Chairman Chiu Jinyi held preliminary discussions in Beijing from April 4 through April 10, 1993, about a meeting between Wang (Daohan) and Koo (Chenfu). They also reached consensus on eight issues regarding the meeting, including time, location, participants, topics, and other related questions. From April 27 through April 29 of that year, the Wang-Koo meeting was held in Singapore, and four agreements were signed: Agreement on a System of Contacts and Talks between the Two Organizations, Agreement on Verification of Cross-Strait Notarized Documents, Agreement on Tracing of and Compensation for [Lost] Cross-Strait Registered Mail, and Joint Agreement of the Wang-Koo Meeting.

The regrettable thing is that, at a time when people on both sides of the strait were hoping that cross-strait relations would continue to move toward the prospects opened up by the Wang-Koo meeting, Lee Teng-hui, leader of the Taiwan regime, moved in the opposite direction and stepped up the pace of dividing the country. The Taiwan regime unilaterally summed up the 1992 Consensus as "one China, separately expressed by each side"; it avoided mentioning that it had confirmed the oral declaration of the one-China principle, the third oral formula proposed by SEF on October 30, 1992, and the resolution of August 1, 1992, on the one-China question by the NUC and the National Unification Guidelines; it distorted the 1992 Consensus as "each speaking for itself" and misled people into believing that the Taiwan regime could make an open interpretation of the one-China principle, thereby creating a basis for its advocacy of dividing the country. Thereafter, Lee Teng-hui's expressions of one-China began to deviate more and more brazenly from the one-China principle.

On November 20, 1993, someone from the Taiwan regime attending the APEC conference in Seattle, Washington, put forth a two Chinas-phase policy. On July 5, 1994, the Taiwan regime made public its Statement on Relations across the Taiwan Straits, saying that "'one China' refers to the historical, geographical, cultural and genealogical China," thereby overtly abandoning the advocacy of one China in the legal sense. The statement gave these explanations of the Taiwan regime's claim that the two sides are equal political entities: "The meaning of a so-called 'political entity' is fairly broad. It might refer to a country, a government or a political organization.... [I]n dealing with cross-straits relations, the relation between the two sides is not one between countries, and it also differs from the usual simple domestic affairs." Lee Teng-hui's "special state-to-state relations" was by this time almost visible on paper. On April 8, 1995, in his speech at the NUC (so-called Lee's Six Points), Lee Teng-hui said that since 1949, "Taiwan and the mainland have been governed by two political entities, neither of which is subservient to the other, thus resulting in a situation whereby the two sides of the straits are separated and separately governed." In July 1996, the brief entitled Participation of the Republic of China in the United Nations, published by Taiwan's Ministry of Foreign Affairs, even more revealingly stated that "China is a neutral historical, cultural and geographical term," and "only after the two sides are unified will there truly be 'one China'." In February 1997, the press office of the Executive Yuan of Taiwan published a brief entitled Looking at the Issue of 'One China,' in which it began to use "a divided China" instead of one China. The brief stated, "Rather than say 'One China,' we should say 'one divided China,' such as Korea now and Germany or Vietnam in the past." On July 9,1999, Lee Teng-hui expressed the theory of two states, arguing that "[s]ince the revision of the Constitution in 1991, the cross-strait relationship has been established as one between states or at least as a special state-to-state relationship."

The facts demonstrate that under the guise of "separately expressed by each side," Lee Teng-hui abandoned the 1992 Consensus, gradually moved away from a one-China policy, destroyed the basis for cross-strait dialogue and consultations, created tremendous difficulties for cross-strait relations, and brought about the straits crisis of 1995–1996 and the cross-straits crisis and deadlock that have existed since July 1999. This is precisely why the mainland cannot agree to describe the 1992 Consensus as "one China separately expressed by each side" or even "the meaning of one China separately expressed by each side." Such a description both distorts the facts and harms cross-straits relations. The ARATS and SEF never engaged in discussions of the political meaning of one China, to say nothing of reaching a consensus that the political meaning of one China would be separately expressed by each side. In other words, the consensus was that each of the two sides would use the format of an oral declaration to show its position of adhering to the one-China principle, and because the meaning of one China was not discussed by the two sides, there was never any consensus on it.[27] A unilateral misinterpretation of the 1992 Consensus will inevitably damage cross-strait relations.

It must be pointed out that some people in Taiwan, particularly the leaders of the new regime, stubbornly deny that in 1992 both sides expressed a position of adherence to one China. Such a contention disregards the facts. By looking at reports in the Taiwan newspapers on the talks between the two organizations, one can readily understand that a responsible person representing the MAC and SEF in the negotiations indicated many times that "our side has always adhered to a 'one-China' policy."[28] On December 3, 1992, in issuing its statement on the Nationalist Party's version of the meaning of one China, the Standing Committee of the party's Central Committee said, "Taiwan independence or 'one China, one Taiwan' are paths which will not work; they are paths which will bring about self-destruction." An editorial in the *Zhongguo Shibao* (*China Times*) of October 29, 1992, also stated, "It must be said that on the position of 'one China,' there is no divergence between the two sides." Another fact that must be pointed out is that, before ARATS and SEF reached their consensus on one China, there was a case in Taiwan in which the Nationalist Party punished a member of the Legislative Council who was a KMT member for violating the one-China principle. In the latter part of September, many members of the Legislative Council, who were also members of the Meeting of Minds (*jisihui*, a second-level organization of the Nationalist Party) in Taiwan's Legislative Yuan, questioned the one-China policy during a general question session. Chen Zhe-nan advocated one China, one Taiwan. Hau Pei-tsun, who was then head of the Executive Yuan, "rebutted him in stern tones," stressing that "a two-Chinas policy will lead Taiwan to a dead end.... If a two-Chinas policy were adopted today, it would bring instant disaster to Taiwan.... One China, one Taiwan is Taiwan independence.... If you don't identify with one China, then don't be a member of the Chinese Nationalist Party." Nationalist Party spokesman Chu Chi-ying indicated that the party adhered to a one-China policy and opposed "one China, one Taiwan." James Soong (Soong Chu-yu), the party's secretary general, emphasized that the one-China policy of the party in power was very explicit. The Nationalist Party's Discipline Committee decided in that case to chastise party members who violated the one-China position with a serious warning.[29] From the facts presented in this chapter, there should be no question that in 1992 both sides and both organizations acknowledged adherence to a one-China position. At the time, preoccupied with consolidating his own power, Lee Teng-hui still needed to stabilize cross-strait relations and had neither the time nor the ability to challenge the one-China principle.

CONCLUSION

The consensus in which both sides of the straits stated their adherence to the one-China principle was reached by ARATS and SEF in 1992 as a result of authorization and mutual efforts. That was the basis, acceptable to both sides, for dialogue and consultations. Without this consensus, the nearly 20 rounds of talks between the two organizations would not have been possible, and the Wang-Koo meeting in Singapore and the four agreements would have been even less possible. After the Wang-Koo meeting, Lee Teng-hui was awed by the momentum that characterized the rapid development of cross-straits relations. He deliberately distorted and destroyed the 1992 Consensus, causing the cross-strait relationship to become turbulent and filled with crises. Since the DPP, which advocates Taiwan independence, assumed control of power, the cross-strait relationship has been mired in an even more dangerous deadlock. Despite this deadlock, the mainland has been making the greatest possible efforts to resolve it peacefully so that the relationship can take a turn for the better and move in a positive direction. Looking at the situation across the strait, this writer thinks that the 1992 Consensus is still the closest point of convergence that can revive dialogue and consultations between the two sides. It must be admitted that the key lies in the acceptance of the one-China principle. The objective existence of one China cannot be changed. In the world today, of the 180-plus member countries of the United Nations, more than 160 have a one-China policy, and this situation will develop further. There is no future for Taiwan independence, which can only bring disaster to our brethren in Taiwan. It is definitely not mainstream public opinion in Taiwan and is repugnant to the hopes of Chinese abroad. As the opening sentence of the National Unification Guidelines explicitly states, "in seeking to build a strong, prosperous country and [promote] long-term development for the people, the Chinese both at home and abroad share the common hope that China will be unified." In light of the broad trends in world developments today, and as the overall strength of the mainland continues to grow, how will our brethren in Taiwan deal with the opportunities and challenges of the twenty-first century? Obviously, the joining of the two sides would be advantageous to both. During the past 50 years, Taiwan has, on the whole, carried out a one-China policy. What harm has that done to our brethren there? On May 15, 2000, Mr. Hau Pei-tsun wrote a piece in *Lianhebao* in which he stated, "Over the past 50-odd years, because we advocated one China, we survived, developed, flourished and grew. Why should we abandon that?" It is Taiwan independence, not the one-China principle, that prevents our brethren in Taiwan from being masters of their own house, threatens the security of Taiwan, and shrinks "Taiwan's international survival space."

The wise man is the one who understands the times. It would not hurt the leadership of the Taiwan regime to look from a higher vantage point, to take the present and long-term interests of our brethren in Taiwan to heart, and to respect and return to the 1992 Consensus. If that were to happen, we could look forward to the resumption of dialogue and consultations between the two sides, which in turn would lead to the peaceful and stable development of cross-strait relations. That would be a blessing for the people of both sides.

APPENDIX A

On the One-China Principle

Before reunification, in handling Cross-Strait affairs and particularly in Cross-Strait negotiations, adhering to the one-China principle means maintaining that there is only one China in the world, that Taiwan is part of China, and that China's sovereignty and territorial integrity cannot be divided.

—From Vice Premier Qian Qichen's speech of January 26, 1998, at a symposium commemorating the third anniversary of President Jiang Zemin's major speech, Continue To Fight To Complete the Great Endeavor of Promoting Our Homeland's Unification

There is only one China in the world, and Taiwan is part of China; at present (China) is not yet unified; both sides should make joint efforts on the basis of the one-China principle to negotiate on equal footing and discuss reunification. A country's sovereignty and territorial integrity cannot be divided, and Taiwan's political status should be discussed in the context of one China.

—From Chairman Wang Daohan's conversation with Mr. Koo Chen-fu in Shanghai on October 14, 1998

Regarding cross-strait relations, the one-China principle that we propose states: There is only one China in the world, the mainland and Taiwan both belong to one China, and China sovereignty and territorial integrity may not be divided.

—From Vice Premier Qian Qichen's remarks of August 25, 2000, during a meeting with a visiting delegation from the *Lianhebao* Group of Taiwan

APPENDIX B

The National Unification Guidelines (Excerpts)

1. Preface: In seeking to build a strong, prosperous country and [promote] long-term development for the people, the unification of China is the common hope of Chinese both at home and abroad. In a rational, peaceful, equal, and mutually beneficial context, both sides of the Taiwan Strait, after a suitable period of earnest exchanges, cooperation, and consultation, should develop a consensus on democracy, freedom, and joint prosperity and together rebuild a unified China.
3. Principles: (1) The mainland and Taiwan are both Chinese territory, and promoting national unification is the common duty of Chinese people.
4. Course: (4) Both sides should put aside hostile stances and, under the one-China principle, solve all disputes through peaceful means.

—Passed at the third meeting of Taiwan's NUC on February 23, 1991, and at meeting number 2223 of the Executive Yuan on March 14, 1991

APPENDIX C

On the Meaning of "One China" (Excerpt)

(1) Both sides of the strait adhere to the principle of "one China," but each side attaches a different meaning to it. The Chinese Communist regime regards "one China" to be "The People's Republic of China" and [holds that] after unification, Taiwan would become a "Special Administrative Region" under its jurisdiction. Our side feels that "one China" should mean the Republic of China, which has existed from its founding in 1912 to the present day; its sovereignty extends to the whole of China, but its present governing power only extends to Taiwan, the Penghu Islands, Quemoy, and Matsu. Taiwan is indeed part of China, but the mainland is also part of China."

—Passed at the eighth meeting of Taiwan's NUC on August 1, 1992

APPENDIX D

Responsible Member of the ARATS Suggests Continuing Talks with Responsible Members of the SEF

A Xinhua reporter learned from the ARATS that on November 3, its Deputy Secretary General Sun Yafu notified SEF Secretary General Chen Jung-chie that the working discussions between the two organizations on "Cross-Strait Usage of Notarized Documents," which had been held in Hong Kong October 28–30, had concluded. He suggested that further talks on related issues be conducted in Beijing or Taiwan, in Xiamen or Quemoy[,] and that responsible members of the two organizations sign a related agreement in one of the aforementioned locations.

It is believed that these working talks in Hong Kong achieved great progress. During the two working discussions on "Cross-Strait Usage of Notarized Documents" and the "Tracing of and Compensation for Lost Cross-Straits Registered Mail," which took place in Beijing during March of this year [2000], the Taiwan side deliberately distorted the ARATS adherence to the one-China principle in functional discussions and [in] its definition of problems arising from Cross-Strait contacts as Chinese matters rather than international matters, saying that these were "adding political topics"; subsequently the SEF unilaterally terminated the discussions. Since the working talks in March ended, responsible members of the State Council's Office of Taiwan Affairs and the ARATS have indicated on numerous occasions that the one-China principle should be expressed in Cross-Strait discussions of functional issues but that for now the political meaning of "one China" need not be raised and the means of expression could be fully discussed; this in fact meant that the means of expression could be either written or oral. During these working talks in Hong Kong, representatives of the SEF proposed a format in which each side would make its own oral declaration of the one-China principle; on November 3, the SEF again wrote to the ARATS, formally notifying it that "each side would express itself through an oral declaration." The ARATS fully respected and accepted the Foundation's proposal, and Deputy Secretary General Sun Yafu telephoned Secretary General Chen Jung-chie and suggested entering into discussions on the specific contents of the oral declarations. This reflects the Association's consistent attitude of seeking mutual respect and truth from facts and not forcing its views on others as well as its sincerity in seeking to reach an accord on the Cross-Strait use of notarized documents.

Our correspondent has learned from sources in the ARATS that when the working meetings in Beijing ended in March, the ARATS promptly presented the Foundation's representatives with a draft agreement that had been revised in accordance with the discussions between the two sides. Prior to the resumption of working talks in Hong Kong, the ARATS wrote to the SEF on September 30 in hopes that (the SEF) would provide written suggestions for changes or a draft as soon as possible, but the SEF did not do so. However, during this round of talks, the SEF raised new requirements regarding the mailing of copies of documents. The ARATS determined that this would take time for study and assessment as well as for consultations with relevant agencies; this (position) was eminently reasonable. Yet the SEF insisted on reaching an agreement in Hong Kong, which was clearly impractical.

As early as September 30 and October 16, the ARATS had written to the SEF, explicitly stating that it would enter into a round of working talks with the SEF in Hong Kong on October 28–29. At the repeated requests of the SEF; the ARATS agreed to extend this by a half day to continue discussions of related issues. During the talks, the ARATS recognized that great progress had been achieved by the Hong Kong talks but that solutions were still needed for some outstanding and some new problems. Therefore, it wrote again to the SEF on October 29, suggesting that after assessing the outcome of the talks, further discussions take place in Beijing or Taiwan, in Xiamen or Quemoy and that responsible members of the two organizations sign an agreement. It appears that whether or not such talks take place soon will be the key to whether or not there will be complete success on Cross-Strait usage of notarized documents, and this bears close watching.

—Xinhua News Agency, November 4, 1992

APPENDIX E

Press Release from the Straits Exchange Foundation, Legal Person (November 3, 1992)

A responsible member of the Chinese Communist ARATS indicated today (November 3) through the Xinhua News Agency that they [ARATS] are willing to "respect and accept" our Foundation's earlier proposal in which each organization is to express the "one-China" principle through an oral declaration, but their Association also indicated that "the specific contents of the oral declarations will be separately discussed."

Our Foundation [said the following:]

1. The talks on practical issues regarding "Document Authentication" and the "Tracing of and Compensation for Lost Cross-Strait Registered Mail" do not involve political subjects. It was only because the ARATS repeatedly insisted during these talks in Hong Kong that there be some "expression" of the "one-China" principle that we obtained the consent of our supervisory body and will accept [the proposition] that each side express itself through an oral declaration. As for the specific content of the oral declaration, our side's expression will be based on the "National

Unification Guidelines" and the resolution passed by the National Unification Council on August 1 of this year.

2. We hope that the Association's staff will return to Hong Kong as soon as possible and will continue and finish the talks on the above two practical issues with our staff who are waiting there.
3. This evening (November 3), we instructed Department Director Shi Hwei-yow and others to remain in Hong Kong for one or two days and to prepare for the resumption of talks. We hope the ARATS will make a decision as soon as possible and will inform us before noon on November 5.

APPENDIX F

Correspondence from the Talks on the Cross-Strait Authentication of Documents

To the Straits Exchange Foundation:

On October 28–30, our Association and representatives from the Chinese Notaries Association and from your Foundation conducted working talks on the Cross-Strait use of notarized documents; at the same time, they exchanged views on the tracing of and compensation for lost Cross-Strait registered mail. In addition to making considerable progress on specific business matters, these working talks also made progress on the question of expressing the one-China principle in Cross-Strait talks on functional issues. This is the result of joint efforts made by all the parties involved.

At the conclusion of the working talks in Beijing in March, we again indicated that specific issues in Cross-Strait contacts are Chinese affairs and should be resolved through discussions in accordance with the one-China principle; in functional talks, as long as both sides demonstrate a basic position of adhering to the one-China principle, the political meaning of "one China" need not be discussed, the format for expressing the one-China principle in functional talks can be fully discussed, and we are willing to listen to the views of your Foundation and of all sectors in Taiwan.

During these working talks, in the context of mutual understanding, your representative adopted the format of having each of our organizations express the one-China principle through an oral declaration and suggested the specific contents to be expressed (see attachment); this included making it clear that both sides of the Strait adhere to the one-China principle, and this content subsequently appeared in various publications in Taiwan. We noted that on November 1, Mr. Shi Hwei-yow released a written statement expressing a position that is consistent with the above suggestion. On November 3, you wrote to notify us formally that you have already obtained the consent of relevant parties in Taiwan for "each side to express itself through an oral declaration." We fully respect and accept your proposal and informed Mr. Chen Jung-chie of this by telephone on November 3.

In order for the talks on the Cross-Strait use of notarized documents to come to fruition as soon as possible, we will now inform you of the key points we intend to include in our oral statement: *Both sides of the Strait adhere to the one-China principle and are making efforts toward national reunification. However, the political meaning of "one China" is not involved in the Cross-Strait functional talks.* Acting in this spirit, the Cross-

Strait use of notarized documents (or other issues under discussion) should be suitably resolved.

We suggest that after we agree on a time to make our oral declarations simultaneously, we continue to discuss, in Beijing or Taiwan, in Xiamen or Quemoy, some specific business matters relating to a draft agreement about which there are differences of opinion and have the agreement signed by responsible members of our two organizations.

(*Signed*) The Association for Relations Across the Taiwan Straits
November 16, 1992

Attachment: the formula for an oral declaration that you proposed on the afternoon of October 30:

"As both sides of the Strait make efforts toward national unification, although they both adhere to a one-China principle, it is understood that there are differences about the meaning of one China. In light of the increasing frequency of nonofficial contacts and in order to protect the rights of people on both sides of the Strait, the authentication of documents should be suitably resolved."

APPENDIX G

Letter from the SEF to the ARATS

To the Association for Relations Across the Taiwan Straits:

We have received your letters of November 16 and 30 about the talks on "Cross-Strait Document Authentication."

Regarding "Cross-Strait Documentation" and the "Tracing of and Compensation for Lost Cross-Strait Registered Mail" being issues between Chinese on both sides of the Strait, this question has been unsettled for a long time. It has not only affected the rights of people on both sides; it has also caused people to begin to question exchanges, which is truly regrettable. We very much welcome receiving the two aforementioned letters from you indicating that [you] "are willing to sign an agreement in a positive spirit" "to enable the matter to be fully resolved."

We have always felt that the functional talks between the two sides should not be related to any political topics, [for] there are differences in how the two sides understand the meaning of "one China." In seeking to find a solution to the problem, we proposed that each side make an oral declaration. As for the specific content of the oral declarations, we have already indicated in our press release of November 3 that we will express ourselves in accordance with the meaning of "one China" in the "National Unification Guidelines" and in the resolution passed by the National Unification Council on August 1 of this year. We have on many occasions stated and explained our position on this subject, and there has been extensive coverage by the media in the territories of Hong Kong, the mainland, and Taiwan on the positions and explanations of both sides.

The most pressing issue at present should be resolving actual problems of a functional nature. Based on the preliminary consensus reached in the Hong Kong talks and taking your views fully into account, we have prepared a draft agreement and delivered it in person to your representatives at the Hong Kong talks. If you find that there are still "differences that have been omitted" in the two drafts on "Cross-Strait Documentation" and the "Tracing of and Compensation for Lost Cross-Strait Registered Mail," please write to us as soon as possible so that we can study the matter.

We attach the greatest importance to the meeting in Singapore between Chairman Koo and Chairman Wang. As for ancillary matters related to the meeting, we will inform you by mail after giving this careful study.

With best wishes,

(*Signed*) The Straits Exchange Foundation, Legal Person
December 3

NOTES

1. Chen Shui-bian's press conference of June 20, 2000. See *Zhongguo Shibao* (*China Times*), 21 June, 2000.
2. See Ouyang Sheng'en, "Farewell, White Gloves-2000 Days of the Straits Exchange Foundation," p. 17.
3. ARATS Executive Vice Chairman Tang Shubei's speech at the panel discussion on the occasion of the first anniversary of the association's founding. See "The Association for Relations Across the Taiwan Straits: Compilation of Major Documents of 1992."
4. Liu Mo, Shao Zhiguang, "Leaving a Fair Footnote to History," *Cross-Straits Relations* 27 (1999).
5. See *Lianhebao* (*United Press Daily*), 24 March, 1992.
6. See *Lianhebao*, 25 March, 1992.
7. Remarks by ARATS Executive Vice Chairman Tang Shubei at a press conference. See *Renmin Ribao* (*People's Daily*) overseas edition, 1 April, 1992.
8. See *Lianhebao*, 28 March, 1992.
9. See note 6.
10. See note 4.
11. See *Lianhebao*, 22 March, 1992.
12. Wang Mingyi, "The Cross-Straits Peace Talks" (*Liang'an hetan*), p. 120.
13. See appendix C.
14. Statement by a responsible person from the ARATS on the publication by the Taiwan regime of a document on the meaning of "one China" in the cross-strait talks on functional affairs, Xinhua News Agency, Beijing, 27 August, 1992.
15. See note 4.
16. Wang Mingyi, "The Cross-Straits Peace Talks" (*Liang'an hetan*), p. 122.
17. Ibid., pp. 124–125.
18. Ibid., pp. 126–127.
19. "Talks Continue Between Responsible Persons from the ARATS and the SEF," Xinhua News Agency, 4 November, 1992.
20. See note 19.
21. See note 4.
22. See appendix D.
23. See appendix E.
24. See *Lianhebao*, 4 November, 1992.

25. See appendix F.
26. SEF Haiwenlu (fa) document no. 81-1045F; see appendix G.
27. See note 4.
28. See *Lianhebao*, 24 March, 1992.
29. See *Zhongguo Shibao* (*China Times*), 6 November, 1992.

Part II

Opportunities for the Future

Chapter 8

Preparing for a Better Time in Cross-Strait Relations: Short-Term Stalemate, Possible Medium-Term Opportunities

David M. Lampton

INTRODUCTION

Breakthroughs, whether in domestic politics or global affairs, require rare alignments of the political and geopolitical stars within and among the involved societies. Such an alignment with respect to cross-strait relations is not in the forecast and not particularly probable during the next two (possibly three) years, although there have been some positive developments in the first half of 2001. One of those positive developments is a United States-China relationship that currently appears on a modestly positive trajectory.

In Taiwan politics today, some argue that President Chen Shui-bian soon will be driven toward acknowledgment of the 1992 Consensus (in which both sides of the strait seemed to subscribe to an ill-defined "one-China" concept to get bilateral, unofficial talks underway). Were this to occur, it would be because of the accumulated needs of political realignment on the island, non-Democratic Progressive Party (DPP) interaction with the People's Republic of China (PRC) political apparatus, and a sagging Taiwan economy (and sagging foreign direct investment into the island) producing business community and popular pressure on Chen for accommodation to PRC one-China demands. Indeed, the National Economic Development Advisory Council met in July and August 2001 and was an important part of this process; Mr.

Chen is under considerable pressure to "seek a common language" with the PRC.[1]

Though this is possible, the more significant and probable opportunities lie in the period beyond March 2004, when elections in Taiwan and the transition to the PRC's fourth generation of leaders will presumably be consolidated.[2] The most immediate task is to lay the conceptual framework now and proceed to develop consensus (a vague road map) so that progress can be made when, and if, the opportunities present themselves in the future—sooner rather than later. It appears to me that a precondition to moving toward a more constructive phase is some type of agreement to go back to the outlines of the 1992 Consensus.[3]

If there is to be a sustainable breakthrough in cross-strait relations beyond the 1992 Consensus issue, it will be because the two sides of the Taiwan Strait can agree upon an open-ended, indeterminate process of cooperation, aimed at gradual "integration" (left undefined), moving from the economic realm to "other" realms.[4] If both sides continue to put the issue of sovereignty front and center, it is hard to foresee a time when the domestic politics of either the PRC or Taiwan will provide space for mutual accommodation. Though the United States cannot produce an agreement, Washington should do what it can to encourage such an open-ended, cooperative process that is premised on vaguely defined "integration," moving first from the economic realm to other realms as conditions permit.

Washington should make it known that such an evolutionary process is fully consistent with American interests (we have no strategic interest in the estrangement or separation of Taiwan from a Chinese mainland that adheres to a policy of peace and development, reform and opening). An evolutionary process of integration would be welcome in East Asia more broadly.

THE CURRENT TRAJECTORY OF U.S.-CHINA RELATIONS

Necessary, but insufficient, conditions for improved cross-strait relations are stable, minimally trustful, and at least modestly productive U.S.-China relations. When relations between Beijing and Washington are tension laden, this creates an environment in which cross-strait tensions tend to rise and become more difficult to manage.

In this respect, the current trajectory of U.S.-China relations is at least minimally supportive of cross-strait progress, after an admittedly rocky start of the administration of George W. Bush that does not need elaboration here. The bureaucracies in both countries now are charged with making the October summit in Beijing a success, China appears finally on the threshold of World Trade Organization (WTO) entry, along with Taiwan, and the generally sagging world economic situation creates a shared mutual interest in keeping two of the better-performing world economies (China and the

United States) in serviceable condition. For the next four months, at least, there will be a continual stream of high-level visitors in both directions that make it likely that the positive momentum can be maintained through the end of this year. Secretary Powell's visit of late July, the release of several American-connected detainees prior to the secretary's visit, and Chinese missions to the United States cumulatively indicate that both countries are endeavoring to make the fall summit in Beijing a success. Moreover, most of the incendiary routine decisions in the relationship (the Geneva Human Rights Commission and Taiwan weapons sales) were dealt with in the first half of this year.

Finally, the net result of the accumulated moves of the Bush administration in its first six months probably did increase the credibility of the American deterrence posture.

Overall, while in the aggregate the current trajectory of the U.S.-China relationship is positive and therefore not an obstacle to cross-strait progress, it probably is not enough to lead to transforming positive developments between Beijing and Taipei.

MISALIGNED STARS IN THE THREE SOCIETIES

Developments during the last seven months in each of the three societies (China's mainland, Taiwan, and the United States) have been complex—some have been more supportive of cross-strait progress than others. On balance, however, probably none of the positive developments are of sufficient strength to overcome the current stalemate. Among the (modestly) positive developments have been President Chen Shui-bian's December 31, 2000, use of the following: "the integration of our economies, trade, and culture can be a starting point for gradually building faith in each other. This, in turn, can be the basis for a new framework of permanent peace and political integration." In that same speech, the president went on to say that, "according to the Constitution of the Republic of China, 'one China' should not be an issue."[5] This phraseology seemingly endorsed the Cross-Party Group's consensus that the constitution under which Chen was elected and swore to defend was a one-China constitution. Other positive developments have included Taiwan's initiative on the Three Mini-Links and the PRC's agreement to proceed with this limited step; a more expansive PRC definition of *one china* from Vice Premier Qian Qichen in January 2001 (there is only one China, China is composed of the mainland and Taiwan, and China's sovereignty and territory cannot be divided); rapidly accelerating economic interdependence across the strait; and debate in both societies about alternate conceptualizations of a stable future structure of association, although the contours of this debate are clearer on Taiwan than on the mainland. Looking to the near future, we can anticipate both the PRC's and Taiwan's accession to the WTO, and we can expect that each side of the strait will have to make efforts to be WTO compatible in their own bilateral economic interaction.

Nonetheless, despite these modestly positive developments, the PRC and Taiwan (as well as the United States) are preoccupied with domestic concerns, and the actual objective with respect to cross-strait relations in each of the three societies currently is not so much to resolve the Taiwan issue or make progress as to keep it from deteriorating into higher levels of conflict while other priorities are addressed.

In the PRC, among the central concerns are preparing for the forthcoming 16th Party Congress in 2002 (meaning agreeing on fourth-generation leadership, among other things) and the National People's Congress meeting the following spring; dealing with agricultural stagnation and widespread drought; coping with urban migration, unemployment, state enterprise reform, and related financial and budgetary issues; and creating some momentum for political change through the vehicle of the three represents. Of course, President Jiang Zemin would like to leave a legacy of progress on the Taiwan issue, but a bigger concern is to avoid what would be seen on the mainland to be retrogression.

In Taiwan, slow economic growth (a 26-year low of 1.06 percent in the first quarter of 2001), a battered stock market (down 48 percent since January 2001), significant unemployment (4.22 percent in June), declining currency value (a 15-year low), and lagging foreign and domestic investment on the island are the paramount preoccupations,[6] along with preparing for the late 2001 Legislative Yuan election in which the DPP hopes to gain seats to facilitate governance (along with as yet unclear impulses toward party realignment within both the KMT and DPP[7]). Former President Lee Teng-hui convened the inaugural meeting of the Taiwan Solidarity Union in August 2001. In terms of external policy Taipei has taken every opportunity to capitalize on early openings in its relations with Washington created by the victory of George W. Bush. We see these efforts in the areas of weapons sales, transit and other visits (President Chen Shui-bian, former President Lee Teng-hui, and Vice-President Annette Lu), and military consultations. Clearly, profitably managing the U.S. account is part of an effort by President Chen Shui-bian to demonstrate to the people of Taiwan that his administration is worthy of a stronger popular mandate and a more supportive legislature.

In Washington preoccupations have been diverse but include slowing growth ("sub-par economic performance," as Federal Reserve Chairman Greenspan said in July 18, 2001, congressional testimony); the presidential transition and all of the predictable bureaucratic, personnel, and policy fights; tax-cut legislation and attendant budget issues; education reform; and health insurance–related legislation. Being a president who won office without a plurality of popular votes, the 2004 U.S. presidential election campaign already is underway, and that election almost certainly will hang on domestic economic issues, most particularly domestic economic performance, as President George Bush, Sr. discovered and his son knows only too well. In the foreign policy realm, early administration foreign policy efforts have been directed to increase support for a new nuclear strategic architecture (missile defense linked to offensive weapons cuts); boosting ties with traditional allies (with limited success thus far); and reconceptualizing, restructuring, and modernizing the American military (already limited by budgetary constraints). With respect to Taiwan policy, the administration's efforts largely have been directed at deterring a possible use of force by the PRC, rather than fundamentally altering the status quo. With respect to China policy, while some initial moves (and incidents like the EP-3 reconnaissance plane forced to land by the Chinese) raised questions about whether or not George W. Bush's policy would remain in the main channel of the preceding six administrations, policy seems to be settling into the same broad streambed as the administration's predecessors. Already, the president's anticipated October trip to the PRC is driving bureaucracies in both countries to come up with positive "deliverables" and although the happenstance of the first six months (the need for a Taiwan weapons sales decision in April and the EP-3 incident, among other things) drove decisions into the Department of Defense arena, anticipated developments and events in the second half of this year have decisions and implementation falling more substantially into the Department of State and White House arenas, fora that (thus far) generally have gravitated more toward continuity with past China policy.

These domestic preoccupations of each of the three societies makes it likely that simply preventing further deterioration of the status quo is likely to remain a higher priority than trying to produce changes when the stars are unfavorably aligned—at least in the near term.

A further characteristic of the current situation reinforces this conclusion and that is that the central cross-strait issue, for both China's mainland and Taiwan, has been sovereignty. As long as the most domestically explosive issue in both societies must be addressed first, little fundamental progress can be anticipated. Neither Taipei nor Beijing has much room for maneuvering within their respective political constellations on the sovereignty issue, and mutual suspicion simply compounds the problems. Nonetheless, the trend toward militarization in the Taiwan Strait makes it imperative to work around this obstacle, and the growing economic integration/interdependence of the two economies creates an opportunity to do so. Let me first examine the ways in which movement from the status quo (when sovereignty is the issue) is difficult and then suggest an alternative approach.

A TYPOLOGY OF CONCEPTS AS RELATED TO SOVEREIGNTY

In thinking about the issue of sovereignty, I found a July 12, 2001, article by DPP legislator Shen Fu-hsiung[8] very useful, more for the typology he suggested than the recommendations he advanced. The following continuum draws heavily on his typology, that describes a spectrum of concepts running from independence of Taiwan through unification.

Unification

- One country
- One country, two systems (Deng Xiaoping, with more flexibility introduced by Jiang Zemin and Qian Qichen)
- Federation
- The divided rule of one China
- One China, divided rule
- One country, two governments
- One China, two countries
- *Status quo* (would be strengthened, not changed, by reaffirmed 1992 Consensus)
- Confederation (Lien Chan?[9])
- Special state-to-state relations (Lee Teng-hui, July 1999)
- Independent commonwealth (James Soong?[10])
- European Union–like arrangement
- British Commonwealth
- State-to-state special relations
- Republic of Taiwan

Independence

A couple of things are notable about this continuum. First, each society has some diversity of advocates for various concepts along this spectrum, though the apparent PRC options are concentrated toward the top of the continuum and options on Taiwan tend toward the bottom. Lee Teng-hui has advocated a special state-to-state, Lien Chan has suggested a confederation, and James Soong has mentioned a quasi-international relationship.[11] Obviously, some fragments of the DPP (not to mention the party's charter) speak of independence. In the PRC, the discussion is much more muted and opaque to outsiders, but there are reports I cannot cite of a debate over whether or not something like a confederal concept would be conceivable or desirable—this, however, has been firmly rebuffed by the spokesperson for the Chinese Foreign Ministry saying, "What we want is reunification, not confederation."[12]

Second, moving beyond the status quo (indeed even reaffirming the status quo through reaffirmation of the 1992 Consensus) to accommodate the preferences of the other side is politically very tough in both societies, because even the slightest move in either direction immediately would be perceived to be a major concession. Sovereignty is the most politically sensitive issue in both societies and tackling it would require the expenditure of huge political capital by leaderships that don't have much—this political capital is needed to address the more pressing domestic issues noted above.

So, although the United States can comfortably live with all of the options on this continuum as long as they are mutually and peacefully agreed upon by the two parties, and although the United States has no enduring interest (strategic or otherwise) in separation, it would not appear to me to be sound policy (or feasible) for the United States to push some alternative that either one or both societies cannot accept under current and likely circumstances for the foreseeable future. So, what might be done, beyond reaffirming the 1992 Consensus?

ALIGN OURSELVES WITH THE POSITIVE FORCES—ECONOMIC

I was in Taiwan (Kaohsiung and Taipei) in late April of this year and had the opportunity to speak with a large number of persons in and out of government and from various political parties on the island. Three things struck me with particular force as they relate to cross-strait relations:

First, I was uniformly told that my previous assumption that Taiwan investment on the mainland was in the U.S. $45 billion range was far too small and that while no one on Taiwan knew for sure, the yearly volume of Taiwan Foreign Direct Investment (FDI) to the mainland had nearly doubled over the last 15 months and that the aggregate accumulated total might well be in the $60 billion to $100 billion range—perhaps more. Indeed, if one considers that the Virgin Islands is listed as the number four foreign direct investor in China for 1999 (many analysts believe that Virgin Islands FDI is substantially Taiwan money), contracting a reported U.S. $3.49 billion and using U.S. $2.66 billion, one gets an idea of the enormity and uncertainty of the capital flows from Taiwan to the PRC.[13]

Second, the first in what has become at least a trickle of public opinion polls (conducted by the Mainland Affairs Council and opposition New Party legislator Elmer Fung) came out in March, April, May, June, and July 2001, indicating an up-tick in Taiwan popular sentiment toward at least considering a future of closer political relationship with the mainland.[14] When in Taiwan, I asked what accounted for this up-tick. Beyond being cautioned about reading too much into these polls given their methodologies, uniformly I was told that the current economic difficulties on the island had created broader popular recognition of the benefits of a stable political and economic relationship across the strait.

Third, the degree of economic interdependence (globalized production chains) across the strait has increased more dramatically than most people have comprehended, perhaps summarized by the fact that 87 percent of global computer motherboard production comes from Taiwan, and about half of this already is actually sourced in the PRC.[15] To be more precise, it is estimated that in 2001 Taiwan will ship about 115 million motherboards overseas. "Last year [2000], domestic and overseas production by Taiwanese mainboard suppliers was 52% and 48%, respectively, according to MIC [Market Intelligence Center]. *Over 96% of the overseas production came from mainland China.* The center predicted that the overseas production rate would outstrip local production this year"[16] (emphasis added).

WHERE DO WE GO FROM HERE?

As I suggested at the outset, it is unlikely that the next six months to three years will see a substantial breakthrough because the domestic political stars in both the PRC and Taiwan are not (and are not likely to be) in favorable alignment. Indeed, domestic political conditions may not be compatible even after this period. This period, however, need not be entirely wasted. Rather, both sides could pursue a nongovernmental, but systematic set of dialogues on what a process of expanding economic cooperation might look like under the right conditions. Our task is to build a shared intellectual apparatus that could be used when the time is ripe.

The preceding developments cumulatively suggest to me that while the issue of sovereignty is very difficult for either the PRC or Taiwan to address now and for the foreseeable future, economic relations is a zone in which mutually beneficial possibilities exist. And, as economic ties and interdependencies increase, the need to develop cooperative frameworks and mechanisms in the legal and other domains will inevitably increase. It is in this context that President Chen Shui-bian's (not repeated) offer of December 2000 to talk about integration with the mainland is of interest and significance. As well, it is in this context, that former Prime Minister Vincent C. Siew's January 22, 2001, speech titled, "Toward the Creation of a 'Cross-Strait Common Market'"[17] also assumes significance. If the two sides can initiate a process of cooperation and dialogue about how to foster economic and other cooperation with the goal of progressively expanding integration, this can be a path around the currently insoluble problem of sovereignty. My suggestion would be to talk about a positive process, a direction, rather than an end state. Start with economics and let the evolution move toward other areas of cooperation and integration as conditions permit over an indeterminate period of time.

My sense is that a process of gradual change could look something like the following: moving from the current (largely ineffective) mini-three links, to discussions of WTO compatibility across the strait and attendant air and sea transportation governance, to sectoral cooperation (e.g., the European Coal and Steel Community), to a common market, to a more explicit political integration. All of this, admittedly, is difficult to conceptualize, much less put into operation, and it would take a long time under even the most favorable conditions. But, unless both sides can at least define a rough road map, only trouble lies ahead. The alternative to pursuing a path of this type is continued and increasingly acute mutual frustration in both Beijing and Taipei as both sides of the strait find no acceptable formula to meaningfully address the issue of sovereignty. Progressive militarization by both sides of the strait will be the inevitable result of this mutual frustration. The United States has neither the internal cohesion nor external capability to push either side into a process such as that described above, although our national interest will be perpetually at risk until a productive cross-strait relationship focused on a process of progressively expanding cooperation is underway. Were such a process to be undertaken, I would guess that the United States could play a very constructive role, one in the interest of both parties. Reaffirming the 1992 Consensus (or something like it) and the reaffirmation of the one-China character of the current Constitution (which has occurred) on Taiwan, however, are what appear to be minimally necessary points of departure if such a hopeful process is to unfold.

NOTES

1. "Taiwan's Chen Says Rivals China, Taiwan Face Economic War," 23 July 2001, FBIS-CHI-2001–0723.
2. Cheng Li, *China's Leaders: The New Generation* (Lanham, MD: Rowman & Littlefield, 2001).
3. Xu Shiquan, "The 1992 Consensus: A Review and Assessment of Consultations between the Association for Relations across the Taiwan Strait and the Straits Exchange Foundation," *American Foreign Policy Interests* 23 (2001), pp. 141–161.
4. In his "Cross Century Remarks" of December 31, 2000, President Chen referred to *integration*, though this word was not repeated thereafter, and about three weeks later Mainland Affairs Commission Chair Tsai Ying-wen seemed to cloud the meaning and implications of the word's use. Ying-jeou Ma, op. cit., p. 149.
5. Chen Shui-bian, "Bridging the New Century: Seeking a New Framework for Cross-Strait Integration," in Chen Shui-bian, *A New Era of Peace and Prosperity: Selected Addresses and Messages* (Taipei: Office of the President, 2001), pp. 40 and 43.
6. "Taiwan's Chen Says Rivals China, Taiwan Face Economic War," 23 July 2001, FBIS-CHI-2001–0723.
7. Shelley Rigger, "Poly Sci 101: Taiwan's Political Evolution," China in the World Press, *ChinaOnline*, 25 July, 2001. Available from the World Wide Web: http://wwwchinaonline.com/commentary_analysis.instreform/newsarchive/secure/2001/jur.
8. Shen Fu-hsiung, "Toward a Common Denominator," *Taipei Times*, 12 July, 2001.
9. Prior to its early August, 2001, Sixteenth National Congress, the Kuomintang, in the voice of Chairman Lien Chan, "temporarily" dropped the confederation proposal. "KMT Shelves Confederation Policy," *South China Morning Post*, 26 July, 2001, p. 8.
10. Soong also used the formulation "quasi-international relationship."
11. Liu Chin-tsai, "A Cross-Strait Common Market?", *Taipei Times*, 23 May, 2001, online edition. Available from the World Wide Web: http://www.taipeitimes.com/news/2001.
12. "KMT Shelves Confederation Policy," *South China Morning Post*, 26 July, 2001, p. 8.
13. *China Business Review*, November-December, 2000. Available from the World Wide Web: http://www.chinabusinessreview.com/foreigninvestment.html.

14. Lawrence Chung, *The Straits Times* (Singapore), 18 July, 2001. Available from the World Wide Web: http://www.nexis.com/research/search/submitViewTagged.

15. Financial Times Information, from China Economic News Service, *Taiwan Economic News*, 30 January, 2001. Available from the World Wide Web: http://www.lexis-nexus.com/universe/document?_ansset=A-WA-A-VZ-MsSEZY-UUW-EEBVU.

16. Financial Times Information, from China Economic News Service, *Taiwan Economic News*, 30 January, 2001. Available from the World Wide Web: http://www.lexis-nexus.com/universe/document?_ansset=A-WA-A-VZ-MsSEZY-UUW-EEBVU.

17. Vincent C. Siew, "Toward the Creation of a 'Cross-Strait Common Market'" (Washington, D.C.: American Enterprise Institute, 2001).

Chapter 9

Growing Cross-Strait Cooperation Despite Political Impasse

Ralph N. Clough

The Taiwan Strait has been calm in recent months. Even though the Taipei-Beijing interaction through the quasi-official Straits Exchange Foundation-Association for Relations across the Taiwan Strait (SEF-ARATS) channel, which the People's Republic of China (PRC) suspended in July 1999 after Lee Teng-hui characterized cross-strait relations as "state-to-state," has not been restored, both governments have pursued moderate policies toward the other. The PRC has turned away from harsh rhetoric and military threats in favor of a united-front policy, using political and economic means to influence the people of Taiwan. Chen Shui-bian has sought to reassure PRC leaders that he will avoid actions that would be interpreted in Beijing as moves toward independence for Taiwan. Both governments are making preparations for membership in the World Trade Organization (WTO), which will require increased economic interaction between the two sides of the strait.

The political impasse continues. The PRC has refused to negotiate with the Chen Shui-bian administration unless Chen accepts the PRC definition of the one-China principle, which Chen has refused to do. Beijing is probably awaiting the results of the December 2001 elections for the Legislative Yuan and for mayors and county magistrates before considering whether any softening of its hard line toward Chen is called for. The entry of both parties into the WTO early in 2002 will increase pressures for some form of cross-strait talks between representatives of the two governments.

The political scene in Taiwan has become more complicated as elections draw closer. Lee Teng-hui has established the Taiwan Solidarity Union (TSU), which will run 30 or 40 candidates for the Legislative Yuan. Lee has expressed the hope that cooperation between newly elected TSU legislators and an increased number of DPP legislators will enable Chen Shui-bian to govern effectively. Lee's pro-DPP stance and his harsh public criticism of the Kuomintang (KMT) have resulted in his being expelled from the party. The KMT, the People First Party (PFP), and the New Party (NP) have agreed on a single candidate to challenge the incumbent DPP magistrate of Taipei county. They have discussed possible cooperation elsewhere to improve prospects for ousting DPP legislators or mayors and magistrates, but how much cooperation will be agreed upon is unclear. Chen has declared his willingness to form a coalition government after the election.

Despite the political impasse over the issue of one China, the governments and people on both sides of the strait have been finding ways to increase cross-strait cooperation. In particular, the trend toward economic cooperation has picked up speed. Examples of increasing cooperation are described below.

THE THREE LINKS

Unlike Lee Teng-hui, who held that the time was not ripe for the establishment of the three links (communication, travel, and shipping), Chen Shui-bian has favored going ahead. In September 2000 he said, "It is about time to have direct shipping links and we must seriously face the issue. We can no longer act like an ostrich and use national security as an excuse." He added that ending the ban on direct links would require negotiations with the mainland. He also instructed Tsai Ying-wen, the chairwoman of the Mainland Affairs Council, to work out plans for opening the mini-links between the offshore islands of Jinmen and Mazu and the mainland.

Despite Chen's willingness to move ahead with the three links, the PRC's insistence on clear-cut acceptance by him of the one-China principle as a precondition for cross-strait talks on any subject seemed, for a time, to block progress. On September 22, however, PRC vice premier Qian Qichen told Chiang Pin-kun, a former head of the Council on Economic Planning and Development in the Lee Teng-hui administration, that the three links issue was not too complicated, but because it involved the one-China issue, the Taiwan-Hong Kong aviation rights model might be adopted technically to solve the matter. Airlines could negotiate with airlines.

Tsai Ying-wen went forward with preparations for the opening of the mini-links on January 2, 2001, even though local officials in Fujian had not been authorized by Beijing to discuss the actual arrangements with their counterparts in Jinmen and Mazu. At the last minute, however, on December 28, a Foreign Ministry spokeswoman in Beijing announced that the PRC would not block the institution of the mini-links, although she criticized the plan as a piecemeal measure. Thus, on January 2, 2001, boats carrying residents of Jinmen and Mazu made the first legal crossings to the mainland since 1949.

Even though representatives of the two governments have not been able to sit down together to work out a detailed agreement on the operation of the mini-links, the number and scope of such exchanges has gradually increased. According to Taiwan's Mainland Affairs Council, as of September 6, 2001, 110 crossings had taken place, 88 by vessels owned by Taiwan companies and 22 by mainland ships. Taiwan residents made 653 visits to Xiamen and Fuzhou, and Chinese from the mainland made 490 visits.[1] On September 5, 2001, the cabinet in Taipei approved expanding the operation of the mini-links to the Penghu Islands in the middle of the Taiwan Strait.

Among those making the direct voyage to Jinmen from the mainland was a 112-member delegation headed by the deputy mayor of Jinjiang to attend the first Jinjiang Trade Fair in Jinmen. In a breakthrough, one ship sailed from Kaohsiung to Xiamen on June 8, with only a brief stop at Jinmen. It carried 363 adherents to a temple in Yunlin county, Taiwan, who took with them the icon of a folk deity that had been taken from a temple in Quanzhou to Taiwan nearly 300 years ago.

The opening of the mini-links is an important step toward the establishment of direct travel and shipping between Taiwan and the mainland. As Qian Qichen has indicated, arrangements can be negotiated between government surrogates, such as shipping associations and airlines. A precedent exists in the successful negotiations for the uninterrupted continuation of shipping and air travel between Taiwan and Hong Kong after Hong Kong became part of the PRC on July 1, 1997. Another precedent was the establishment in 1997 of a transshipment center in Kaohsiung as the result of negotiations between shipping associations in Taiwan and on the mainland. This arrangement allows direct shipments between Kaohsiung and the mainland ports of Xiamen and Fuzhou of goods originating in or destined for third areas—not passing through Taiwan customs.[2] In August 2001 the Republic of China (ROC) government approved the transshipment by air to third countries overseas of goods arriving at the transshipment area from the China mainland.

In preparation for the establishment of the three links, a 12-member delegation of civil aviation administrators headed by Yeh Igan, director of the Huadong Civil Aviation Bureau under the Civil Aviation Administration of China, arrived in Taiwan in December 2000 for a 10-day fact-finding visit in preparation for the establishment of direct air links. The principal Taiwan air carriers have already opened liaison offices on the mainland and formed close ties with their mainland associates. Once the two governments have reached agreement on the three links, airlines on both sides of the strait will be prepared to move quickly to take advantage of the potentially highly lucrative cross-strait routes.

In August 2001, work began on the Gaoqi airfreight terminal in Xiamen, in which four Taiwan air companies have agreed to invest $14 million, 49 percent of the cost of the terminal, which will start operations in 2003. The Xiamen government will provide the other 51 percent.

In September 2001, Taiwan's China Airlines bought a 25 percent stake in the PRC's first specialized air cargo company, China Cargo Airlines, Ltd.

A biennial seminar on cross-strait shipping services, which was established in 1991 by the mainland's China Association for Shipping across the Taiwan Strait and Taiwan's Chinese Maritime Transportation Research Association, but suspended after 1997, was resumed in September 2001. A 50-member Taiwan delegation, including shipping executives, harbor officials, and scholars, took part in the seminar held in Shenzhen. Two officials of Taiwan's Ministry of Transportation and Communication attended as advisers.

FIBER-OPTIC CABLES

The least discussed of the three links is cross-strait communication. PRC officials have proposed setting up a fiber-optic cable across the strait, but the government in Taiwan has maintained its position that communication must be indirect. Consequently, mail, telephone, and fax messages are routed through Hong Kong or other places, requiring extra payments for this indirect service.

Taipei has not objected, however, to being connected to international cable networks that provide a link between Taiwan and the mainland. For example, Taiwan's state-run Chunghwa Telecom Company invested $36 million for a 2.39 percent share in the world's longest undersea cable network, running 40,000 kilometers from western Europe, through the Mediterranean, skirting the Middle East and the Asian continent, and winding up in Australia. This submarine cable, known as the SEA-ME-WE 3 cable network, was connected to the first of two stations in Taiwan in May 1999. In June 1999 Chunghwa signed a memorandum of understanding for developing a high-capacity fiber-optic submarine cable linking seven Asian countries and territories, the Asia-Pacific Cable Network 2 (APCN-2). It will connect Taiwan, mainland China, Hong Kong, Korea, Japan, Malaysia, and Singapore. Still another submarine cable is the America-Asia Network (ANN), which will link the United States with mainland China, Taiwan, Korea, and Japan. Construction of this cable, incorporating the most advanced technology, was agreed upon by the communications carriers concerned in October 2000 and is to be completed during 2002.

MEDIA

For several years the two principal privately owned newspapers in Taiwan, the *China Times* and the *United Daily News*, have stationed correspondents in Beijing, rotating them every two or three months, but correspondents from mainland newspapers (all government owned) have visited Taiwan only occasionally, for not more than a week or two at a time.

On September 22, 2000, in the interview with Chiang Pin-kun mentioned above, Qian Qichen suggested that mainland correspondents be permitted to reside in Taiwan on the same rotating basis as Taiwan correspondents in Beijing. Three correspondents from the mainland's *Xinhua* news agency promptly applied to the government in Taiwan for permission to be stationed there for a month. On November 10 the Government Information Office and the Mainland Affairs Council (MAC) announced that correspondents from the mainland would be admitted for one-month stays in Taipei. Each news bureau, newspaper, TV or radio station would be limited to two correspondents at a time. Vice Chairman Lin Chong-pin of the MAC said that "this was only our first step. We will continue to take further steps if the new policy generates positive interaction across the Taiwan Strait."[3] Zhu Zhongliang, deputy editor-in-chief of *Xinhua's* Shanghai bureau, welcomed Taiwan's new measures and said that *Xinhua* hoped to open a branch in Taiwan in the not-too-distant future. On February 8, 2000, the first two *Xinhua* reporters arrived in Taipei for a month's stay.

CROSS-STRAIT TRAVEL

The growing economic integration of the two sides of the strait has led to visits back and forth by senior government officials and former officials, despite the political impasse. In early December 2000, a group headed by Zhang Qi, a senior official of the PRC's Ministry of Information Industry visited Taiwan to promote exchange and cooperation in that industry. Later that month, a 39-member delegation headed by Zhang Jingan, director of the China Torch High Tech Development Center under the Ministry of Science and Technology, attended a two-day seminar in Taipei. Zhang told the seminar that joint development of technology and new products would ensure a win-win situation for the mainland and Taiwan.

In December Shih Yen-hsiang, director of Taiwan's Industrial Development Bureau of the Ministry of Economic Affairs, made a fact-finding tour of southeastern China arranged by Taiwanese investors on the mainland. Also in December, John Chang, a former secretary-general of the KMT and now head of a recently established association to promote Taiwan business on the mainland, made an eight-day visit there.

John Chang's visit, while aimed at furthering cross-strait economic cooperation, also had a political purpose. He exchanged views with Wang Daohan, chairman of ARATS, on cross-strait relations. Chang was one of several former high KMT officials whose visits were encouraged by the PRC government because, unlike Chen Shui-bian, they had declared support for the eventual unification of Taiwan with mainland China. The most prominent of such visitors was Wu Po-hsiung, a vice president of the KMT and a former secretary-general of the president's office and minister of interior. In November 2000 Wu met with Qian Qichen, Chinese Communist Party (CCP) politburo member

Huang Ju, as well as Wang Daohan. Another November visitor was Liang Su-yung, a KMT member and former speaker of the Legislative Yuan.

In January 2001, the vice mayor of Shanghai, Feng Guoqin, visited Taipei. The mayor of Taipei, Ma Ying-jeou, proposed that the two cities hold regular meetings between officials to expand exchanges, and he expressed the hope that the Taipei city government might later set up a representative office in Shanghai. Feng said that the PRC authorities would study these proposals, and he invited Ma to visit Shanghai. In a prompt response to Feng's visit, Taipei's deputy mayor, Pai Hsiu-hsiung, visited Shanghai in February 2001.

In January 2001, Vice President Annette Lu announced that beginning July 1, 500,000 tourists from the mainland would be allowed to visit Taiwan. By June 30, 2001, the MAC had completed the planning and the drafts of laws and regulations concerning the travel of mainland tourists to Taiwan. On July 9, however, the MAC said that detailed arrangements would be "subject to cross-strait negotiations, which we cannot make public for the time being."[4] As of October 1, 2001, mainland tourist travel to Taiwan had not yet begun.

In September 2001 the PRC's finance minister met in Suzhou with Taipei's finance minister to discuss preparations for the APEC meeting scheduled for October in Shanghai.

PETROLEUM EXPLORATION

Cooperation in petroleum exploration between the two state oil companies, the mainland's China National Offshore Oil Company (CNOOC) and Taipei's China Petroleum Corporation (CPC), which began in 1996 near Pratas Island in the South China Sea, was suspended after Liu Teng-hui announced his two states theory in July 1999. Wei Liucheng, chairman and CEO of CNOOC disclosed in Hong Kong in August 2001 that he planned to visit Taipei in November to finalize details of an agreement to resume the joint exploration project.[5]

ACADEMIC COOPERATION

In 1997 the Ministry of Education proposed to recognize the degrees earned by students from Taiwan at selected mainland universities. At that time the Executive Yuan shelved the proposal. Now, with more than 10,000 students from Taiwan in mainland universities, demands for recognition of mainland degrees have grown louder. Many Taiwan students believe that their chances for a job with a Taiwan-invested company on the mainland will be better if they have a mainland degree. The current minister of education, Ovid Tzeng, agreeing that the time is ripe for change, has revived the proposal and set in motion the preparation of detailed regulations.

In another move to increase cross-strait academic cooperation, the Legislative Yuan has authorized mainlanders to accept teaching positions in Taiwan.

In October 2000, the MAC relaxed restrictions on mainland educational and cultural and high-tech visitors, allowing them to reside in Taiwan as long as three years.

CROSS-STRAIT TRADE AND INVESTMENT

The expected entry into the WTO in early 2002 by both the PRC and Taiwan have caused Taiwan's entrepreneurs to step up their investment in the mainland. Mainland investment, which had doubled in 2000 over the previous year, continued to grow strongly in 2001.

The Ministry of Economic Affairs reported an increase in the first six months of 23 percent over the same period in 2000, to $1.4 billion.[6]

Demands by business that the Chen administration ease restrictions on cross-strait trade and investment became more insistent as the months passed. Responding to these pressures, which were intensified by a severe slump in Taiwan's economy, the Economic Development Advisory Commission (EDAC) in August 2001 recommended replacing Lee Teng-hui's go slow, be patient policy on mainland investment with a policy of active openness and effective management, intended to expand cross-strait economic relations. The recommendations of the commission, which included top business leaders, government officials, and scholars, reflected a consensus between the ruling party and the opposition that a more robust cross-strait economic relationship was needed to revive economic growth in Taiwan. Chen Shuibian and leaders of the opposition parties expressed support for the EDAC recommendations, which included ending the ban on direct postal links, taking steps to permit the establishment of direct shipping and air travel, easing restrictions on Taiwan investment on the mainland, and permitting mainland investment in Taiwan real estate.

INFORMATION INDUSTRY

During the year 2000, the integration of information industry manufacturing between Taiwan and mainland China proceeded apace. During 2003, according to Taiwan's Institute of Information Industry, 38.6 percent of Taiwan companies' information technology hardware was produced in mainland China. The Institute predicted that this figure would rise to 51 percent in 2001. The institute also noted that mainland China in the year 2000 edged out Taiwan for the first time as a global producer of information industry hardware ($25.5 billion versus $23.2 billion), but 72 percent of that total came from Taiwan companies' manufacturing bases on the mainland.

The heads of Taiwan's leading information industry companies acknowledged the government's concern that excessive transfer of manufacturing to mainland China would endanger Taiwan's economy. They declared, however, that in order to be successful in the fiercely competitive global market, some of them had no choice but to shift increasingly advanced technology manufacturing to the mainland. For example, although the government banned production of notebook computers on the mainland by Taiwan companies, all of the leading producers of notebook computers have invested in mainland factories to turn out computer components. They have urged the government to lift the ban on notebook production on the mainland, and some of them are already expanding their facilities there in the expectation that the ban will be lifted. Increasing worldwide demand for notebook computers has put heavy pressure on the Taiwan suppliers of original equipment manufacturer notebooks to companies such as Dell, Sharp, and Compaq to increase production and reduce costs.

Even the producers of semiconductors, who have no present plans to shift their capital-intensive, high-technology production to the mainland, foresee a time when that will be necessary. Morris Chang, chairman of the Taiwan Semiconductor Manufacturing Company (TSMC), told a seminar in November that the global marketing strategies of Taiwan's semiconductor manufacturers make inevitable their eventual investment in the mainland. If they do not extend their business network into the mainland, Chang said, they will gradually lose their international competitiveness.[7]

The involvement of Taiwanese businessmen in integrated circuit manufacturing on the mainland has already begun in a $1.6 billion computer chip plant being built in Shanghai. This project has attracted much attention because it is a joint venture, the vice chairman of which is Jiang Mianheng, the son of Jiang Zemin, and the president and CEO is Winston Wang, the son of Wang Yung-ching, head of Taiwan's Formosa Plastic Group. Winston Wang has declared that no Taiwan money is going into this plant and that he has no personal financial stake in it. This plant will produce eight-inch silicon wafers with 0.25-micron circuitry, technologically well behind the twelve-inch, 0.13-micron circuitry, the standard for the latest wafer fab plants being built by TSMC and United Microelectronics Corp (UMC).[8]

The growing cross-strait cooperation in the information industry was highlighted by the presence of a strong mainland China delegation at the Computex Taipei 2001 computer exposition in June. The mainland delegation included Yang Yuanqing, president of the PRC's leading computer company, the Legend Group, Yang Yuhang, director of Great Wall Broadband Network Service Co., Yin Yiping, director of China Telecom's Telecommunication Department, Zhang Daming, director of China International Electronic Commerce Center, and Lin Li, director of the Economic Information Center of the State Economic and Trade Commission.[9]

Legend president Yang Yuanqing told the press that Legend would increase its cooperation with its Taiwan business partners, First International Computer (FIC), Compac, and Mitac. Legend expects to more than double its production of notebook computers in 2001 to 250,000, outsourcing most of it to these Taiwan companies. Yang said that the Taiwan partners provide good product design, manufacturing, and services, whereas Legend focuses on the marketing of its name-brand products in mainland China's rapidly growing market for notebook computers. Legend is establishing a notebook computer assembly plant in Shanghai to facilitate cooperation with Taiwan companies.[10]

Yang Yuhang, president of Great Wall Broadband Network Service Co., which is setting up a broadband network in the PRC, said that his company expected to purchase most of its local area network equipment from Taiwan companies, such as D-Link Corp. and Accton Technology Corp.

Taiwan's business leaders recognize that in order to exploit the advantages of operating in mainland China, but to avoid being absorbed by that giant economy, they must keep their most technologically advanced production and their design and marketing centers in Taiwan. They can also maintain their global leadership in certain branches of the information industry by collaborating with technologically advanced companies elsewhere. For example, UMC is not only building new 12-inch wafer fab plants in Taiwan, it also has two joint-venture wafer fab plants in Japan and has just announced plans to build a $2 billion, 12-inch chip foundry in Singapore, in a joint venture with a European chipmaker. TSMC has also built a foundry in Singapore in a joint venture with Philips Semiconductor.

CROSS-STRAIT COMMON MARKET

Vincent Siew, a former premier of the ROC and current vice chairman of the KMT, has advanced a striking new proposal: the establishment of a cross-strait common market that would lead in time to the political integration of Taiwan and mainland China. He made this proposal in an article in the *Asian Wall Street Journal* in November 2000 and elaborated on it in a speech at the American Enterprise Institute in Washington, D.C., on January 22, 2001.

Mr. Siew believes that by setting the goal of a cross-strait common market, the two sides could take full advantage of the complementary nature of the two economies and move step by step toward that goal, which would also pave the way for political integration. He called attention to the similarity between his proposal and President Chen Shui-bian's New Year's speech, in which Chen referred to the integration of the two economies as a basis for "a new framework of permanent peace and political integration." Siew called on Americans to strongly support this endeavor. Asked whether the PRC had responded to his proposal, as presented in the *Asian Wall Street Journal* in November, Siew said that so far there had been no negative response.

CONCLUSIONS

Will the relatively moderate policies of the two governments and the trend toward greater cross-strait cooperation continue during the remainder of 2001, even though the political impasse remains unresolved?

Vice Premier Qian Qichen, in his speech of January 22, 2001, on the sixth anniversary of Jiang Zemin's Eight-Point Proposal on reunification, adopted a moderate tone, indicating that the PRC would press ahead with its united-front policy, even offering to work with former proindependence individuals to improve cross-strait relations, if they abandoned their separatist stance. Nowhere in the speech did Qian repeat the mantra that the PRC reserved the right to use force to accomplish reunification. He did, however, demand that Chen Shui-bian specifically acknowledge the one-China principle and the 1992 Consensus on that principle between SEF and ARATS. He also said that in Taiwan, since March 2000, "the struggle between separatism and anti-separatism has become sharper and more complex" and he calls for a "sense of urgency" in order to accomplish reunification at an early date.

The PRC's defense white paper of October 2000 took a harder line on the Taiwan issue, asserting that "The Taiwan Straits situation is complicated and grim." The white paper concluded that because "hegemonism and power politics still exist and are further developing, and in particular the basis for the country's peaceful reunification is seriously imperiled, China will have to enhance its capability to defend its sovereignty and security by military means."

Although Chen Shui-bian tried in his inaugural address to assure the PRC that he would not make any move toward independence and his administration has taken various steps to improve cross-strait interaction, a specific acceptance by him of the one-China principle as demanded by the PRC seems unlikely. In his effort to win a maximum number of Legislative Yuan seats in December, Chen cannot afford to alienate irretrievably the significant segment of the DPP that is firmly proindependence.

Thus, it seems probable that the political impasse will not be resolved this year. The PRC will maintain pressure on Chen, while waiting to see whether changes in Taiwan politics and the results of its united-front policy will improve prospects for reunification.

Meanwhile, cross-strait economic integration and other forms of cooperation will continue. The two governments will be compelled to find ways of dealing with each other in order to make progress toward opening the three links and to make the adjustments required by membership in the WTO.

The stress on economic cooperation by Qian Qichen, Chen Shui-bian, and Vincent Siew suggest a growing cross-strait consensus on this trend. As Qian put it: "As we enter the new century, faced with the trend of economic globalization and fierce competition, and faced with the progress of science and technology which is changing with each passing day, the compatriots on both sides of the strait should all the more link hands in cooperation to meet the challenges together and make both of them winners in mutual benefit in the economy and in science and technology."

Vincent Siew's common market proposal also cites economic globalization as creating a strong incentive for both sides of the strait to cooperate in the progressive integration of their economies, which in turn could lead to a step-by-step integration of politics. Chen Shui-bian's New Year's speech refers to the integration of the two economies, trade, and culture as a starting point for creating the basis for a new framework of permanent peace and political integration.

Despite the apparent consensus on the inevitability of a trend toward economic integration leading to eventual political integration, the two sides differ on the pace of that process. Qian calls for reunification at an early date, while Chen and Siew clearly envisage a prolonged, step-by-step process. It seems probable, however, that so long as the PRC perceives the general trend moving toward eventual unification and Taiwan leaders make no move toward independence, the PRC will not try to impose a solution by resorting to military force.

An important external factor is the policy of the United States. As Qian declared, "We resolutely oppose all intervention by foreign forces in China's settlement of the Taiwan problem." It would be highly desirable for the new U.S. administration to express support for the trends toward cooperation between the two sides of the strait, aligning itself with the powerful forces arising from the globalization of the world economy that are drawing mainland China and Taiwan together. To overemphasize the balance of military forces in the Taiwan Strait would be in the long run a losing game for Taiwan. Taiwan's security is best ensured by the growing network of economic interdependence and other forms of cross-strait cooperation that people on both sides of the strait perceive as mutually beneficial.

NOTES

1. Taipei, Central News Agency, 20 September, 2001.
2. During the first 10 months of 1999, 1,400 voyages between Kaohsiung and Xiamen and Fuzhou carried 284,000 TEU's (20-foot equivalent units), an increase of 37.8 percent over the same period of 1998 (Xinhua, 21 November 21, 1999). During 2,000 shipments between Xiamen and Kaohsiung rose to 1,060,000 TEU's, with an average of 14 sailings daily between the two ports (*Central Daily News*, 13 February, 2001).
3. *China Post*, 11 November, 2000.
4. "MAC News Briefing," 9 July, 2001, p. 3.
5. *China Post*, 29 August, 2001.
6. Nomura, *Asia Insight*, 5 September, 2001, p. 30.
7. *China Post*, 29, November, 2000.
8. *New York Times*, 29 November, 2000.
9. *China Post*, 1 June, 2001.
10. *China Post*, 8 June, 2001.

CHAPTER 10

Chen Administration Acts to Expand Cross-Strait Economic Relations

Ralph N. Clough

Two developments during the past six months have demonstrated a determination by the Chen administration to expand economic relations with mainland China, despite the continuing political impasse. These developments were the recommendations by the Economic Development Advisory Conference (EDAC), endorsed by President Chen, and the admission of Taiwan to the World Trade Organization (WTO).

The EDAC, composed of 120 business leaders, government officials, academics, and representatives of the ruling and opposition parties, presided over by Chen Shui-bian himself, reached a consensus in late August 2001 on 322 proposals. The willingness of the opposition parties to participate and the ability of EDAC to reach a consensus on a large number of proposals reflected a deep concern among the participants at Taiwan's severe economic recession and the need to act to revive the economy.

EASING RESTRICTIONS ON CROSS-STRAIT INVESTMENT

On November 8, 2001, the Republic of China cabinet announced that the previous go slow, be patient policy toward mainland investment would be replaced by a new policy defined as "active opening, effective management." A number of EDAC recommendations concerning mainland investment were adopted. The new policy lifted the $50 million limit on single investment projects on the mainland, simplified the process for seeking approval of investments under 20 million, authorized Taiwan banks, through their off-shore banking units, to deal directly with mainland financial institutions (thus permitting entrepreneurs to send funds directly across the strait, rather than through a third place), and exempted mainland investments from double taxation. To increase the flow of capital investment into Taiwan, the previous total ban on investment from mainland China is being lifted, with investment being allowed initially in Taiwan real estate.

The Chen administration has recognized that cross-strait trade and investment policy must be an integral part of Taiwan's global economic strategy. To compete effectively in the world marketplace, Taiwan's entrepreneurs must be able to take full advantage of the mainland's cheaper land and labor and its massive market. Chairwoman Tsai Ing-wen of the Mainland Affairs Council (MAC) pointed out that the transfer of Taiwan's labor-intensive manufacturing to the mainland had resulted in the upgrading of Taiwan's industry. Now, 55.8 percent of Taiwan's exports were high-tech products and industrial hollowing-out was no longer a major concern. She warned, however, that it would continue to be important for Taiwan's industries to keep their roots in Taiwan.[1]

ADJUSTING TO MEMBERSHIP IN THE WTO

By January 1, 2002, both the People's Republic of China (PRC) and Taiwan had become members of the WTO. Both will have to make substantial adjustments in their trade regulations in order to comply with WTO requirements. Taiwan officials recognize that lowering import restrictions on imports from the China mainland will result in a considerable increase in imports, especially in agricultural products, with a damaging impact on Taiwan's farmers. To limit that impact, investment from Taiwan has been banned in the production of hogs, chickens, pond-raised fish, and other agricultural products that can now enter Taiwan from the mainland under WTO rules. The impact on Taiwan's economy will not be entirely negative, however. Taiwan authorities expect that the PRC's membership in the WTO will open opportunities for an increase in Taiwan's exports to the mainland and participation in service industries there.

In a talk at Twin Oaks in Washington, D.C., on December 4, 2001, Tsai Ing-wen stressed that both Beijing and Taipei would have to adjust to the globalizing trend and to the membership of both in the WTO. She expected that the process would be difficult, taking several years to complete. To bring Taiwan's trade with China in line with its trade with other countries, Taipei would begin with unilateral actions, without consultation with the Beijing; however, eventually, with respect to some topics, consultation with Beijing would be essential. She hoped that the authorities there would be flexible enough to sit down with Taiwan representatives to discuss differences.

CROSS-STRAIT TRAVEL

Since 1987 when large-scale travel from Taiwan to mainland China began, the government in Taipei has maintained tight restrictions on travel in the reverse direction. Restrictions were necessary to prevent the mainland, already one of the most crowded areas on earth with its population of 23 million, from being flooded by immigrants from among the 1.3 billion Chinese on the mainland. Pressures have been growing, however, to ease the restrictions. Business people married on the mainland wanted to bring their spouses and children to Taiwan. Companies with factories on the mainland wanted to bring technicians to Taiwan for training. The tourist industry, suffering from Taiwan's economic recession, wanted to open the door to mainland tourists. The Chen administration responded by taking several steps to modify immigration strictures.

As of August 2001, some 120,000 marriages had taken place between people from the two sides of the Taiwan Strait.[2] During the three years from 1998 to 2001, the number of spouses admitted to Taiwan for permanent residence was limited to 3,600 per year. Spouses admitted to Taiwan from the mainland were not allowed to take jobs. From January 1 to March 19, 2001, 346 mainland spouses were expelled for working illegally in Taiwan. Growing criticism resulted in modification of this restrictive policy in April 2001. Mainland spouses are now allowed to work if their Taiwan spouse came from a low-income family, was 65 or older, was mentally or physically disabled, or suffered from serious disease or injury. In August 2001 the MAC announced that the quota for the admission of mainland spouses would be raised beginning in 2002.[3]

In October 2001 Taipei relaxed the restrictions on the travel of merchants and business professionals from mainland China. Professionals need only to have worked in their present posts for three months instead of one year. They could reside in Taiwan for up to six years, instead of the previous three-year limit. They needed to file their entry applications only five days in advance, instead of two months. These decisions responded to suggestions by the American Chamber of Commerce in Taipei and the European Council of Commerce and Trade, making it easier for multinational corporations to operate out of Taiwan. Requirements for the admission of mainland Chinese merchants were reduced from average annual cross-strait purchases of $500,000 to $300,000 or single-visit purchases of $100,000 instead of $200,000. Their entry permits would also be processed in five days instead of two months.[4]

Vice President Annette Lu had announced in January 2001 that beginning on July 1, 500,000 tourists from mainland China would be admitted to Taiwan. On July 9, however, the MAC announced that detailed arrangements would be "subject to cross-strait negotiations, which we cannot make public for the time being."[5] Finally, Tsai Ing-wen announced that mainland Chinese who were studying abroad or were permanent residents of foreign countries would be admitted to Taiwan as tourists, beginning January 2, 2002. These tourists would have to travel in groups, their visits would be limited to 10 days, and a limit of 1,000 per day would be imposed.[6]

PETROLEUM PROJECT COOPERATION

The China Petroleum Corporation (CPC) of Taiwan and the China National Offshore Oil Corporation (CNOOC) of mainland China agreed in December 2001 to resume the joint petroleum exploration project originally agreed upon in July 1996, but suspended after Lee Teng-hui's July 1999 characterization of cross-strait relations as state-to-state relations. The two state-owned corporations now will invest up to $20 million in a 50-50 joint venture registered in a third country. Signature of the agreement was expected to take place in late December in Kaohsiung during an annual industry conference there that would permit drilling to begin as early as January 2002.[7]

INFORMATION INDUSTRY MANUFACTURING CONTINUES TO SHIFT TO THE MAINLAND

Taiwan's government-backed China External Trade Development Council (CETRA) led a semiconductor trade mission to mainland China in December 2001 to promote cooperation between companies on the two sides of the Taiwan Strait. It is the first time that CETRA has gone to the mainland to promote sales of Taiwan's semiconductor products. Seven of Taiwan's leading semiconductor companies held seminars in Beijing for 800 representatives of mainland semiconductor-related business.[8]

In December 2001 the Ministry of Economic Affairs in Taipei announced that the ban on investment on the mainland for the manufacture of 122 information technology products would be lifted. Among the 122 products were notebook computers, DVD players, and mobile phones. Notebook computer manufacturers, who for a long time had been manufacturing computer components in their mainland factories, now will be able to assemble notebook computers there, both for export and for sale on the growing mainland market.[9] Taiwan's Institute of Information Industry predicted that mainland factories of Taiwan's companies will produce two million notebook computers in 2002, 15 percent of their estimated production of 14 million units.[10]

Until recently, Taiwan had assembled liquid crystal display (LCD) monitors with LCD panels imported from Japan. Gradually, Taiwan manufacturers acquired the technology and during 2000 produced nearly $3 billion worth of LCD panels in Taiwan. Some LCD manufacturing has already moved to mainland China following the established pattern of higher technology flowing from Japan to Taiwan and then on to the mainland.

Since 1996, Taiwan's producers of motherboards have been establishing plants on the mainland. By 1998, 60 percent of the value of motherboards produced by Taiwan companies came from their mainland plants.[11] Asustek, Taiwan's largest motherboard manufacturer has shifted part of its production to the mainland, as have all of Taiwan's other principal motherboard manufacturers. In September 2001, one of them, Gigabyte Technology Co., announced that it was entering into a joint venture with Legend Holdings, the PRC's leading computer company, to produce motherboards on the mainland. Each of the partners will hold a 50 percent interest in the joint venture, which, by combining the production of their existing factories, will produce nine million motherboards annually, making it the third largest manufacturer of motherboards in the world, after Taiwan's Asustek and Elitegroup Computer Systems Company. By joining with Legend, Gigabyte will gain preferred access to China's growing computer market.[12]

Silicon wafer foundries have been among Taiwan's high-tech industries in which mainland investment has been banned, but the EDAC recommended that the ban on 8-inch chip foundries be lifted. In December 2001, Morris Chang, chairman of Taiwan Semiconductor Manufacturing Co. (TSMC), the world's largest contract manufacturer of chips, urged the government to act on this recommendation. He said that even though the mainland microchip market was relatively small, the global semiconductor industry was in a slump. Though there was no need for Taiwan companies to set up 8-inch foundries on the mainland in the near future, China's semiconductor industry would grow rapidly during the coming five years and Taiwan companies would have to position themselves to participate in it. Chang predicted that within 10 years the mainland's integrated circuit design industry might exceed that of Taiwan. TSMC itself has opened a liaison office in Shanghai to explore business relationships with potential foundry suppliers and markets on the mainland, appointing a senior official from TSMC North America to head the office.[13]

Robert Tsao, the head of TSMC's chief rival in Taiwan, the United Microelectronics Corp. (UMC), visited Shanghai in August to explore the possibility of selling 8-inch used foundry equipment to semiconductor manufacturers in mainland China. TSMC officials revealed that their company also had been assessing the prospect for selling some of its used machinery to the mainland.[14]

The PRC is pressing hard to surpass Taiwan in semiconductor production. Its wafer foundries currently turn out only 4-inch, 5-inch, and 8-inch wafers, but three new plants under construction will produce both 8-inch and 12-inch wafers, although Taiwan will still hold an advantage with the world's most advanced 8-inch and 12-inch manufacturing equipment. Its foundries currently account for 13.5 percent of global production. Taiwan also exceeds mainland China in design houses, with 140 in Hsinchu Science-Based Industrial Park, compared with only 21 in Shanghai.

Nevertheless, the PRC has plans to make the Shanghai area the largest semiconductor base in the world and has attracted semiconductor firms from Taiwan, Japan, and the United States to the Zhangjiang High Technology

Park in the Pudong district. Dr. Gong Wang of Taiwan's Industrial Technology Research Institute points out that Taiwan and the PRC are competing strenuously for technology, capital, well-trained high-caliber engineers, and investment environment in building their semiconductor bases.[15]

THREE LINKS

At the panel presentation at Twin Oaks on December 4, 2001, Tsai Ing-wen said that "if we need three links for cross-strait trade, we will find ways to accomplish this." Some progress was evident in devising ways to continue and expand cross-strait trade and travel, despite inability to agree on instituting the full three links.

Taiwan-Hong Kong aviation relations, which had been extended for six months after the previous five-year agreement expired on July 1, 2001, continued into the beginning of the new year, even though no new multiyear agreement had been signed. The delay apparently resulted from differences over whether the new agreement could be negotiated entirely by unofficial organizations, as preferred by Beijing, or would include participation by the MAC, as desired by Taipei.

On October 12, 2001, the MAC reported that the PRC had gradually relaxed its restrictions on visits to Jinmen and Mazu by mainland ships and people under the mini-links program. By the end of September, mainland ships had made 27 voyages to the two offshore islands, and 524 people from the mainland had made the trip. Taiwan vessels made 96 voyages to mainland ports and 8,703 persons from the islands visited the mainland.[16]

On September 5, 2001, the cabinet approved expanding the operation of the mini-links to the Penghu Islands in the middle of the Taiwan Strait. In December the PRC invited two magistrates-elect from Jinmen and Mazu to go to Beijing to discuss cooperation on the mini-links, which Taipei welcomed as an indication that Beijing was becoming more proactive in promoting exchanges through the mini-links.

Taipei altered its regulations to make possible some cross-strait direct shipment via the transshipment center in Kaohsiung, but Tsai Ing-wen said that this was not enough and means should be found to expand it.

Tsai said that establishing a cross-strait air link was the most difficult. She said that once such links had been established, trips by people from Taiwan to the mainland would increase from the current three million per year to five million. Cross-strait negotiations on an air link have been delayed, not only by differences between Beijing and Taipei as to the institutions to be empowered to negotiate, but also by the difficulty of reaching a consensus among Taiwan agencies as to how to prevent opening of cross-strait air travel from endangering Taiwan's security.

Other indications of movement toward opening the three links include the purchase by Taiwan's China Air Lines of a 25 percent stake in a newly established mainland air cargo company, the purchase of a 49 percent stake by four Taiwan air companies in a new airfreight terminal in Xiamen, and the resumption of a biannual seminar on cross-strait shipping services. The seminar, originally established in 1991, but suspended since 1997, was cosponsored by Taiwan's Chinese Maritime Research Association and the mainland's Association for Shipping across the Taiwan Strait and held in Shenzhen in September 2001. Two low-level officials from Taiwan's Ministry of Transportation and Communication attended the seminar.[17]

CONCLUSIONS

Though neither Jiang Zemin nor Chen Shui-bian has been willing to meet the other's terms for the opening of a political dialogue between their representatives, both have favored the expansion of cross-strait economic relations. Membership of both economies in the WTO will further movement in that direction, although it will take time to make the necessary adjustments.

Yielding to business pressures, Chen Shui-bian has consented to the replacement of Lee Teng-hui's policy of "no haste, be patient" regarding Taiwan's investment on the mainland with a new policy designated as active opening, effective management. The new policy reflects Chen's espousal of the middle way in his governance of Taiwan. Carrying out "active opening," the government relaxed restrictions on mainland investment, whereas through "effective management" it moved gradually and carefully on the three links and the admission of mainland tourists to Taiwan. Chen sought a balanced cross-strait policy that would enhance Taiwan's ability to prosper in the global trend toward interdependence without imperiling Taiwan's security or his own political position and prospects.

Taiwan and the PRC are in a transitional period in cross-strait relations. The Chen administration is seeking ways of taking advantage of its election gains in the Legislative Yuan to improve its ability to govern. Leaders in the PRC are probably still mulling over the implications of the Taiwan election for their own cross-strait policy. Both governments need time to adjust to their membership in the WTO. In the meantime, business enterprises on both sides of the strait will be finding way to expand cross-strait economic relations in anticipation of an upturn in the global economy in 2002.

NOTES

1. *New York Times*, 8 November, 2001; *Taipei Journal*, 23 November, 2001.
2. *Taipei Journal*, 18 August, 2001.
3. *China Post*, 10 April and 11 August, 2001.
4. Taipei, *Central News Agency*, 12 and 29 October, 2001; Taipei, *Associated Press*, 29 October, 2001.
5. *Mainland Affairs Council News Briefing*, 9 July, 2001, p. 5.
6. Taipei, *Associated Press*, 23 November, 2001; *China Post*, 18 December, 2001.

7. *Wall Street Journal*, 19 December, 2001.
8. *China Post*, 5 December, 2001.
9. *Reuters*, 30 November, 2001; *China Post*, 1 December, 2001.
10. Taipei, *Central News Agency*, 26 November, 2001.
11. *Taipei Journal*, 20 September, 2001.
12. *Financial Times*, 16 September, 2001; *China Post*, 20 September, 2001.
13. *China Post*, 6 October, 18 December, 2001.
14. *China Post*, 3 September, 2001.
15. *China Post*, 13 December, 2001.
16. MAC press conference, 12 October, 2001.
17. Taipei, *Central News Agency*, 9 September, 2001.

Chapter 11

Outlook for Economic Relations between the Chinese Mainland and Taiwan After Joining the World Trade Organization

Yu Xintian

DEEPENING OF CROSS-STRAIT ECONOMIC INTERDEPENDENCE

In the past 10 years, Taiwan business people have entered the mainland on a large scale and cross-strait economic interdependence has increasingly been enhanced. According to the mainland's official data, by 2000 Taiwan-invested enterprises on the mainland had reached 47,000, with contractual investment of U.S. $48.66 billion and actual investment of U.S. $26.38 billion. But according to the estimate of Taiwan's central bank, Taiwan's investment in the mainland had hit U.S. $70 billion. Economic circles have even estimated the investment at U.S. $100 billion. Driven by a large amount of investment, the total trade volume between the two sides of the strait in 2000 created a record high. According to the mainland's official statistics, the trade volume reached U.S. $30.53 billion, up 30.1 percent over the previous year, whereas according to Taiwan's statistics, it hit U.S. $32.38 billion. The cross-strait accumulated total trade volume had amounted to U.S. $190.93 billion, of which the mainland's export to Taiwan was U.S. $31.04 billion. Taiwan had become the fifth-largest trade partner and the second-largest import market of the mainland. The mainland had become the second-largest export market and the largest source of trade surplus for Taiwan. The proportion of the cross-strait trade in Taiwan's trade had risen from 1.7 percent in 1982 to 11.1 percent in 2000. In the same period, the proportion of Taiwan's export to the mainland in its total export had gone up to 17 percent from 0.88 percent.[1]

The development of cross-strait economic and trade relations not only has been stepped up in quantity but also has undergone qualitative changes in structure. First, the main force of Taiwanese business movement westward has transferred from the traditional industries to industries such as petrochemistry and computers. And their traditional industries entering the mainland have turned from shoe, hardware, and toy manufacturing in the initial stage to electrical household appliances, bicycles, and textiles. Petrochemistry, Taiwan's important pillar industry, has begun to transfer to the mainland. High-tech electronic information industry has moved to the mainland for production in all aspects. The output value of Taiwan-invested computer hardware has accounted for 72 percent of the mainland's total output value of these goods. Most of companies hold that where there is market, there is investment. When global economic competition becomes fiercer and producing cost must be reduced, entrepreneurs can only invest in the mainland. Besides, the mainland itself has an increasing internal demand market.

Second, a new pattern of division of labor has been formed, that is, production and supply on the mainland and marketing in Taiwan. A considerable part of Taiwan's export products are produced on the mainland, for example, 30.9 percent in electronic information industry.

Third, Taiwan's businesses have transferred their manufacturing centers to the mainland; in recent years they have also gradually moved their research and development centers to the mainland because of a shortage of high-tech talent on the island. Universities and colleges on the mainland are able to train 145,000 computer engineers, whereas only 4,000 may be trained in Taiwan. Taiwan-funded research and development centers are mainly concentrated in Beijing, Shanghai, Suzhou, Guangzhou, and Xi'an in cooperation with Qinghua University, Jiaotong University, and Fudan University.

Last, investment has developed from odd enterprises to enterprise groups to joined development zones. In the past, one or two enterprises didn't get anywhere, whereas now core enterprises bring along related upstream and downstream businesses, forming a complete business environment. Taiwan-invested special zones have gradually taken shape through a more than 10-year development period; for instance, there are more than 13,800 foreign-investment enterprises in Dongwan, Guangdong, most of which come from Taiwan. In metropolitan Shanghai, it is estimated that there are 300,000 Taiwanese business people and a few schools for their children.

This phenomenon is of great significance. I. Wallerstein, U.S. initiator of world system theory, said to a journalist with Taiwan's *United Daily News* that, after WWII, there were four countries divided by the Cold War in the world:

Germany, Vietnam, Korea, and China. Germany and Vietnam have been reunified in varying ways. Compared with them, China's divided region is unbalanced, especially in population distribution. He predicted that the two sides across the Taiwan Strait would be reunified in the coming 20 years. He held that in fact the two sides had been reunified in their economies, which was an important step. If Taiwanese business people want to do business on the mainland, they will naturally exert pressures on Taiwan's government and ruling party, which may change Taiwan's political spectrum.[2]

Influenced by the recession of the U.S. and world economy, Taiwan's economy is continuing to sink. The economic growth rate in 2001 will be –2.12 percent, the first negative growth rate in history. It is estimated that the annual nongovernmental investment will drop by 23.8 percent and civil consumption will grow by 1.28 percent, the largest drop since 1956. Besides, although the trade surplus may be reduced, the number of the unemployed may continue to increase, and the local government's financial deficit may get worse. It is estimated that the economic growth rate for 2002 would be 2.23 percent.[3] The mainland's economic growth rate will be about 7 percent. Its attraction for Taiwan's businesses will increase.

CROSS-STRAITS ECONOMIC RELATIONS AFTER THE WORLD TRADE ORGANIZATION ENTRY

After successively joining the World Trade Organization (WTO), the opportunity for complementary and mutual benefit for the two sides across the Taiwan Strait will be expanded, their economic contacts will be more frequent, and a more effective system of division of labor and cooperation may possibly be formed. The reason is that they have common standards for their economic and trade activities. Though there may seem to be many problems now, and the formation of the system will take a very long time, large transnational corporations in the world have drawn up strategic plans according to such recognition. It is almost unavoidable that the development of Taiwan will take the mainland as its hinterland.

Firstly, Taiwan's investment in the mainland will expand from giving priority to manufacturing industry to tertiary industries such as finance, insurance, telecommunications, and tourism, making a significant breakthrough in cross-strait economic relations. After joining the WTO, cross-strait trade and fund contacts will increase by a large margin, the demands for circulating and allocating funds will be more urgent, and Taiwan's commercial banks will inevitably set up branches on the mainland. Taiwan's Ministry of Finance considers that nine banks conforming to its standards have applied to the authorities for operation on the mainland. In fact, Taiwan's First Commercial Bank entered the mainland through Hong Kong at the beginning of 1997 and made money in the first year.[4] Funds from the mainland and Taiwan will be invested in each other's stock markets, and economic interaction between the two sides will be closer.

The per capita insurance revenue on the mainland (RMB 127 yuan in 2000) is far lower than the world's average (RMB 360 yuan in 2000), and the ratio of insurance revenue to gross domestic product (1.8 percent in 2000) is also far lower than the world's average (6 percent to 7 percent). Considering that the potential of the insurance market on the mainland is so huge, no wonder Taiwan's companies eye it covetously and scramble for it. This action will greatly stimulate Taiwan's tertiary industry, promote Taiwan's industrial upgrading, and help establish a new cross-strait industrial system of division of labor.

Secondly, cross-strait investment and trade will gradually move from the current one-way pattern into a two-way one. In the past 10 years, only Taiwanese businesses have invested in the mainland, because the Taiwan authorities have not yet allowed the mainland's investment into the island. In accordance with the WTO's rules, the artificial limitations will be relaxed or lifted. On October 31, 2001, Taiwan's Executive Yuan passed the WTO-related bills, and various service industries such as legal, accounting, and real estate will open much wider to the outside world. Not only foreigners will be involved, but also the mainland's talents.[5] Visiting Taiwan in June 2001, Legend Group, a leading computer authority on the mainland, expressed that Taiwan's companies will be its main external-processing partners, and the scale of placing orders will be enormous.[6]

Thirdly, after joining the WTO, three direct links across the strait will be hard to avoid. Without three direct links, cross-strait trade has had to go through a third location. According to the estimates of Taiwan's aviation circles, the cross-strait air passenger-cargo transport market will create a business opportunity of $40 billion new Taiwan dollars each year.[7] After WTO entry, faced with increasingly fierce competition in the world, reduction of transportation cost will certainly be put on the agenda. The Chinese government's stance is that the three direct links don't have to be resolved through the WTO, and they are part of the internal economic and trade relations within one China, which the Taiwan side does not recognize after stalling for a long time. For this reason, the Chinese government has adopted a flexible policy, advocating that as long as Taipei recognizes that the so-called three links are part of internal affairs of one country, they can be operated at the nongovernmental and enterprise levels and Taipei need not first recognize "one China."

Though cross-strait economic and trade development is an economic behavior, it must have governmental support. In this regard, there are many obstacles on the Taiwan side. First of all, the Taiwan authorities have at last replaced the go slow, be patient policy with an active opening up, effective management policy. But when formulating specific policies, they are not always resigned to it and really are unwilling to open. At first, Taiwan authorities said that the upper limit of U.S. $50 million of investment in the mainland would be lifted, which is welcome, but they also said that an investment of over U.S. $20 million would be examined as a special case, which means the limit is more severe.[8] Even Taiwan's economic circles are worried about much "management" but no "opening-up." Second, the excuse that the Taiwan authorities set up defenses to prevent the mainland's cheap goods from pounding the Taiwan market also does not hold water. In the past 10 years, Taiwan's trade surplus has hit U.S. $130 billion, of which U.S. $20 billion occurred in 2000. Therefore, increase of import from the mainland is inevitable. This increase can give Taiwan consumers more benefits. Last, the Taiwan authorities take "hollowed industries" as the threat and require the industries to "be rooted in Taiwan." This is also completely off the point. The go slow, be patient policy and southward movement policy implemented by the Taiwan authorities for so many years have failed to impede the upsurge of Taiwanese business investment in the mainland. This explains that the economic trend likely to continue. Those industries already having no superiority in Taiwan must be transferred outward, of course, which can make Taiwan a designing, marketing, training, and financial center in division of labor. Taiwan can also join hands with the mainland to develop new technologies, industrialize them, and explore overseas markets with the aid of excellent name brands. It can also rely on its superiority in high-tech, finance, and talent to act as an intermediary for foreign enterprises' entry into the mainland and cooperation with the latter.[9] Only by opening Taiwan to the outside world can the industries be rooted in the island. Where is the world layout without the cross-strait layout? Chen Shui-bian said that Taiwan must "plough Taiwan deep and lay out the whole world." Yu Zongxian, an academician of the Central Research Institution, put forward whether Taiwan will actually accept globalization or concentrate its attention on cultivating localization and whether it will regard the mainland as the hinterland of its development or limit itself to the island. If Taiwan remains undecided, it will lose the opportunity for its economic recovery.[10] People of sagacity have all seen the opportunity for development on the mainland, whereas only the Taiwan authorities are still lost in political consideration. Not long ago, the European Chamber of Commerce in Taiwan issued its annual suggestions. It held that after joining the WTO, the chances for development of the mainland's market would be far larger than that of Taiwan. If Taiwan wants to keep its superiority in economic competition, it must implement reforms and accelerate the cross-strait three direct links.[11] Taiwan has let the this chance slip by. As is known to all, the initial development of the mainland's economy was propelled by Hong Kong capital, which is the reason why it accounts for over 50 percent of the total foreign investment on the mainland. Later, Taiwan investment arrived. But with the acceleration of the mainland's market in line with the international market, European and U.S. investment occupy the largest proportion of foreign investment. This shows that in the past 10 years, Taiwan has missed the best opportunity to develop itself through economic and trade interaction. If Taiwan still regards WTO entry as a political platform rather than an economic one, it will not catch up in the future.

U.S. POLICY TOWARD CROSS-STRAIT ECONOMIC INTERACTION AFTER THE WTO ENTRY

On November 11, 2001, participating in UN general debates, U.S. President Bush extended a welcome to the two sides of the Taiwan Strait into the WTO. He said, "I believe that the entry of China and Taiwan into the WTO will be conducive to consolidating the global trade system and promoting world economic growth." The United States will adopt a constructive attitude, join hands with the two economies, and assist them in meeting challenges to honor their commitments to the WTO. On November 9, C. Barshevsky, former U.S. trade representative, wrote an article that appeared in *The Washington Post* discussing the following advantages of the WTO entry of the two sides across the strait. The first advantage is that the two sides will have a new and unique institutional means of discussing economic issues, one that doesn't raise questions of sovereignty. These means will make the extremely huge informal trade and investment relationship between the two sides across the strait more stable and closer. The two sides can also rely on this mechanism to enhance mutual trust and find common interests. The second is the WTO entry will be beneficial to U.S. export to the mainland, which is still growing by 20 percent. It is estimated that, including Hong Kong, U.S. export to the Chinese mainland equals its export to Germany. The Chinese mainland has become the fifth-largest export market for the United States. The third advantage is that it will complement strengthened human rights on the Chinese mainland. The fourth advantage is it will help strengthen Asia-Pacific peace and security. Though the differences in Sino-U.S. relations will not disappear for this reason, it will reduce chances of conflicts and further develop the common interests between them. This is correct.

The United States has close economic ties with both the Chinese mainland and Taiwan. Handling Sino-U.S. relations after the WTO entry of the two sides across the strait not only involves U.S. economic interests but also is of vital importance to U.S. security interests in this region. To this end, I put forward the following suggestions.

First, the United States should and can promote the interaction of cross-strait economic and trade relations and encourage the two sides to move toward economic integration. As is known to all, the Chinese mainland joined the WTO in the capacity of the People's Republic of China, a sovereign state, whereas Taiwan was in the name of a "separate customs territory within a sovereign state." Taiwan tried every possible way to internationalize the cross-strait relations in the WTO, but it was in vain. The Chinese mainland has worked out flexible policies and adopted enterprise-to-enterprise and a nongovernment-to-nongovernment approach to accelerate cross-strait economic integration. The mainland's economic level is much lower than that of Taiwan, but it actively opens itself to Taiwan. On the contrary, Taiwan is really a closed society. If there are more common interests and interdependence between the two sides across the strait, it will be conducive to common development and prosperity. If the United States gives support, it will certainly create more business opportunities for U.S. entrepreneurs.

Second, the United States can give the Chinese mainland more help, including in the fields of economy, trade, finance, technology, and talent training, in responding to challenges after joining the WTO. This measure will not only support the Chinese mainland's development but also produce an indirect effect on cross-strait economic integration. No matter how the Taiwan authorities place restrictions, Taiwanese business investment in the mainland is irresistible. Besides, polls show that more and more young Taiwan elite will come to the mainland to seek the opportunity to work and develop. Currently, there are 100,000 cross-strait married couples, and the figure is increasing. If the Chinese mainland's economy can maintain sustained, stable, and healthy development, it will be beneficial to Taiwan economy and to Asian development and contribute to U.S. economic recovery. Giving help at a critical moment will not only enable the United States to occupy a bigger share in China's more healthy market, but also will enable it to gain a huge repayment. In this sense, helping China is helping the United States itself.

Third, the United States can support the integration of the Chinese mainland with the East Asian economy and spur Taiwan to join the integration. Predicated on the global recession deepened by the September 11, 2001, incident, conducting economic structural reforms and recovering economic vitality is imminent. East Asian countries should base their economic development on domestic and regional demands. The United States should not worry about being excluded from East Asia, because all the Asian countries are closely related to the U.S. economy. Furthermore, U.S. support for regional cooperation will only strengthen its influence on the region. East Asian countries all actively export to the United States, while the United States absorbs only one-fourth of this region's export; trade between East Asian countries accounts for 50 percent.[12] China is considering setting up a free trade zone covering the mainland, Hong Kong, and Macao, and a free trade zone with the Association of Southeast Asian Nations (ASEAN) 10 by 2010. Taiwan is trying to join the ASEAN 10 through Singapore, which is really seeking from afar what lies close at hand. It is the most convenient path for Taiwan to join the free trade zone of the mainland, Hong Kong, and Macao. If the Taiwan authorities are unwilling, they can consider a free trade zone with the mainland alone or similar arrangements to share the results of cooperative development. Nicholas Lardy, U.S. economist, pointed out that the China is not only a major country introducing foreign investment but also a major country investing abroad. Calculated in the realm of the world, China ranks eighth, whereas the top seven are all developed countries. In other words, China is among the best of developing countries in investing overseas.

He suggested that Taiwan should take advantage of the opportunity to seek a win-win cooperation basis and should not struggle with the mainland. He held that the WTO entry of the two sides across the strait will help relax the tension in the Taiwan Strait, enhance the living standard of the people on the mainland, and be conducive to U.S. economic and political interests. This may be rated as a win-win gain for the three parties.[13, 14]

Lastly, U.S. support of the economic integration between the two sides across the strait will also help the two sides to have more self-confidence and mutual trust and expand and consolidate their base of dialogue. From a long-term point of view, this is a road full of hopes that is beneficial to U.S. politics and economy. For example, there will be a lot of large-scale infrastructure projects in the three direct links. U.S. support will make the people across the strait have greater understanding of the constructive role of the United States, and the United States will gain economic repayment. Its political and economic effects are far greater than sales of arms to Taiwan.

NOTES

1. Mainland Affairs Council, "Monthly Statistics of Cross-Straits Economy," October 2000, p. 24. Available online at http://www.mac.gov.tw.
2. *United Daily News* (Taiwan), 8 October, 2001.
3. *Ta Kung Bao*, 26 November, 2001.
4. *Economic XXX* (Hong Kong), 22 October, 2001.
5. *United Daily News* (Taiwan), 1 November, 2001.
6. *China Electronics Daily*, 31 June, 2001.
7. *Central Daily News* (Taiwan), 31 October, 2001.
8. *United Daily News* (Taiwan), 7 November, 2001.
9. Ibid., 15 November, 2001.
10. Ibid., 5 November, 2001.
11. Ibid., 23 November, 2001.
12. *China Times* (Taiwan), 12 November, 2001.
13. *United Daily News* (Taiwan), 16 December, 2001.
14. *China Times* (Taiwan), 12 November, 2001.

CHAPTER 12

The Cross-Strait Balance and Its Implications for U.S. Policy

David A. Shlapak

INTRODUCTION

Though the political situation across the Taiwan Strait seems driven by a recurring cycle of tension and relaxation, the military forces on both sides consistently regard one other with a wary eye. The Chinese People's Liberation Army (PLA) stands as Beijing's ultimate deterrent to Taiwanese independence, whereas the armed forces of the Republic of China (ROC) prepare to defend their island against any assault from the mainland.

Both China and Taiwan are engaged in ongoing programs of military modernization. On China's side, these efforts are aimed at increasing Beijing's freedom of action vis-à-vis Taiwan by both augmenting the PLA's capabilities to take successful offensive action against the island and making it more difficult and costly for any external power—especially the United States—to intervene in a cross-strait clash. For Taiwan's part, its military is focused on countering this evolving threat.

This chapter attempts to briefly address three topics. First, it assesses the state of each side's military modernization program. Second, it discusses the cross-strait military balance and presents some thoughts on the kinds of threats China might realistically pose to Taiwan in the near term. The chapter concludes with suggestions for how U.S. policy can help promote a stable military balance between Beijing and Taipei.

MILITARY MODERNIZATION IN CHINA AND TAIWAN

Although upgrading China's defense capabilities was proclaimed as one of the Four Modernizations promulgated in 1973, Chinese real defense spending did not enjoy significant growth until the 1990s. Fueled by China's dramatic economic expansion, real military expenditures then began to grow steadily, increasing by over half between 1991 and 1998. China's military budget has continued to grow since, including a nearly 18 percent increase for the past year, the largest rise of the decade in real terms. Taken in all, the resources available to the PLA have increased significantly—perhaps by 80 percent or more—since 1990.

It is important, however, to see these dramatic spending increases in the appropriate context. For most of the 1990s, China's defense budget went up more or less in parallel with the country's rate of overall economic growth, and even today its military spending almost certainly remains right around 3 percent of the country's gross domestic product. Furthermore, some of the recent large increases in the official defense budget are almost certainly intended to offset losses in off-the-books income being incurred by the PLA as it withdraws from the civilian economy per Jiang Zemin's directive in July 1998. In other words, China is hardly embarked on a reckless military buildup. All indications are that internal stability and economic growth remain the primary goals of the Chinese leadership; increased military power, although important, continues to be a secondary goal to be pursued in a measured and affordable manner.

At the same time that we should not overestimate the pace of China's defense modernization we also should not underestimate the magnitude of the task at hand. Beijing faces a monumental job in improving its military infrastructure and capabilities. Doctrinally, the PLA has made an important transformation, evolving from planning for a "people's war"—relying on a massive peasant army of "rifles and millet" to overwhelm an attacking enemy in a prolonged campaign fought in the vast hinterlands of China's immense territory—to focusing on what the Chinese call "local wars under high tech conditions" (LWUHTC), conflicts that will call for rapid offensive operations conducted beyond China's borders. The new doctrine radically alters the demands placed on the PLA, calling for it to develop land, sea, and air power projection capabilities beyond anything it has attained previously. Succeeding in a complex LWUHTC will require that the PLA substantially revamp itself in virtually every important aspect, including its force structure, command and control and logistics systems, and training procedures.

The massive Chinese military has been likened to a boxer with short arms and slow feet, and more than a decade of concerted effort has produced only slow progress in correcting its manifold deficiencies. Despite numerous programs to build modern military equipment at home and procure it abroad, the PLA in 2001 is still largely equipped with tanks, fighters, and warships based on 40- to 50-year-old Soviet designs. Much of its order of battle is two or three technological generations behind counterpart weapons fielded by the United States and Taiwan.

This is not to say that meaningful improvements have not taken place. The Chinese have acquired a number of advanced weapons from Russia, including

Su-27 fighter aircraft, Su-30MK multirole fighter-bombers, KILO attack submarines, and Sovremenny destroyers. China has also undertaken licensed production of the Su-27 and is reportedly developing a new indigenous fighter (the J-10) and three submarine classes (the diesel-powered Song and two nuclear subs, the Type-93 attack boat and the Type-94 strategic-missile submarine). Though many of these systems are still not operational, and those that are in the PLA inventory have in some cases experienced teething pains as the troops have learned how to operate and maintain them, if carried to completion, such programs should greatly improve the hardware dimension of China's military power.

China has also proven itself capable of designing and producing high-quality ballistic missiles. According to reports, China may have as many as 350 short- and medium-range missiles stationed within range of targets in Taiwan and may also be nearing deployment of its first mobile, solid-propellant intercontinental ballistic missile, the DF-31, which was first flight tested in 1999. China is also reportedly embarked on a high-priority effort to develop land-attack cruise missiles (LACMs), air-launched versions of which could be operational around 2005. LACMs could pose a qualitatively new problem for Taiwan since carrier aircraft could conceivably fly to locations north, south, and even east of the island before launching their missiles, thus presenting an all-azimuth threat to defenses that have typically been oriented westward, toward the mainland.

Perhaps most importantly, China has begun to revamp the PLA's institutional side as well. The army's disentangling from the civilian economy, undertaken in the name of improved military effectiveness, has already been mentioned. Also, the PLA has slimmed down substantially over the past decade and plans to shed additional manpower in coming years; so-called fist units, intended to be the leading edge of the ground forces' rapid-response capability, have been formed in most military regions. Training programs have been revised and become more demanding and realistic, and new logistics and command and control (C2) infrastructures—better suited to supporting the LWUHTC doctrine—are reportedly being put in place.

In all of these areas, however, China is starting from the bottom of very steep learning curves. Building modern logistics and C2 systems will be a long and very expensive process. Development of the operational-level doctrines needed to support the overall LWUHTC concept will proceed slowly, particularly because Chinese thinking on the vital topic of joint operations remains in its infancy. Despite changes in training curricula and standards, many PLA exercises remain highly stylized and scripted, and the army, navy, and air force continue to have difficulty working closely together. And, even with the ongoing infusion of Russian-built equipment, Beijing's arsenal will remain dominated by antiquated, obsolete weapons for years to come, and deficiencies in maintenance and training will likely limit the operational usefulness of its most modern platforms. The spotty historical performance of indigenous arms production efforts—it has in the past taken the Chinese more than a decade to even reverse-engineer existing weapons systems—suggests that it will be many years, if ever, before Beijing can be militarily self-reliant in any meaningful way. The PLA's modernization program will therefore continue to depend in large measure on episodic and expensive purchases from sometimes-unpredictable foreign suppliers.

For the next 10–20 years, then, the Chinese military will see modest, gradual improvements in capability but will also continue to struggle to overcome its many problems. By 2020 the PLA will almost certainly be a higher-quality force than it is today—smaller in size than at present and still limited in capability compared with the U.S. military—but with at least some forces capable of undertaking power projection operations along China's immediate periphery.

On the other side of the Taiwan Strait, modernization is also proceeding at a moderate pace. For many years, Taiwan's defense programs have been constrained by Taipei's inability to procure armaments on the open world market like a so-called normal country. Wanting to restrain Taiwan's military capabilities, Beijing has consistently pressured arms-exporting nations such as France, Germany, and the Netherlands to forego or severely limit sales to Taiwan. Sino-U.S. relations have also been adversely affected on a number of occasions by strident Chinese opposition to proposed transfers of American arms to Taiwan. These pressures have made it almost impossible in the past for Taiwan to acquire submarines, for example, for its navy. In addition, the Taiwanese economy, while less affected than many others in the region by the Asian financial crisis of 1997–98, has been hammered by the steep downturn in the global high-tech sector over the past 18 months. With gross domestic product (GDP) stagnating and many economists predicting the onset of a serious global recession that would further dampen demand for the Silicon Island's exports, the ROC military may find itself with fewer resources with which to address the island's growing defense needs. Taken together, these two factors are likely to continue to restrict the pace and extent of Taiwan's military modernization.

To be sure, Taiwan's military is starting from a higher base than is the PLA; on average, Taiwanese equipment is more modern and its troops better-trained than their mainland counterparts. Like the PLA, however, the Taiwan military has suffered from institutional problems. In particular, foreign arms purchases have frequently been pursued as much for their symbolic value, indicating the selling country's support for Taiwanese security, as they were for the actual capabilities the new weapons added to the ROC's arsenal. Therefore, acquisitions have often focused on high-visibility, big-ticket items—American fighters, French frigates, and the like—and neglected other critical but less-glamorous aspects of military power such as training, spare parts, and support. Ongoing reforms within the Taiwan Ministry of National Defense (MND) and armed forces have promise for helping correct these problems, but it will take years for the ROC military to completely overcome the legacy of past decisions.

At this writing, Taiwan continues to acquire and integrate new weapons into its force structure. For example, in August 2001, the commander of the ROC Air Force (ROCAF) announced that two wings of F-16 fighters would at last become operational in early 2002. Taiwan has also reportedly decided to purchase the four ex-U.S. Navy Kidd-class guided missile destroyers that the Bush administration offered to Taipei in April 2001; when they enter ROC Navy service, the Kidds will be the most advanced and well-balanced surface combatants on either side of the Taiwan Strait. Taiwan's tactical C2 system would be measurably improved by the proposed purchase of 50 U.S. Joint Tactical Information Distribution System (JTIDS) terminals and associated hardware and software. The United States has also agreed to sell Taiwan 12 P-3 Orion antisubmarine warfare (ASW) aircraft and to assist Taiwan in acquiring up to eight badly needed diesel-powered attack submarines.

THE CHINA-TAIWAN MILITARY BALANCE AND CHINESE OPTIONS

China's leadership sees maintaining its claim to sovereignty over Taiwan as critical to regime survival, and Beijing is committed to having a credible ability to use force against Taiwan should it come to regard such action as necessary. How do the militaries of the two sides stack up against one another, and what options for using force against Taiwan does China have?

The mainland certainly enjoys a significant numerical advantage over Taiwan in every meaningful category of weaponry. The PLA Air Force, for example, fields over 3,000 fighter and attack aircraft versus about 500 for Taiwan, the Chinese navy has more than 30 operational submarines as against 2 for Taiwan, and so forth. Though Beijing could not bring all of this combat power to bear in a conflict with Taiwan, it would certainly enjoy a significant edge in numbers as well as a much greater potential to rapidly make good its combat losses.

Significantly offsetting China's numerical superiority is Taiwan's overall qualitative advantage. As noted earlier, Taiwan's military is by and large fitted out with weapons and equipment that are considerably more modern than the majority of the gear fielded by the PLA, and the island's forces are also better trained than their mainland counterparts. The average Taiwanese air force pilot, for example, flies about 150–180 hours each year compared with around 100 hours for a PLA aviator; that difference would have a substantial impact of the outcome of any air-to-air combat between the two sides.

One much-discussed cross-strait scenario involves a Chinese attempt to invade and occupy Taiwan. In a prior study, the author and two colleagues examined such a contingency in detail, focusing on a large-scale Chinese attack in the period between 2005 and 2010.

The analysis envisaged large-scale Chinese air and missile attacks lasting several days coupled with a major naval battle for control of the waters of the Taiwan Strait. Within this basic context, we studied almost 2,000 different campaigns, varying such critical factors as the size and modernization level of Chinese forces, the relative training levels of the two sides, the extent of direct U.S. involvement in the defense of Taiwan, and so on. We evaluated each of these cases to determine whether China could gain a meaningful level of air or sea superiority. Chinese control of the air and sea would at minimum leave Taiwan at Beijing's mercy and would go a long way toward enabling China to invade the island; Chinese inability to win the air and naval battles, on the other hand, would virtually preclude any prospect of their occupying Taiwan.

Our broad findings were consistent with what has been the general wisdom on this topic: by and large the PLA appears unlikely to be able to achieve the degree of air and maritime superiority required to lay Taiwan open for invasion. However, our research did identify a number of key factors that had sizeable impacts on the likelihood of a successful defense by the Taiwanese. Here we highlight four.

First, our analysis assumed that Taiwan's will to resist would not crumble at the first touch of Chinese steel. Though our assessment showed that the effectiveness of Taiwan's military forces was somewhat degraded by China's air and missile attacks, we assumed that the ROC would fight on; there was no catastrophic collapse of national will. Though this was an almost automatic assumption to make for this kind of assessment—after all, there's little point to a war game if one side chooses not to fight—in the real world, Taiwan's willingness to sustain a costly battle against the mainland is an important consideration that should be taken into account in any assessment of the cross-strait military balance.

On an operational level, Taiwan's military, and especially its air and air defense forces, needs to take steps to ensure that it has the ability to continue fighting effectively even after absorbing heavy Chinese attacks. The analysis indicates that there is great leverage available to Taiwan from passively protecting its military infrastructure to ensure that the ROC air force, in particular, can continue to operate while sustaining ongoing missile and air strikes. Fairly straightforward steps in this direction, such as improved hardening for fuel supplies and maintenance facilities and more and better equipment and training for rapid runway repair, could significantly blunt the military effects of China's missile arsenal for at least the next decade.

Similarly, a successful defense will require that Taiwan's C2 system be both capable and robust. To fight outnumbered and win, the Taiwanese need to maximize the effectiveness of their smaller forces, which means being able to employ them where and when needed. Improvements in early warning and battle management as well as survivability could have major payoffs for Taiwan. The acquisition and integration of JTIDS will be a helpful step in this direction as would purchasing additional AWACS-type aircraft and the upgrading of the ROCAF's existing E-2T Hawkeye radar planes. Also, Taiwan needs a modern identification friend or foe system to permit it to more effectively knit together the army's surface-to-air defenses with the fleet of air force interceptors.

Finally, the United States could play a crucial role in helping Taiwan defend itself. Across all cases studied, Taiwan left on its own had only about a 50-50 chance of denying air control to the Chinese. Adding a single U.S. fighter wing flying from bases in Japan or one carrier battle group operating in the open ocean east of Taiwan raised the defense's success rate to about 65 percent. Small increments of U.S. forces, such as a squadron of bombers armed with antiship missiles stationed on Guam and two or three attack submarines operating near the strait appeared to have similarly disproportionate impacts on the naval war. That such modest amounts of U.S. combat power could make such a difference was perhaps the most interesting and surprising result of the study.

If an outright invasion of Taiwan would be high-risk gambit for China, Beijing may have more attractive options at lower levels of violence. Taiwan's economy is highly dependent on maritime trade; its exports totaled over $148 billion in 2000, representing more than 38 percent of its GDP. Imported energy is also vital to Taiwan; more than 99 percent of its coal and oil and almost 95 percent of its natural gas come from foreign suppliers. It seems possible, then, that China could attempt to coerce Taiwan by interdicting or threatening to interdict commercial shipping going to and from Taiwan.

The PLA navy enjoys an overwhelming numerical advantage in submarines, and its most advanced KILO submarines are very capable weapons for either open ocean or littoral operations. Furthermore, the waters of the Taiwan Strait are shallow and noisy, making them a very poor environment for ASW operations. Chinese submarines could exploit these advantages to directly attack ships near Taiwan's handful of ports or lay underwater mines that, when activated, could sink or disable even large freighters or tankers. Mines could also be laid by air, from surface vessels, or even covertly, from commercial vessels; Iran used the latter tactic effectively against tanker traffic in the Persian Gulf during its war with Iraq. Just the threat of submarine or mine attacks could raise insurance rates to prohibitive levels or deter shipping operators from approaching Taiwan's waters altogether; the impact on Taiwan's trade-driven economy of any significant reduction in seaborne commerce would be immediate and dramatic. Taiwan requires greatly improved ASW and countermine warfare capabilities if it is to be able to neutralize this potentially catastrophic threat. Though the P-3, submarine, and countermine helicopter acquisitions agreed on between the United States and Taiwan in April 2001 will help address this threat, it will be many years before these platforms are fully operational in the ROC military. Even then, countering sea mines may remain a problem for Taiwan unless steps are taken to improve its capabilities in that area.

China's surface-to-surface missile force, which is likely to include cruise as well as ballistic missiles within the next decade, constitutes another threat to Taiwan, and one that is likely to grow in severity in the coming years. With projected increases in the numbers of deployed missiles as well as expected improvements in their quality, by 2010 or so this arsenal will likely be able to hold at risk a variety of key economic and military targets throughout Taiwan. Countering China's missiles will require a multifaceted response in which active defenses will certainly play a role. In the near to mid-term, however, Taiwan should invest a substantial amount of energy and resources in passive defenses, such as hardening key military and economic facilities such as airbases and petroleum storage sites. Large industrial facilities such as semiconductor factories will remain vulnerable—although selected passive measures may somewhat increase their survivability as well—but maximizing the level of protection given to those assets that can be hardened will permit such active defenses as are available to be concentrated around critical softer targets.

China could also employ special operations forces (SOFs) against critical infrastructure targets in Taiwan. The ROC's electrical power grid, for example, is notoriously unreliable; the 1999 collapse of a single high-tension tower in central Taiwan in an earthquake-induced landslide blacked out 80 percent of the island. Two months later an earthquake knocked out a single substation; much of Taiwan was plunged into darkness, and power shortages continued for several weeks afterward. SOFs could also be used against other economic or military targets, either independently or as part of a larger Chinese pressure campaign.

CONCLUSIONS AND IMPLICATIONS FOR U.S. POLICY

From what we have seen of China and Taiwan's respective modernization programs, three general observations can be made.

First, while both sides are working hard to upgrade their military capabilities, neither is embarked on the kind of breakneck or crash program that could upset the overall cross-strait balance in the near to mid-term. China has the material potential to significantly increase its rate of external arms acquisition should it decide to devote more spending to the military, but,

- the PLA will likely continue to experience difficulties assimilating and operating advanced weaponry because of limitations in training, maintenance, and doctrine; and
- China's indigenous arms industry is showing few signs of making the kinds of breakthroughs in development and production capabilities that would be needed to enable the mainland to become self-reliant in equipping its military.

For its part, Taiwan's ability to modernize its armed forces will continue to be constrained by the reluctance of its foreign suppliers, including the United

States, to provide Taipei with the full range of equipment that it appears to desire. Taiwan's own laboratories and factories are capable of fulfilling some but by no means all of the ROC's requirements; in this regard, the Taiwanese military finds itself in the same boat as the PLA.

A second point is that China's ability to use force against Taiwan is and will probably continue to be circumscribed by shortfalls in important capabilities. It is unlikely that China will soon be able to credibly threaten the invasion and occupation of Taiwan; the PLA appears unable to gain the necessary air and sea superiority, and except under the most favorable circumstances, it would have trouble transporting sufficient forces across the strait to overcome serious Taiwanese resistance. Instead, the PRC's most credible threats will be at lower levels of violence, with military power being employed to coerce rather than conquer Taiwan. China has several options at these lower rungs of the escalation ladder, including mining or blockade of Taiwanese commerce or limited missile or SOF attacks directed against important economic or military targets on the island.

It is difficult to predict how effective coercive attacks would be at changing Taiwanese behavior; the historical record is inconclusive with regard to such tactics. What can be said, however, is that to at least some extent, China's weakness on the upper end of the violence scale should reduce the efficacy of any coercive strategy. The only military option that guarantees China control of Taiwan is to seize and hold the island; China's inability to credibly threaten such an undertaking essentially caps the threat that the PLA can present to Taipei and denies it escalation dominance. Absent the risk of invasion, a Taiwan willing to absorb whatever blows China can deliver could conceivably defeat even a sustained and violent campaign of coercion. Whether or not Taiwan could or would be able to do so is, of course, an open question.

A third point is that in the long term, the advantage in the cross-strait military balance may lie with the PRC. To a certain extent, the limitations on China's military power are self-imposed; should Beijing choose to put significantly more emphasis on modernizing its armed forces, its huge economy and relatively free access to the cash-and-carry international arms market would seem likely, over time, to give the mainland an edge over Taiwan. If accelerated modernization of hardware were accompanied by institutional reforms both within the PLA and in its supporting industrial base, the improvement of the PLA's military position could eventually be sufficient to upset the political balance between Beijing and Taipei and dramatically destabilize the cross-strait situation.

From a U.S. perspective, this outcome—indeed, any destabilization in the China-Taiwan relationship—is one to be avoided. The United States has consistently maintained that the denouement of the cross-strait situation, whether unification or no, should be arrived at through peaceful means. Furthermore, the Bush administration has gone farther than its predecessors in asserting the U.S. commitment to support Taiwan in the event of an unprovoked attack from the mainland, meaning that a clash between China and Taiwan is likely to embroil American forces as well. To the extent, then, that a reasonable correlation of forces between the two sides is a necessary, though certainly not sufficient, condition for keeping peace between the mainland and Taiwan, Washington has a clear stake in sustaining that military balance.

In April 2001, President Bush indicated his intent to terminate the existing process by which the United States reviews Taiwan's requests for military assistance on an annual basis. Instead, Bush said, the United States would provide arms to Taiwan as needed. By avoiding a yearly decision on weapons sales, this policy change removes what had become an recurring neuralgic point in Sino-U.S. relations, potentially reducing the visibility of U.S.-Taiwan defense cooperation while putting it broadly on the same footing as other foreign military sales activities. This normalization promises continued support for Taiwanese defense needs while perhaps reducing the contentiousness of the arms transfer process.

Taiwan could benefit from U.S. assistance in many areas, including a number of less visible ones. The U.S. could, for example, help improve the ROC military's passive defenses to enhance survivability and operability in the event of Chinese air or missile attack. U.S. advice would also be valuable in helping along Taiwan's nascent MND reforms, as well as in improving training and maintenance programs and C2 procedures and equipment. Taiwan requires significant improvements in its doctrine for joint, all-arms warfare; here, too, the United States could provide valuable assistance. All of these are ways of helping the Taiwan military get maximum bang for the bucks it has already invested in assembling a fairly formidable collection of modern equipment.

As far as new weapons systems are concerned, the United States should ensure that Taiwan's advantage in air power remains unchallenged by the PRC. Steps in this direction could include the actual provision of AIM-120 advanced medium-range air-to-air missiles to the ROCAF and the sale of more, and more capable, E-2 airborne radar and C2 aircraft. The United States should also help Taiwan acquire the most advanced available technologies for countering sea mines, which pose a very real threat to the island's commercial lifeline. Additional mine-clearing ships and helicopters are needed, as is better training.

Finally, the United States will eventually need to make a decision regarding how to deal with China's missile buildup opposite Taiwan. In particular, the question of how much to assist Taipei in deploying a reasonably effective ballistic missile defense (BMD) will have to be addressed. At present the point is somewhat moot, as all available BMD systems are of only limited operational effectiveness. However, as more capable interceptors are developed and fielded, the issue of whether to provide them to Taiwan—with all the friction such a decision would almost certainly produce in Sino-U.S. relations—will have to be confronted.

Recent events in the United States and central Asia have shifted American and global attention away from the western Pacific in general and the China-Taiwan confrontation in particular. U.S. efforts to gain Chinese cooperation in a campaign against terrorism may even open the door to a dramatic improvement in relations between Washington and Beijing. Nevertheless, until either China forswears the use of force against Taiwan or the United States abandons its half-century-long commitment to support the security of that vibrant island democracy, the Taiwan Strait will remain a potentially dangerous flashpoint between the Pacific region's two greatest powers. Avoiding war between China and Taiwan is mainly a political challenge, but it has an important security component. Helping ensure that the present, fairly stable, military balance across the strait remains intact into the future seems likely to remain a core component of U.S. strategy toward this important and volatile situation.

CHAPTER 13

Cross-Strait Confidence Building: The Case for Military Confidence-Building Measures

Bonnie S. Glaser

INTRODUCTION: WHY CROSS-STRAIT CONFIDENCE-BUILDING MEASURES ARE NEEDED

Political relations across the Taiwan Strait remain at an impasse, and prospects for resumption of cross-strait dialogue are dim, at least in the near term. Beijing continues to insist that Taiwan President Chen Shui-bian accept the existence of one China as a precondition for reopening talks. President Chen has raised the possibility of a future one China and also has talked about the creation of a "new framework of permanent peace and political integration." He remains unwilling, however, to consider returning to the 1992 Consensus on one China that was reached by representatives of the two sides in Singapore almost a decade ago. Since Chen's election as president, the mainland has adhered to a policy of "listening to his words and watching his deeds." Barring a radical shift in Chen's policy toward cross-strait relations, Beijing is unlikely to abandon this approach. Thus, a near-term breakthrough in cross-strait relations is unlikely.

Despite the lack of progress on the political front, cross-strait trade and economic ties are growing apace, and people-to-people contacts are expanding. In January 2001, Taipei opened the three mini-links of direct trade, transport, and postal services between its outlying Kinmen and Matsu islets with selected Fujian ports. Direct links are likely to be gradually broadened following both sides' entry into the World Trade Organization. Two-way trade between the mainland and Taiwan reached $30 billion in 2000, making Taiwan China's sixth-largest trading partner. Taiwanese firms have invested a total of U.S. $50 billion in the mainland since the late 1980s. One-fifth of that amount has been invested in the past two years. Investment will likely increase in the wake of Taipei's decision in August 2001 to gradually lift controls on cross-strait economic and trade exchanges, including scrapping the $50 million ceiling on individual mainland investment cases. The People's Republic of China (PRC) benefits from the infusion of Taiwanese capital, technology, and managerial and marketing skills, whereas Taiwanese firms depend increasingly on access to the mainland as a market and production base.

The expansion of trade and economic and social contacts across the Taiwan Strait should provide reason to be cautiously optimistic that a peaceful solution between the people on both sides of the strait can eventually be worked out. Any optimism must be tempered, however, in view of the apparent acceleration of the militarization of the relationship between China and Taiwan. The PRC is developing the capability to apply military pressure on Taiwan, not only through deployment of ballistic missiles, but also through development of conventional air and naval forces as well as land-attack cruise missiles. In addition, China seeks the capability to deter the United States from intervening in a crisis on Taiwan's behalf. Beijing continues to refuse to renounce the use of force against Taiwan because it views the threat of force as the only effective means of deterring Taipei from declaring independence. To meet the growing military threat and resist coercion from China, Taiwan is seeking to acquire more advanced weapons systems, including the Aegis combat system as well as missile defense capabilities. Moreover, there is discussion in Taiwan about the need to develop counteroffensive capabilities to deter and defend against an attack by the mainland.

The crisis in the Taiwan Strait in 1996 when China fired missiles into the waters off Taiwan underscored the danger of growing tensions between Beijing and Taipei. Since cross-strait relations remain unstable, a repetition of that crisis is easily imaginable. In addition, the possibility that an accident could escalate to conflict is growing. Increased sorties by the PRC and Taiwan fighters in the Taiwan Strait—including jets occasionally crossing the midline that demarcates the air space of the two sides either inadvertently or deliberately—pose such a risk, especially in the absence of a communications link between the two militaries that could be employed in a crisis to clarify both sides' intentions.

It is in the interests of Washington, Beijing, and Taipei to prevent armed conflict in the Taiwan Strait and, if possible, slow the trend toward a costly and potentially destabilizing arms competition. Construction of a stable set of cross-strait relationships can serve to ease tension and inhibit crisis. This is already taking place to a limited extent in the economic and cultural spheres.

To make further progress in this direction, steps might be taken between the two defense establishments to build trust and minimize the chances of an armed clash arising from misunderstanding or miscalculation. The implementation of cross-strait military confidence-building measures would serve this end and would be a win-win achievement for Taiwan and the mainland.

While negotiations of thorny political issues such as sovereignty will be arduous, especially in the near term, confidence-building measures (CBMs) are relatively easy to negotiate and to implement. They can be tacit and informal and based on mutual consensus without formal, legally binding agreements. As such, they are ideally suited to the Taiwan situation. Cross-strait CBMs could begin with an initial phase of unilateral declaratory measures that evolves into a succession of reciprocal declaratory statements and actions. This could be followed by modest, easy-to-negotiate bilateral initiatives and gradually build to more complicated and advanced measures. Substantial progress in the implementation of military CBMs and the creation of a genuine confidence-building dynamic presupposes significant improvement in political relations between the two sides, however.

This chapter begins addressing the subject of cross-strait confidence building by discussing definitions of CBMs and providing a brief history of CBMs in Europe and their application in the Asia-Pacific region. This is followed by some examples of CBMs between nonstate parties. Subsequent sections assess factors that complicate cross-strait confidence building, PRC wariness of cross-strait CBMs and military confidence building with Taiwan, and prevailing incentives for China to proceed with CBMs despite its concerns. The risks and benefits for Taiwan in pursuing cross-strait CBMs are subsequently analyzed, and the positions of the Taiwan government past and present on implementing cross-strait CBMs are discussed. The role of the United States in a cross-strait confidence-building process is also addressed. Finally, a road map of possible cross-strait CBMs is presented in three phases, beginning with unilateral, declaratory measures and preliminary military CBMs aimed at reducing the risk of conflict due to miscalculation or accident. Mid- and long-term phases consisting of more advanced CBMs are outlined that presuppose an improved political atmosphere as well as a higher degree of trust across the strait than currently exists.

DEFINING CBMS

There is no single, universally accepted definition of CBMs, which are also sometimes referred to as confidence- and security-building measures (CSBMs). Some definitions are quite broad, encompassing a multitude of trust-building initiatives across the spectrum of relations between two hostile states or parties. The Confidence and Security Building Measures Working Group of the Council for Security Cooperation in the Asia-Pacific (CSCAP) uses an expansive definition that includes "both formal and informal measures, whether unilateral, bilateral or multilateral, that address, prevent, or resolve uncertainties among states, including both military and political elements."[1] In this definition, CSBMs include virtually any measures that contribute to a reduction of misperception, suspicion, and uncertainty. These measures do not necessarily have to be directly concerned with security, but their combined impact contributes to a lessening of tension and an increase in trust.[2]

CBMs can also be defined more narrowly as initiatives designed to make military intentions more explicit by increasing transparency and predictability, thus reducing the risk of accident or miscalculation.[3] This objective is achieved by such steps as the exchange of information about each other's military activities and doctrine, contacts between militaries, and communication measures such as the setting up of hot lines and the establishment of conflict-prevention centers. Notification and mutual observation of military maneuvers and missile tests can also be beneficial in building trust. Once confidence levels have reached a relatively advanced stage, constraining military operations can also play an important role. However, constraining measures in the CBM context are not binding to the extent that legal treaties are and therefore must be differentiated from arms control/limitation measures.

The history of confidence-building efforts demonstrates that CBMs need to be tailored to the distinctive geographical, political, and cultural environments prevailing in a given region or situation. In the European experience, CSBMs have focused more narrowly on initiatives in the military/security sphere. In the Asia-Pacific region, both narrowly defined military measures and more broadly defined political, economic, humanitarian, and environmental measures have been applied.

Taipei and Beijing can benefit greatly from the implementation of CBMs that avert misperception and misunderstanding that can escalate to military conflict. The establishment of communication links (hot lines) between the two militaries could substantively contribute to the avoidance of miscalculation in a crisis. In addition, an explicit agreement on rules of engagement for jet fighters that includes refraining from flying across the invisible central line of the strait or conducting provocative flights against each other could minimize the risk of an air battle breaking out due to misjudgments made by pilots. More fundamentally, however, the cross-strait situation requires an approach that can alter the existing hostile images and perceptions. Gradual steps are needed that can transform negative perceptions and build a less-hostile and eventually cooperative relationship.

A prerequisite for successful implementation of CBMs is that both sides believe that it is in their national interest to reduce uncertainties, avert accidents that could escalate to conflict, and make relations more predictable. There must be political will to proceed. For the process of confidence building to get underway between Beijing and Taipei, both must hold the judgment that the benefits to be gained outweigh the risks associated with cooperation or the unilateral advantages to be gained by not cooperating. As Ralph Cossa has noted, "CBMs must be viewed in 'win-win' not 'win-lose' terms."[4]

A BRIEF HISTORY OF CBMS

CBMs were sporadically used in the first half of the twentieth century as a means of reducing tension and increasing transparency of military intentions. European militaries allowed observers from other states to watch exercises prior to World War I, and the Versailles Treaty included provisions establishing military liaisons to increase Allied coordination. Though historians differ about what early efforts constitute CBMs, many agree that overtures by the United States to the Soviet Union, beginning in the 1950s, represent the first significant generation of CBMs.

In 1955, President Dwight D. Eisenhower proposed the Open Skies Treaty, an agreement permitting overflights of military facilities and exchanges of blueprints. Though the Soviet Union rejected this offer at the time, it is regarded as one of the first efforts to promote military transparency during the Cold War. The United States also proposed a hot line with the Soviet Union to improve crisis management after the Cuban missile crisis. Along the same vein, the United States and Soviet Union signed several agreements in the early 1970s to reduce the risk of accidental nuclear conflict by improving nuclear infrastructure, early-warning systems, and communication channels. CBMs played a critical role in avoiding conflict and building trust in East-West relations.

These bilateral efforts were only a precursor to the watershed event in the history of CBMs—the signing of the Helsinki Final Act in 1975 by the members of the Conference on Security and Cooperation in Europe (CSCE), a multilateral organization encompassing all of Europe besides Albania and including the United States, Canada, and the Soviet Union. In the Helsinki Final Act, the CSCE agreed to institutionalize confidence-building measures as a means of promoting European security. Specifically, the Helsinki Final Act required prior notification of military exercises of a certain size and exchange of observers. Though these provisions were not strictly adhered to, these meetings and future discussions spurred the Conference on Confidence and Security Building Measures and Disarmament in Europe in Stockholm, the most extensive CBM agreement ever reached.

After two years of negotiations, the Document of the Stockholm Conference was signed in 1986. The document outlines five CBMs: prior notification of military activities, observation of military activities, annual calendars, and verification and compliance. The Stockholm Document is especially significant because it included extensive verification procedures that created a greater level of enforcement to CBMs with far-reaching implications for European militaries.

The United States and Soviet Union continued to experiment during the late 1980s with CBM-type agreements. These agreements built on earlier attempts to reduce the nuclear danger by establishing nuclear risk-reduction centers to improve information exchange. These efforts at reducing East-West tension continued in the early 1990s with the signing of several agreements in Vienna that provided additional notification requirements on military exercises and added some constraints on allowable military movements.

In the post–Cold War period, nations and parties in other regions sought to adapt the European experience to their own situations and implemented CBMs to reduce uncertainty and avoid unintended conflicts. States and hostile parties in the Middle East, South Asia, Latin America, Africa, central Asia, and the Asia-Pacific have employed CBMs to promote stability.

ASIA-PACIFIC CBMS

CBMs have been widely employed in the Asia-Pacific region in unilateral, bilateral, and multilateral contexts. In contrast to the European approach to CBMs, Asia-Pacific states have opted for largely informal attempts to foster dialogue instead of binding agreements. Asian nations have created several multilateral fora to discuss issues of regional concern. The primary multilateral track I efforts include the Association of Southeast Asian Nations (ASEAN) and its larger cousin, the ASEAN Regional Forum (ARF), a multilateral forum for security dialogue that was created in 1994. Both are consensus-driven organizations that have taken a gradual approach to CBMs and preventive diplomacy.[5] The ARF has focused its efforts on several important security issues in the Asia-Pacific region, including piracy, environmental threats, and maritime shipping coordination. ASEAN ministers concluded an agreement in 1996 to establish a regional code of conduct for the South China Sea to enable multilateral cooperation against piracy and drug trafficking without involving disputed territorial claims. ASEAN members are currently working on formulating a broader code of conduct to deal with disputes.

Nongovernmental actors have also played an important role in CBMs in the Asia-Pacific region. The Council for Security Cooperation in the Asia Pacific (CSCAP) is one of the largest nongovernmental, track II efforts to encourage dialogue by regional experts on Asia-Pacific security challenges. In February 2001, CSCAP issued a memorandum on Cooperation for Law and Order at Sea, which was written by members of its working group on maritime CBMs. Other regional track II efforts include the Northeast Asia Cooperation Dialogue and the South China Sea Informal Meeting. Both groups provide a setting for informal dialogue on their respective issues.

Asian nations have also conducted CBMs bilaterally. Singapore and Malaysia signed a Memorandum of Understanding in 1995 that established the Malaysia-Singapore Defence Forum, an institutionalized military dialogue where high-level officials discuss areas to improve defense cooperation and interaction. Singapore and Malaysia have used these contacts to reduce lingering suspicion after their political separation in 1965 and to coordinate greater levels of joint defense cooperation and training.[6]

Japan has also been active in using CBMs to reduce regional tension, often through declaratory measures. During the Cold War, Japan largely relied on unilateral declarations renouncing war and nuclear weapons to attempt to allay regional fears of a resurgent Japanese military. Japan has continued these declaratory statements, while also pursuing bilateral CBMs. Despite lingering territorial disputes and the absence of a peace treaty, Japan and Russia have established annual policy-planning talks along with ministerial and military exchanges. Partly as a result of these discussions, Japan and Russia signed an Incidents at Sea Agreement in 1993 and have also engaged in maritime search and rescue cooperation.[7] These efforts to facilitate dialogue between the two nations have reduced tensions and made cooperation in other disputed areas of the relationship more feasible.

Japan and South Korea have also engaged in military CBMs in the 1990s, primarily in the naval arena. South Korea made its maiden port call to Japan in 1994, and the two nations established a military hot line soon after. These initial steps led to regularized ministerial meetings and academic exchanges. Contacts between Japan and South Korea's military have grown in recent years as formal dialogue at higher levels and commitments to joint naval exercises have been undertaken.

In addition to East Asia, CBMs have also been widely used in South Asia. The dispute between India and Pakistan over Kashmir is an explosive territorial conflict that has sparked three wars and is generally regarded as posing the most dangerous threat of nuclear conflict in the near term. The nuclear detonations by India and Pakistan in 1998 only highlight the importance of injecting confidence into the India-Pakistan relationship. India and Pakistan have experimented with CBMs in the past to quell tensions resulting from intensified violence in Kashmir. Specifically, India and Pakistan have signed agreements to provide advance notice of military exercises, prevent violations of air space, and conduct operations in border areas.[8]

Mainland China was opposed to CBMs until the mid-1980s, but since then has gradually implemented confidence-building measures with the United States as well as with many neighboring countries. This shift is likely a result of Beijing's recognition that CBMs can be beneficial in the creation and preservation of a peaceful international environment that China deems essential for its economic development. Since the early 1990s, China and the United States have established a series of CBMs, including high-level military exchanges, military academic exchanges, reciprocal visits of naval warships, and functional military exchanges. In June 1998, Jiang Zemin and Bill Clinton signed an agreement to not target each other with their strategic nuclear weapons. In January 1998, the two sides signed a Military Maritime Consultative Agreement, which calls for convening an annual meeting and for the establishment of working groups to discuss issues of mutual concern with the aim of preventing possible crises on the high seas. In the past decade, China has also implemented CBMs with India and Russia, bilaterally, as well as with Kazakhstan, Kyrgyzstan, and Tajikistan.

CBMS INVOLVING NONSTATE PARTIES

CBMs are not limited to sovereign states and have achieved some degree of success when applied between hostile parties where one or both sides are not sovereign entities. Specifically, parties to disputes, often substate political representatives or quasi-state governments, have engaged in low-level dialogue and preliminary exchanges of information in an effort to build trust and establish lines of communication. The general goal of these exchanges has been to increase the political comfort level of the parties and provide a basis for future discussion and cooperation. Over time, these informal networks can instill an operational-level trust that may spur more formalized and structural agreements. Instances in which CBMs have been implemented between hostile parties in which either one or both participants have not been sovereign states have taken place in Europe, the Middle East, Africa, and Latin America. Although these confidence-building measures have not resolved the underlying disputes in these areas, they have contributed to a reduction of violence and in some cases created an atmosphere conducive to negotiations toward a more lasting settlement.

The conflict over the political status of Northern Ireland is historically one of the most hotly contested political disputes. The United Kingdom and various nonstate representatives of the inhabitants of Northern Ireland, particularly Sinn Fein and the Ulster Unionists, have achieved substantial progress in recent years in addressing the governance of Northern Ireland, partly due to the contribution made by CBMs. The United Kingdom and political factions within Northern Ireland have engaged in extensive CBMs to create the necessary political will and trust to initiate and follow through with the Ulster peace process and implement the Good Friday Agreement. Early CBMs included secret dialogue between the Irish Republican Army (IRA) and an emissary of the British Government from 1990 to 1993 and later public talks between John Hume and Gerry Adams, which kick-started the process in 1993 and 1994. Both sides used declaratory pledges of nonviolence to convince the opposing sides of their willingness to compromise. The IRA declared a series of cease-fires in response to British attempts to scale back Britain's military presence in Northern Ireland, eliminate internment powers, and increase the rights of inhabitants.

Following the signing of the Good Friday Agreement in 1998, both sides have gradually moved toward implementation of their obligations. In the Northern Ireland case, U.S. mediation has played a crucial role in encouraging public statements supporting a nonviolent resolution of the dispute.

Small-scale moves have been used to boost confidence and indicate a willingness to honor the agreement. Recently, the IRA has allowed inspections of arms bunkers by international weapons inspectors to signal their commitment to decommissioning weapons, a critical step in removing the threat of force from the political dispute over Northern Ireland. Though these efforts fall short of formal verifiable decommissioning, they are nevertheless an important step in convincing the United Kingdom of the IRA's desire for peace. The Northern Ireland example illustrates the critical role of initial dialogue for increasing understanding and the importance of CBMs throughout the process of negotiation and implementation.

Israel's negotiations with the Palestine Liberation Organization (PLO) provide another prime example of CBMs between a state and a nonstate political representative of the population. Stretching back to the Camp David Accords of 1978, it was agreed that Israel, Jordan, Egypt, and representatives of the Palestinian people should participate in negotiations on the resolution of the Palestinian problem. Real negotiations with the PLO did not materialize until 1993, when Israeli Prime Minister Rabin and Yasir Arafat signed the Declaration of Principles, which contained a statement on mutual legitimate existence, thus in effect recognizing the PLO as the legal representative of the Palestinian people. In a gesture aimed at building trust, Israel released Palestinian political prisoners. This initial agreement led to the Interim Agreement on the West Bank and Gaza Strip in 1995, which included a Palestinian pledge to revoke those articles of its covenant calling for the destruction of Israel. These early efforts, along with steps by the Israeli police and military forces to moderate their treatment of Palestinians and increase freedom of movement, helped engender trust between the two sides and provided a modicum of political will necessary to reach a broader agreement.

Unfortunately, these efforts have unraveled in recent years. The assassination of Prime Minister Rabin dealt a serious blow to supporters of the peace process within Israel and eliminated one of the few Israeli politicians with sufficient stature and willingness to advance the peace process. The efforts of his successor, Prime Minister Ehud Barak, were met with substantial public skepticism, and a renewed campaign of terror has undermined the efforts of diplomacy and confidence building. The failure of CBMs to promote an enduring peace and build confidence between Israel and the PLO demonstrates the potential pitfalls involved and underscores the necessity that both parties have political will to proceed and are committed to the confidence-building process.

FACTORS THAT COMPLICATE CROSS-STRAIT CONFIDENCE BUILDING

There are factors in the cross-strait situation that make the implementation of CBMs especially challenging. These factors need to be understood, but they do not necessarily pose insurmountable obstacles to progress.

- China and Taiwan have asymmetrical threat perceptions. Taipei is concerned about a military attack launched by the mainland and is also worried that the Chinese may use military means to coerce the island into accepting the PRC's terms for political negotiations. Beijing is fearful that Taiwan is drifting toward separation from the mainland and may eventually declare formal independence. The PRC views its military buildup against the island, in part, as necessary to deter such an outcome.
- There is a huge disparity between the two sides' military forces, both in terms of numbers and in power projection capability (as well as nuclear capability). China has developed and deployed offensive military capabilities against Taiwan. Taipei primarily has defensive weapons and capabilities.
- China has so far judged that its interests are best served by keeping Taiwan off balance, rather than by enhancing Taiwan's sense of security.
- China views the threat of force as essential to deter Taiwan independence, which is an obstacle to agreement that neither side will initiate use of force against the other. Beijing outlined the conditions under which it would resort to force against Taiwan in its white paper on Taiwan that was released in February 2000.
- Beijing insists that the cross-strait relationship is an internal affair. China opposes international mediation efforts, which may rule out the possibility of external diplomatic assistance and, possibly, third-party verification of CBMs.
- China is not inclined to be transparent in the field of military affairs, although the Chinese have made some progress in this regard in recent years. China has published two white papers on national defense, the first in 1998 and the second in 2000. In 1995, it published a white paper on China's arms control and disarmament. Taipei has increased transparency by publishing white papers on national defense every two years since 1992 that, by comparison, contain more detailed facts and figures about its armed forces and defense budget.
- Taipei has had little opportunity to develop expertise in arms control. Since it is not recognized internationally as an independent, sovereign state, Taiwan has not been able to participate in multilateral arms control fora such as the Conference on Disarmament. It is not a signatory to international arms control treaties nor a member of treaty-based intergovernmental organizations related to arms control. It has had no experience in negotiating or implementing CBMs with China or any other country. This lack of knowledge and experience has resulted in skepticism and suspicion about the benefits of arms control for Taiwan and may hamper the process of pursuing CBMs across the strait.

By contrast, the PRC has gained substantial experience in arms control in the past decade. The process of acceding to the Non-Proliferation Treaty (NPT) in 1992, signing the Chemical Weapons Convention (CWC) in 1993, negotiating and signing the Comprehensive Test Ban Treaty (CTBT) in 1996, and participating in the Conference on Disarmament in Geneva has provided Chinese officials with a great deal of knowledge about international arms control norms and practices. U.S.-Chinese discussions of arms control and nonproliferation have also significantly contributed to China's understanding of these issues. China has also gained experience in CBMs through the negotiation and implementation of the Shanghai Accord with Russia and the Central Asian Republics (Kazakhstan, Kyrgyzstan, and Tajikistan) and the New Delhi Accord with India. These agreements have resulted in programs for military exchanges and various border agreements, including the establishments of hot lines, border demarcation negotiations, prior notification, and restriction of military maneuvers and troop movements along the borders.

MANAGING CHINESE CONCERNS AND POTENTIAL REACTIONS

China is likely to resist discussion of CBMs with Taiwan, at least initially. Since CBMs historically have been most often applied between two sovereign states and Beijing's CBM experience has been confined to its relations with other sovereign states, China will fear that the very act of agreeing to hold CBM talks with Taiwan would bestow upon Taipei an actual international position or provide opportunities for Taipei to promote itself as an independent country in the international arena. Beijing may seek to obtain a statement from Taiwan on the existence of one China as a precondition to engaging in CBM discussions.

The Chinese may also be wary that U.S. efforts to promote cross-strait CBMs are part of a broader strategy to perpetuate the separation of Taiwan from the mainland. There is a widely held assumption in China that the United States opposes reunification of Taiwan with the mainland and that American policies are aimed at either preserving the status quo or supporting Taiwan independence. In a worst-case scenario, Chinese concerns could adversely affect Beijing's cooperation with Washington in arms control and nonproliferation since China continues to link U.S. policies toward Taiwan with Chinese willingness to cooperate on proliferation and arms control matters.

If progress toward cross-strait CBM implementation is to be achieved, it is therefore important to understand Chinese concerns and then consider whether and how to assuage Chinese worries. To persuade Beijing of its sincerity in embarking on a confidence-building process across the strait, Taiwan should avoid using CBMs to elevate its international status or promote the island's existence as a separate state. This would undermine the entire confidence-building process, even though it might be politically popular domestically. It would also risk sending the signal to Washington that Taipei is not seriously interested in stabilizing the situation across the strait. Instead, Taipei should seek to craft CBM proposals with an eye to strengthening China's perception that Taiwan is not seeking the establishment of two separate states. Taiwan should also be willing to refrain from trying to participate in ongoing multilateral CBMs and dialogues from which Beijing has excluded Taipei until progress is made bilaterally. Statements of U.S. support for cross-strait CBMs should stress the goals of boosting confidence and understanding between China and

Taiwan and minimizing the possibility of conflict resulting from miscalculation or accident.

China will also likely suspect that U.S. support for arms control education and training for Taiwan officials is linked to an effort to forge closer U.S.-Taiwan military ties. The Chinese already fear that the United States and Taiwan are covertly planning to develop operational military links. This concern has been fueled in part by discussion of U.S. provision of advanced theater missile defense systems to Taiwan and Taipei's interest in acquiring Aegis-equipped destroyers that may serve as a future platform for upper-tier Theater Missile Defense (TMD). A transparent approach with Beijing that emphasizes the limits of U.S. involvement and the benefits for Taiwan and China of employing CBMs to enhance cross-strait stability may ease Chinese concerns to some extent.

INCENTIVES FOR CHINA TO ENGAGE IN CBMS WITH TAIWAN

Though Beijing will no doubt have reservations and suspicions, the Chinese leadership also has reasons to view the opening of a dialogue and subsequent implementation of cross-strait military CBMs as potentially beneficial to Chinese interests. First, the preservation of peace and stability in China's periphery remains the backbone for the country's stable economic development. Beijing and Taipei both share a strong interest in minimizing the risk of accidental war in the Taiwan Strait. Second, engaging in cross-strait CBMs could shore up domestic support for the Chinese leadership, especially if the confidence-building process is perceived internally as promoting reunification with Taiwan. Third, cross-strait CBMs would diminish the concerns of the people on Taiwan about China's bellicose intentions toward the island that have been especially prominent since the 1995–96 missile firings. Beijing asserts that its one country, two systems proposal is intended to reassure the people on Taiwan that they can preserve their way of life and remain secure. If China truly seeks to strengthen the sense of security of Taiwan's people, then CBMs are a good means to achieve that goal.

A fourth benefit for Beijing in implementing military CBMs with Taiwan is the promotion of dialogue and interaction between the Taiwan and PRC militaries. In the past few years, the expansion of contact across the strait has been limited primarily to academics, business people, scientists, and cultural and tour groups. Initiating contact between the two sides' militaries will provide a new channel for cross-strait interaction. Moreover, under Beijing's one country, two systems proposal for reunification, Taiwan would retain its military forces after reuniting with the mainland. The early promotion of mutual contact between the two defense establishments to lay the groundwork for future cooperation and coordination should therefore be in Chinese interests. A fifth advantage of CBMs for China is the possibility that significant progress in confidence building between the two sides of the strait, if accompanied by a reduction in the Chinese military threat to the island, would, over time, reduce pressure on the United States from Taipei as well as from members of Congress to sell more weapons to Taiwan.

The Chinese are not irrevocably opposed to engaging in cross-strait military CBMs. In fact, prior to former Taiwan President Lee Teng-hui's public remark characterizing relations between Taiwan and China as those between two sovereign states in July 1999, the People's Liberation Army (PLA) was conducting research into cross-strait CBMs and the possibility of opening contacts with Taiwan's military. According to a senior colonel from China's National Defense University, the PLA sees an opportunity in the development of cross-strait military contacts to bolster the role of the Taiwan military, which, like the PLA, is staunchly opposed to independence for the island. The same senior colonel pointed to the common position held by Beijing and Taipei on Chinese ownership of the Spratly Islands as a basis for dialogue between the PLA and the Taiwan military.[9]

In an unpublished paper, another retired PLA senior colonel from the General Staff advocated that both sides of the strait explore CBMs in the political, economic, and military realms.[10] Some of the specific CBMs he cited include the establishment of a hot line between leaders as well as local commanders, the conduct of joint military exercises in the coastal strait areas, the provision of advance notification of major military exercises and military deployments, the conduct of regular visits by senior military leaders, the holding of port calls for naval ships, the exchange of observers to military exercises of the other side, cooperation in maritime safety measures and the establishment of joint rescue procedures, and joint reaffirmation of the no-flying line in the center of the Taiwan Strait. The precondition for pursuit of CBMs, according to the retired PLA officer, is Taiwan's acceptance of Beijing's one-China principle.

In the same unpublished paper, the retired PLA officer put forward his view that the mainland should agree to freeze its deployment of Short Range Ballistic Missiles (SRBMs) along the coast in exchange for a Taiwan declaration to freeze its purchase of military weapons from abroad. Though such a trade-off would not place limits on the mainland's growing air and naval threats to Taiwan and thus would not be in Taipei's interests, it nevertheless holds out the possibility that mutual constraint measures could be negotiated if and when there is a high level of confidence attained between the two sides of the strait. Although it is uncertain whether the PLA officers' views and recommendations are shared by others in the PLA or the senior Chinese leadership, it is nevertheless significant that some PLA experts are considering cross-strait CBMs and are making specific suggestions in internally circulated papers.

BENEFITS AND RISKS FOR TAIWAN

The negotiation and implementation of military cross-strait CBMs should be done gradually and cautiously. Comprehensive assessments should be conducted of each proposed CBM, including the possible dangers that any measure could pose for Taiwan's national security. Only CBMs with a good chance of successful implementation should be pursued to reinforce the overall objective of increasing mutual confidence and reliability. In general, however, CBMs involve few risks. They are informal and not binding so can be halted if deemed necessary in response to a violation or provocation from the other side.

Like China, Taiwan would profit from the implementation of CBMs that reduce the risk of miscalculation and escalation of incidents in the air or at sea. The opening of a dialogue between the two sides' militaries could lessen misunderstanding and remove misperceptions. Advocacy of CBMs by Taipei, along with positive declaratory statements demonstrating Taiwan's sincere intentions, will put pressure on China to appear more reasonable in the eyes of the international community. Taiwan's declared interest in discussing cross-strait CBMs with the mainland would no doubt be viewed by the United States as a constructive step that is conducive to the easing of tension between the two sides of the strait.

Backing a CBM agenda with the mainland will also likely receive domestic approval in Taiwan. Public opinion polls show that the majority of the Taiwan people support reduced tension with China and hope that their government will improve cross-strait relations. Of course, if there is no reciprocity from the mainland, then the Taiwan government could be vulnerable to charges of making too many concessions to Beijing. Therefore, Taipei should proceed slowly, in a step-by-step manner. President Chen Shui-bian has already followed a course of seeking to persuade Beijing of Taiwan's good will toward the mainland. Confidence-building initiatives would be compatible with this policy.

Specific military CBMs could carry small risks. For example, information exchange can be used to spread disinformation that would provide China with an advantage in a military crisis. There is also the risk that information being passed is incomplete, for example on weapons inventories, but the sharing of partial information is still preferable to the provision of no data at all. Agreement on measures that constrain the military activities and deployments of both sides, which would likely only be considered at an advanced stage, holds the risk of cheating or violations and thus should include appropriate verification provisions.

Of greatest concern to Taipei is probably the possibility that the implementation of CBMs with mainland China may result in reduced support in the United States for selling arms to Taiwan. If a pattern of confidence building across the strait takes hold and the PRC military threat to the island begins to ease, it is inevitable that the issue will come to the fore of whether and how United States arms sales to Taiwan should be modified to contribute to the process of improving cross-strait relations. The mainland will almost certainly argue that continued advanced weapons sales to Taiwan are undermining the positive trend in cross-strait relations. Beijing's urgency to reduce U.S. weapons sales to Taiwan would, however, likely diminish if the political atmosphere in cross-strait relations has improved and CBMs are being implemented.

Cross-strait CBMs that establish communication channels, provide for greater transparency of military activities, procurements, and deployments, and improve maritime safety will not likely have any appreciable impact on political support in the United States for arms sales to Taiwan. If the PRC indicates a willingness to lessen the military threat it poses to Taiwan by such steps as reducing its power projection forces and deployments opposite the island, then the issue of whether to modify or curtail U.S. weapons sales may arise. Chinese willingness to take such major steps, however, would likely presuppose an advanced degree of reconciliation between the two sides and a possible agreement on political arrangements.

FACTORS FAVORABLE TO CBM IMPLEMENTATION ACROSS THE STRAIT

The extensive European experience of confidence building through the CSCE process suggests that CBMs simply cannot work in the absence of a political decision to attempt to alter the negative security relationship between the relevant parties. There must be a shared desire to move, however slowly, from misunderstanding and suspicion, to mutual reassurance, and, from there, toward active cooperation. CBMs are tools to help promote positive interactions in the pursuit of a new security relationship.

Although the process of cross-strait discussion and implementation of bilateral CBMs will no doubt be long and arduous, there are reasons that the two sides may find compelling to initiate a process of confidence building:

- There is no hostility between the people on either side of the strait. They have a similar origin, culture, and language. With the exception of small number of aboriginal people, the vast majority of Taiwan's 22 million inhabitants are of Han Chinese ancestry. Eight percent of those immigrated to Taiwan from the mainland in the beginning of the sixteenth century; 20 percent arrived after the Communists defeated the Nationalist government in 1949. Taiwan culture has its roots in the mainland, and both peoples speak the same language (along with other dialects).
- People-to-people interaction between China and Taiwan has been expanding rapidly, especially in the business and cultural fields. Trade and economic relations have also continuously increased in the past decade. Politically, China has assiduously sought to develop contacts with Taiwan's opposition parties in the past year. Developing contact between the two militaries can be viewed as an extension of the process underway of broadening cross-strait contacts.
- Both seek to avoid war and increase economic prosperity. Escalation to conflict is bound to harm economic development on both sides of the strait. The proximity of the PRC's and Taiwan's naval and air forces operating in and around the strait increases the likelihood of accidental encounters. The modernization of PRC forces will further raise the chances of accidents occurring between the two sides' military

forces. The absence of effective communication channels and mechanisms for crisis management significantly increases the possibility of conflict as a consequence of misunderstanding or miscalculation.

- China's recent emphasis on making positive overtures to those in Taiwan who favor one China and wooing Taiwan investors shows a recognition that reliance on military threats and bellicose rhetoric undermines Beijing's goal of peaceful reunification.
- Whereas in the past Beijing agreed to open negotiations with Taiwan as a provincial government, China's new position that both the mainland and Taiwan are part of one China suggests that China will accept Taiwan as an equal partner at the negotiating table. This should make discussion and implementation of CBMs easier than in the past.
- Initial contacts between the two militaries have already taken place with the visits of retired military officers from Taiwan to the mainland to hold discussions with military and civilian specialists at such institutions as the PLA's National Defense University and the PLA General Staff's China Institute of International Strategic Studies.

TAIWAN'S POSITION ON CROSS-STRAIT MILITARY CBMS

Taiwan President Chen Shui-bian has expressed interest in the establishment of a mutual CBM with China. In his election victory speech on March 18, 2000, President Chen explicitly endorsed the pursuit of cross-strait military CBMs, stating that "[w]ith the prerequisite of ensuring state security and the people's interests, we are willing to negotiate on cross-strait direct transportation and trade links, investment, a peace agreement, a military mutual-confidence-building mechanism, and other issues." Since his inauguration, President Chen has called for "the establishment of a Taiwan Strait conflict management and prevention mechanism to maintain regional peace and stability."[11]

Prior to Chen Shui-bian's election, his Democratic Progressive Party published a white paper on national defense that included a lengthy section on cross-strait CBMs.[12] CBMs were portrayed as a means of averting conflict as a result of accident or miscalculation as well as an instrument to build trust and foster good will between the two sides of the strait. The white paper specifically espoused the implementation of transparency measures, including prior notification of military exercises and troop movements, exchange of military information, and open publication of military research and weapons purchases and sales. It also called for the implementation of maritime safety measures, including maritime emergency assistance and cooperation to capture maritime criminals and handle fishing disputes. Other CBMs, such as the establishment of a military hot line, exchanges of military personnel, and jointly working out rules of engagement for Taiwan and PRC forces, were also mentioned in the white paper.[13]

Taiwan's leading opposition party, the Kuomintang (KMT), also favors discussing cross-strait CBMs with the mainland. When President Lee Teng-hui was still in office, he stated on April 9, 1999, that "there are many mechanisms that can be used to achieve peace across the Taiwan Strait. We can also discuss military issues, including the possibility of using military CBMs." A year earlier, Premier Vincent Siew had first proposed exchanging information on military exercises with the mainland and establishing military CBMs to promote military transparency and avoid miscalculation.[14] KMT presidential candidate in the 2000 elections Lien Chan also endorsed negotiation of CBMs with the mainland. "While intensifying our defense war readiness to cope with the worst case of war, I deeply hope in the future for an active development and building of cross-strait military confidence-building forces," Lien Chan said. "Through engagement and understanding between the concerned personnel, I aspire to resolve conflict, even setting up a notification and verification system and hot line for mutual military exercises, to avoid unnecessary irritation and overreaction.[15]

Taiwan military leaders have also spoken out in favor of implementing cross-strait CBMs and cooperating with the PLA. For example, Defense Minister Wu Shi-wen noted that although the two sides of the Taiwan Strait have not established a military dialogue mechanism, there is room for cross-strait CBMs. Wu specifically called for the two sides to begin cooperating in non-political humanitarian operations such as emergency rescue or maritime and air disaster relief work. "The two sides could then gradually forge mutual trust through cooperation in both non-military and military fields," he added.[16] Taiwan's most recent national defense white paper, released in August 2000, mentioned for the first time the military's plan to promote the establishment of a mutual trust mechanism with mainland China's PLA.[17]

On July 6, 2000, Taiwan's Ministry of National Defense sponsored a seminar on the proposed establishment of a mechanism for military exchanges across the Taiwan Strait. The seminar brought together government officials, industry executives, scholars, and experts to discuss the feasibility of establishing a cross-strait military mutual trust mechanism as part of overall cross-strait CBMs. The agenda also included the possible impact of the proposed cross-strait military mutual trust mechanism on the Republic of China's national security. According to a Ministry of National Defense spokesperson, the seminar marked just an initial step in mulling the feasibility of developing a military exchange or mutual trust mechanism with mainland China.[18]

ROLE OF THE UNITED STATES IN PROMOTING CROSS-STRAIT CBMS

The role of the United States in facilitating the discussion and implementation of CBMs between Beijing and Taipei should be extremely limited. Washington should not mediate between the two sides, nor should the United States propose specific CBMs for consideration. The U.S. approach should be evenhanded, and any assistance provided by the United States should be offered to both sides. For example, the United States could help both China and Taiwan take advantage of educational opportunities in the United States to gain more expertise in arms control theory and practice in preparation for the possible opening of a Taiwan-China dialogue on CBMs. This is especially important in the case of Taiwan, which has had little, if any, training and experience in CBMs. Experts from both sides of the strait could jointly attend CBM courses at private institutions such as the Monterey Institute of International Studies or participate in CBM workshops at the Cooperative Monitoring Center at Sandia Laboratories.

The United States could also facilitate the establishment and development of contacts between the Taiwan and PRC militaries by providing a forum for discussion. Washington could encourage an American-based think tank to bring together experts from Taiwan and China in a track II conference to discuss cross-strait CBMs. Participants from both sides of the strait could include military scholars and retired military officers to explore specific CBMs that might be acceptable to both sides.

One reason that the United States should not aggressively push a CBM agenda is that doing so could create a perception in Taiwan that Washington is putting undue pressure on Taipei to negotiate with the mainland. This could make the Taiwan government vulnerable to charges that its policies have resulted in a U.S. decision to no longer abide by the Six Assurances. The Six Assurances, which successive U.S. administrations have annually reaffirmed since the signing of the August 17 Communiqué with the PRC in 1982, state that Washington (1) has not agreed to set a date for ending arms sales to Taiwan; (2) will not hold prior consultations with mainland China on arms sales to Taiwan; (3) will not revise the Taiwan Relations Act; (4) will not play any mediation role between Taipei and Beijing; (5) has not altered its position regarding Taiwan's sovereignty; and (6) will not exert pressure on Taipei to enter into negotiations with mainland China.

A ROAD MAP OF MILITARY CBMS

Confidence building is most successfully pursued as a step-by-step process that, in the early stages, focuses on unilateral declaratory measures. Once the two parties have engaged in a succession of reciprocal declaratory statements and actions, then the stage is set for preliminary bilateral efforts. Early bilateral measures should include relatively modest, easy-to-negotiate initiatives that do not exceed the level of political rapprochement existing between parties. No timetable should be set for progress toward more ambitious CBMs. Only those CBMs that have a reasonable chance of being approved by both sides should be proposed and discussed to avoid increasing suspicions.[19]

Below is a menu of options for possible cross-strait CBMs in three phases, short-term, medium term, and long term. Phase one is divided into two parts: declaratory initiatives and options for cross-strait military CBMs that can be considered at the present time in the absence of a significant reduction of political tensions across the strait. Phase two options assume improvement in the larger political relationship between Beijing and Taipei. Phase three options include ambitious CBMs that would require a high level of trust between the two sides.

Phase One: Declaratory Initiatives

Declaratory measures are public statements that set out one party's position on a particular issue in such a way that it reassures the other party. They usually begin as unilateral initiatives and, over time, may be reciprocated by the other side, thereby promoting a broader confidence-building dynamic. Declaratory measures pose little or no risk to national security, but can serve important political ends, both domestically and internationally. Statements that clarify one side's position or intentions put the onus on the other side to respond in kind. They also remove any excuse that the other side may have for stepping up military pressure or relying on harsh political tactics. Declaratory CBMs often win praise from the international community and earn respect from abroad for the national leader that is responsible for issuing them. Moreover, declaratory CBMs have the potential to generate public support or to muffle domestic criticism. As Michael Krepon and Jenny Drezin note in their writings on declaratory diplomacy, "The right combinations of words, symbolic gestures, and actions can mobilize support and isolate recalcitrant forces at home and across troubled borders."[20] Krepon and Drezin also point out that national leaders can use declaratory initiatives to fashion an image of self-confidence rather than weakness.

To be effective in persuading the other side of one's commitment to confidence building, proclamations of reassurance must be believable. They may also require accompanying action, especially when mistrust is deep and long-standing. Krepon and Drezin explain that "Declaratory CBMs need to jar pre-existing mindsets, an especially difficult task, which is why reinforcing actions are essential.... Leaders who wish to reconcile with adversaries cannot depend on words alone; they must undertake a coherent and comprehensive strategy that demonstrates 'credible commitment.' Political risk taking for reassurance can demonstrate credibility."

Understanding the psychology of the other side is imperative for declaratory CBMs to be successful. A common language, culture, and history, such as that which prevails in cross-strait relations, provides an especially favorable environment for declaratory CBMs to be used effectively. A national leader's choice of wording determines whether his statement signals good will and sincerity or is merely empty rhetoric. As an example of a successful declaratory CBM, Egyptian President Anwar Sadat delivered a speech before the Israeli Knesset in 1977 in which he used empathetic language in making an appeal to the common interests of both sides to break down differences between Arabs and Israelis. Sadat sought to heal wounds and build common ground by speaking of tragedies experienced by both sides and shared bereavement resulting from past wars.

Taiwan President Chen Shui-bian has made declaratory statements aimed at reassuring mainland China and building trust across the strait on several occasions, both before and after his election victory in March 2000. In his inauguration speech, for example, President Chen pledged that as long as the Chinese Communist Party regime has no intention to use military force against Taiwan, he would not declare independence, he would not change the national title, he would not push forth the inclusion of the state-to-state description in the Constitution, and he would not promote a referendum to change the status quo in regard to the question of independence or unification. In addition, he promised that the abolition of the National Reunification Council or the National Reunification Guidelines would not be an issue.[21]

In President Chen's New Year's address on December 31, 2000, he similarly attempted to convey good will to the mainland. Chen expressed his belief "that the people on the two sides of the Strait share the same roots as well as the common goal of coexistence and co-prosperity" and noted that both sides had indicated "the wish to live under the same roof." Taking advantage of the common language used by both sides of the Strait, President Chen appealed to the PRC to jointly search "for a new framework of lasting peace and political integration between the two sides."[22]

There are also historical examples in which Taipei employed declaratory CBMs and followed with unilateral reinforcing actions. In 1987 Taiwan lifted martial law, and in 1991 terminated the "period of mobilization against communist rebellion," marking an end to Taipei's stated aim of retaking the mainland by force. Subsequently, Taiwan gradually reduced its military forces deployed on Kinmen and Matsu, started publication of a white paper on national defense, and began public announcements of all major military exercises. In another instance of a unilateral good will gesture to the mainland, on the eve of Taiwan negotiator Ku Chen-fu's visit to China in 1997, Taipei cancelled a major annual military exercise to create an amicable atmosphere for the visit.

Beijing has used declaratory measures in its policy toward Taiwan, as well. Chinese President Jiang Zemin's 1995 Eight-Point Proposal for reunification included the statement that "Chinese will not fight Chinese." As noted above, in August 2000 Chinese Vice Premier Qian Qichen signaled that Beijing would deal with Taipei as an equal negotiating partner by declaring that Taiwan and the mainland are both part of China. The PRC has also frequently employed declaratory statements in the nuclear sphere, for example by declaring in the wake of its first nuclear test in 1964 that China would never initiate use of nuclear weapons against a nuclear power and would never employ nuclear weapons against a non-nuclear state. In a joint declaratory measure, Russia and China pledged in 1994 not to use nuclear weapons against each other and not to target each other with nuclear weapons.

Both sides of the strait could consider the following declaratory CBMs to advance the confidence-building process to a higher stage:

- China could forswear the use of military force against Taiwan except under the sole condition that Taipei declares de jure independence. If Beijing refuses to relinquish the use of force, then it could at least emphasize its preference for a peaceful solution and rely on peaceful means to achieve that objective. Taipei, if unwilling to rule out independence as an option, could agree not to hold a national referendum on the island's status for a set period, perhaps 10 years.
- Both sides could publicly express their intention to resolve disputes peacefully and eventually to sign a joint statement ending hostilities across the Taiwan Strait.
- Beijing could state orally, or include in its white paper on national defense, a position that Taiwan is covered by China's pledge not to initiate first use of nuclear weapons. Taipei could, in turn, forswear the development of nuclear weapons.
- Taipei could express a willingness to limit its acquisition of more advanced missile defense systems if Beijing agrees to freeze its deployments of short-range ballistic missiles and pull back those already deployed out of range of the island.

Phase One: Near-Term Cross-Strait Military CBMs

Gradually Develop Military-to-Military Contacts

- Conduct informal exchanges between the two sides to discuss security issues.[23] This could begin with visits of retired military officers and civilian national security experts. Active-duty officers could be included as trust is built on both sides. Discussion topics could include broader Asia-Pacific security issues such as the South China Sea, Korea, and Japan. Track II conferences could provide an opportunity for military personnel to meet each other and to exchange perspectives and information. Such conferences could be held on either side of the strait or in the United States under sponsorship of an American think tank. Both the PLA and Taiwan military currently participate in conferences on international security issues, but only rarely do they participate together. The PLA has not permitted Taiwan military officers to attend conferences held on the mainland, but it has invited national security academics and retired Taiwan military officers to Beijing to exchange views.
- Assign military representatives to Taiwan's Straits Exchange Foundation (SEF) and China's Association for Relations across the Taiwan Strait (ARATS) to serve as liaisons. They could be used to pass information prior to the installation of a hot line between the two militaries. Eventually, a working group could be set up in the SEF-ARATS channel for discussion of CBMs.
- Establish contacts between the PRC and Taiwan military personnel in third countries. Both Beijing and Taipei post defense representatives in their respective overseas embassies and representative offices. These individuals could regularly meet and exchange views.
- Send active-duty military officers from both China and Taiwan at the same time to American think tanks and universities. So far, this has taken place at the Atlantic Council of the United States. Both sides could also send military officers to the

Asia-Pacific Center in Honolulu, the Monterey Institute of International Studies, the Stimson Center, the Kennedy School of Government at Harvard, and so on. This would enable the two militaries to have regular contact with members of the other side's military. Joint projects could be considered between Taiwan and Chinese military officers on subjects of common interest, such as Japan's military strategy or South China Sea security.

Develop Maritime Cooperation

- Expand cooperation in naval and maritime activities where there are shared interests. The navies of China and Taiwan are engaged in many activities that relate to maintaining the safety of the waters and security in the Taiwan Strait. They engage in pollution control, conduct search and rescue operations, curb piracy and smuggling, provide assistance for natural resource exploration, and conduct fisheries patrols in addition to their wartime activities and exercises. Collaborative efforts between China and Taiwan in some of these naval and maritime activities where their interests converge can provide habits of cooperation that can play a role in building trust.[24] Specific proposals include the following:
    - Hold a track II conference to study the cooperative models of other navies to monitor and control marine pollution and curb smuggling through the sea. Discussions would focus on practical steps to implement cooperation between the navies.
    - Undertake joint scientific and technical projects to study ocean currents and flows, weather patterns, and movements of fish.
    - Cooperate in environmental management activities such as countering marine pollution. This could include planning for cooperative responses to oil spills and other environmental disasters.
    - Establish cooperation between maritime agencies from China and Taiwan to solve the issue of fishermen being caught crossing into each other's territory.
    - Cooperate to curb smuggling and otherwise maintain cross-strait security. Due to the unique geographical and political background of the Taiwan Strait, there have always been areas where there are no patrols, thus resulting in security gaps in the strait's maritime space. Criminals have been able to take advantage of such gaps, posing dangers to travelers passing through the strait. In 1998, the Fujian border defense corps, which is responsible for guarding the 3,300-kilometer coastline, proposed exploring with Taiwan the possibility of jointly maintaining cross-strait security and cooperation.[25]
    - Set up maritime risk-reduction centers in both countries to exchange information.

Set Up Direct Communication Links

- Establish communication links, beginning at lower levels. Such links could be set up between commanders of naval vessels or commanders of units facing one another across the strait. The recent steps taken by Korea and Japan could be instructive in this regard.[26] Such communication links would carry symbolic importance as well as substantively contribute to the avoidance of miscalculation in a crisis.

Most hot-line agreements provide for meetings between the two sides to review the functioning of the communications link and suggest upgrades or changes. The creation of such a committee would provide another forum in which to expand contacts between the two militaries.

A civilian hot line already exists between China and Taiwan, providing a precedent in this area. In November 1997, the Taipei-based China Rescue Association and its mainland counterpart, the China Marine Rescue Center, set up a hot line to facilitate marine rescue work in the Taiwan Strait. Under the agreement, when accidents occur in the Taiwan Strait involving the ships of either Taiwan and the mainland, the ships in distress and the rescuing ships may use the hot line to request assistance and ask for permission to enter the waters and harbors of the other side. The hot line operates 24 hours a day.[27]

Establish Rules of the Road and Communication Measures in the Event of Dangerous Military Incidents

- Negotiate an agreement aimed at preventing dangerous military activities and containing their consequences if they occur. Such an agreement would include codes of conduct for military forces and mandate modes of consultation and communication in crises. An INCSEA agreement was signed by the United States and the Soviet Union in 1972 and an accord on Dangerous Military Incidents was signed in 1989. In January 1998 China and the United States signed the Agreement between the Department of Defense of the United States of America and the Ministry of National Defense of the People's Republic of China on Establishing a Consultation Mechanism to Strengthen Military Maritime Safety. According to the agreement, the agenda items of their maritime and air forces may include, among other items: measures to promote safe maritime practices and establish mutual trust such as search and rescue, communications procedures when ships encounter each other, interpretation of the rules of the nautical road, and avoidance of accidents at sea. The PLA Navy and the U.S. Navy subsequently conducted two search and rescue exercises, the first in December 1998 and the most recent in December 2000.

Agree on Explicit Rules of Engagement

- Reach an explicit agreement barring either side from crossing the midline of the strait. In the Taiwan Strait, the Taiwan Air Force and the PLA Air Force have maintained a tacit agreement on an invisible central line of the strait, and neither side has conducted any provocative flights against the other. According to a November 29, 1998, article in Taipei's *Tzu-Li Wan-Pao*, "since the end of air battles over the Taiwan Strait in 1958, when carrying out patrol duties during ordinary times, our fighters have always kept a distance of thirty sea miles from the mainland's coast, while the Chinese Communist fighters usually carry out their duties close to their own coast line. Maintaining a tacit agreement on an invisible central line of the Strait, neither side has conducted any provocative flights against each other, so as to prevent an air battle from breaking out due to misjudgments made by their pilots."[28] Violations of this tacit agreement have occurred, heightening concern about possible conflict triggered by an aerial fight accident. A more explicit agreement that includes verification provisions to confirm compliance would lessen the possibility of escalation to war resulting from an accident.

Phase Two: Mid-Term Cross-Strait CBMs

Institute a Program of Regular Military Exchanges

- Regularly exchange delegations from military academic research institutions.
- Exchange visits to military bases and conduct reciprocal visits to naval platforms.
- Exchange visits by high-ranking military officials to engage in security dialogues.

Conduct Data and Information Exchanges

- Provide prior notification of military exercise plans, including dates and scales of exercises. This notification could include missile tests, as well. Though both sides currently announce most exercises in advance through their respective defense or government spokespeople, it would be a confidence-building initiative for each side to formally provide such notice directly to the other side, perhaps through the SEF-ARATS channel initially. In addition, more detail could be provided. As has been done in Europe, agreements could be made to specify the amount of lead time for announcements, and then lead time could be gradually increased.
- Exchange information on armament inventories, weapons procurement, number of military personnel, and so on. Both sides could provide briefings on their respective defense budgets.
- Exchange intelligence on regional security, especially areas of territorial dispute with other countries such as the Spratly Islands. The two militaries can collect geographical and historical information to bolster their claims and coordinate on how to approach other claimants.

Establish a Joint Military Communication Link and Leadership Hot Line

- Set up hot lines to provide communication channels between senior military and government leaders.

Expand Maritime and Naval Cooperation

- Conduct joint projects, such as development of South China Sea resources.
- Exchange port visits and visits of coast guard and naval officers.
- Engage in cooperative Sea Lanes of Communication (SLOC) monitoring.
- Hold joint military exercises to practice search and rescue procedures. Cooperate in search and rescue operations.

Establish Risk-Reduction Centers

- Set up permanent centers in Taiwan and China to support the implementation of CBMs and other bilateral agreements.

Phase Three: Long-Term Cross-Strait Military CBMs

Assuming that Taiwan and China establish a pattern of trust and cooperation along with a degree of political understanding, CBMs can proceed to a more advanced level. The two sides could consider implementation of constraint measures, which are aimed at keeping certain types and levels of each side's military forces at a distance from one another. Constraint measures that prevent emplacement of large numbers of troops and weapons in a specified zone aim to limit the ability of parties to mount large-scale offensives.

Establish Keep-Out Zones

- Define a demilitarized zone and a military buffer zone in the Taiwan Strait in which specified military activities are prohibited.

Agree on Limits for Military Exercises and Deployments

- Establish limits on the number and location of deployments of ballistic missiles and ballistic missile defense systems.
- Set restrictions on the types, scale, frequency, and timing of military exercises. Establish long lead times for conducting large-scale exercises that involve movement of certain levels of troops and equipment. Agree not to hold exercises in important air routes, sea lines, and at sensitive political times.

Implement Verification Measures

Verification measures are designed to collect data or provide first-hand access to confirm or verify a party's compliance with an agreement. This could include verification of the accuracy of data exchanges and compliance with restrictions on weapons deployments or troop movements. Verification measures can also provide early warning of potentially destabilizing activities. Inspections can be carried out jointly or by third parties. Verification is likely less important at the early stages of confidence building and would become relevant only once the process reaches a mature stage.

- Conduct on-site inspection visits to factories and military bases.
- Carry out aerial inspections and ground-based electronic sensoring.

Sign a Non–Use of Force Agreement

In the case of China and Taiwan, an advanced stage of mutual trust would likely need to be attained before an accord could be reached committing both sides to refrain from using force against the other. Such an accord would likely presuppose an agreement on broader political issues between Taipei and Beijing. In the near term, both sides could consider signing a conditional, limited-term non–use of force agreement in which Taipei would forego a declaration of independence for a specified number of years and Beijing would promise to not initiate the use of force against Taiwan unless it declared independence.

CONCLUSION

The relationship between China and Taiwan remains deeply mistrustful and highly unstable. A political resolution of cross-strait differences is unlikely in the near term. Gradual steps are needed that can transform negative perceptions and build a less-hostile and eventually cooperative relationship. Confidence-building initiatives that reduce misperception, uncertainty, and suspicion should be considered by both sides to enhance cross-strait stability. As a first step, Beijing and Taipei should engage in a reciprocal process of unilateral, declaratory CBMs. Preliminary CBMs in the military sphere should be implemented to reduce the risk of conflict due to miscalculation or accident. As the political relationship improves, more ambitious CBMs can be contemplated.

NOTES

1. Ralph A. Cossa, "Cross-Strait Confidence Building: Taking the Next Step."
2. A similarly all-embracing definition of CBMs is "a myriad of political, economic, and environmental arrangements which are themselves not concerned with security, but which in sum indirectly probably contribute more to regional confidence and security than those measures specifically designed for that purpose." See Desmond Ball, "The Most Promising CSBMs for the Asia-Pacific Region." Paper prepared for Conference on the Asia-Pacific Region: Links Between Economic and Security Relations, organized by the Institute of Global Conflict and Cooperation, University of San Diego, California, May, 1993.
3. M. Susan Pedersen and Stanley Weeks, "A Survey of Confidence and Security Building Measures." In *Asia Pacific Confidence and Security Building Measures*, Vol. XVII, No. 3, ed. Ralph A. Cossa (Washington, D.C.: CSIS Significant Issue Series, 1995).
4. Ralph A. Cossa, "Cross-Strait Confidence Building: Taking the Next Step."
5. The Henry L. Stimson Center, Confidence Building Measures Project. Available from the World Wide Web: http://www.stimson.org/cbm/china/track1.htm.
6. Robert Karniol, "Forum offers new era of Singapore/Malaysia." *Jane's Defence Weekly* 23 (1995).
7. Benjamin Self, "Confidence-Building Measures in Japanese Security Policy." In "Investigating CBMs in the Asia Pacific Region," May 1999, report 28. Available from the World Wide Web: www.stimson.org.

8. Sony Devabhaktuni, Mathew C.J. Rudolph, and Michael Newbill. Key Developments in CBMs between India and Pakistan." In *Global Confidence Building New Tools for Troubled Regions*, eds. Michael Krepon, Michael Newbill, Khurshid Khoja, and Jenny S. Drezin (1992) pp. 189–196.

9. Off-the-record discussion at a conference on Sino-U.S. security relations held in May 1999.

10. The unpublished paper was shared with this author on the understanding that the retired PLA officer's name would not be revealed.

11. Meeting with C. Daniel Mote, president of the University of Maryland, October 26, 2000, Central News Agency, FBIS, 26 October, 2000.

12. DPP "White Paper on National Defense," November 23, 1999.

13. The DPP paper on policy toward the PRC also endorsed the implementation of CBMs, noting that "Taiwan and China should as soon as possible open negotiations in regard to confidence-building measures." The text noted that: "We admit that in regard to the present situation in bilateral intercourse, in speaking of building comprehensive and concrete confidence building measures [CBM], we still have many obstacles to overcome. However, as for maritime safety and cooperation, and transparency measures, the difficulty in fact is relatively small; this is because the function of the CBMs is to lessen to a great degree, through dialogue and cooperation, the possibility of war, representing a focus on the safety of people's lives, and according with common universal values. Thus, we hold that having somewhat limited topics from the start in regard to the challenges and conflicts from the political situations on both sides, and these issues as the chief topics and goals of the negotiations, is a fairly realistic method "White Paper on Chinese Policy Into New Century," *Democratic Progressive Party*, 9 November 1999.

14. Cited in "Taiwan's Olive Branches" on the Taiwan Mainland Affairs Council home page, December 2000. Available from the World Wide Web: http://www.mac.gov.tw/english/MacPolicy/policy10/olive98.htm.

15. Text of speech by Lien Chan on "Defense Strategy and Defense Building for the New Century." *Chung-Yang Jih-Pao*, FBIS, 9 December, 1999.

16. Sofia Wu, "MND Cultivating Manpower for Cross-Strait Military Exchanges," Central News Agency, 27 September, 2000.

17. "Taiwan: Defence Report Emphasizes Combat Capabilities, Trust Mechanism," Central News Agency, 8 August, 2000.

18. Papers were delivered at the conference on four topics: (1) prospects for establishing a cross-strait military mutual trust mechanism; (2) cross-strait relations and the proposed military exchange mechanism; (3) international confidence-building measures; and (4) mainland China's stance and views on confidence-building measures, were discussed during the one-day seminar. "Seminar Held on Military Exchanges with Mainland," Central News Agency, 6 July, 2000.

19. Margaret (Peggy) Mason, "Confidence Building in the Asia Pacific Region: Prospects and Problems," *Asia Pacific Confidence and Security Building Measures*, Vol. XVII, No. 3, ed. Ralph A. Cossa (Washington, D.C.: CSIS Significant Issue Series, 1995).

20. Michael Krepon and Jenny S. Drezin, "Declaratory Diplomacy and Confidence Building." In *Declaratory Diplomacy: Rhetorical Initiatives and Confidence Building*, Stimson Report No. 27, eds. Michael Krepon, Jenny S. Drezin, and Michael Newbill (May 1999).

21. Taipei Government Information Office, WWW-Text in English at http://www.gio.gov.tw, 20 May 2000.

22. The first Chinese character President Chen used in the term "integration" (*tonghe*) is no doubt deliberately the same as the first Chinese character used in the term "unification" (*tongyi*). Taipei Office of the President of the Republic of China, WWW-Text in Chinese at http://www.gio.gov.tw, 31 December 2000.

23. Many of these CBMs have been proposed in earlier articles on cross-strait military CBMs. See, for example, Ken Allen, "Military Confidence-Building Measures across the Taiwan Strait"; Major General Tyson Fu, "A Preliminary Proposal for Military 'Confidence-Building Measures' Across the Taiwan Straits," prepared for the International Forum on Peace and Security of the Taiwan Strait, cosponsored by the 21st Century Foundation of Taiwan and the American Enterprise Institute, July 26–27, 1999, Taipei; and L. Celeste Johnson, "Military Confidence Building Measures between Taiwan and the People's Republic of China," May 1999.

24. Lieutenant Commander Duk-Ki Kim, "Cooperative Maritime Security in Northeast Asia," *Naval War College Review* 50, no. 1 (Winter 1999).

25. "Fujian Seeks Taiwan Cooperation on Fighting Crimes at Sea," *Beijing Zhongguo Xinwen She*, FBIS-CHI-98–040, 6 February, 1998, cited in Ken Allen, "Military Confidence-Building Measures across the Taiwan Strait."

26. Victor Cha, "Positive and Preventative Rationales for Korea-Japan Security Cooperation," in *U.S., Korea, Japan Relations: Building Toward a "Virtual Alliance,"* ed. Ralph A. Cossa (Washington, D.C.: CSIS Significant Issue Series, 1999), cited in Cossa, "Cross-Strait Confidence Building: Taking the Next Step."

27. "Hot line to Facilitate Rescue Work in Taiwan Strait," Central News Agency, FBIS-CHI-97–329, 25 November, 1997, cited in Allen, "Military Confidence-Building Measures across the Taiwan Strait."

28. "Mainland Fighters Said to Appear Above Taiwan Straits," *Taipei Tzu-Li Wan Pao*, FBIS, 29 November, 1998, cited in Allen, "Military Confidence-Building Measures across the Taiwan Strait."

Part III

Since the Taiwan Elections, December 2001

Chapter 14

More of the Same Despite an Election and a War

Nancy Bernkopf Tucker

The results of the Taiwan elections in December 2001 are both reassuring and disturbing in promising more of the same in Taiwan, across the strait and in relations with the United States. This election did not herald a political revolution, did not solve burdensome and distracting problems, and did not even forecast a path in Taiwan for much-needed political, economic, or spiritual healing in the days and months to come. Though Taiwan is faced by dire threats externally from China and internally from partisanship and inexperience, the electorate neither panicked nor rallied around the center. Moreover, even though the continuing disintegration of the Kuomintang (KMT) is of historical significance, the fact that the broader pan-blue alliance of KMT, People's First Party, and New Party supporters shares many of the conservative proclivities of the old KMT means that Taiwan's political agenda will alter only the margins. The changed alignments in the Legislative Yuan (LY) may give Chen Shui-bian's administration the ability to enact some of its priorities, but cleaning up corruption, restructuring the government, let alone engaging China constructively, will remain very difficult.

It is critical to recognize that, above all, this election did not comprise a referendum on cross-strait relations, as much as the opposition tried to make that a key issue. The voting public has not deviated from its desire to sustain the status quo—driving the prounification New Party from power in the LY and giving the fledgling Taiwan Solidarity Union (TSU) a boost more as a tribute to Lee Teng-hui than because of a sudden surge in favor of independence. In fact, Taiwan's voters, by granting the Democratic Progressive Party (DPP)/TSU candidates strong support, indicated that for many on the island there continues to be a disjunction between trade with and investment on the mainland and future political integration with China. Beijing's recent wait-and-see strategy has assumed that economic ties would help to undermine Chen and inevitably produce political union, relieving it of the need to use military coercion. These elections and evolving economic conditions (including a revival of the U.S. economy, a reduction in Taiwan's mainland investing, and a diversification of Taiwan's economy into service industries) may prompt Beijing to begin to rethink the efficacy of relying on economic dependence to solve its Taiwan problem.

Meanwhile, reactions to the election in Beijing and Washington were muted. Beijing is increasingly preoccupied with its own succession politics and the demands of pressing economic readjustment needed to meet the obligations of World Trade Organization (WTO) accession. At the same time, the focus of the U.S. government, with its almost single-minded dedication to the post–9/11 war on terrorism and the fighting in Afghanistan, minimizes the energy left for worrying about China-Taiwan relations.

This is not to say that the results of the election campaign did not come as a shock to Beijing. Although the Chinese Communist regime did not expose itself to the humiliation of previous elections where it baldly attempted to intimidate the voters, first into abandoning Lee Teng-hui (1996) and then into opposing the irresponsible Chen Shui-bian (2000), Beijing did, nevertheless, miscalculate again. During the months following the presidential victory of Chen and the DPP, Beijing adopted a united-front policy, courting Chen's opponents by inviting them to the mainland where they were feted and flattered. Beijing did not understand that Taiwan's democrats were embarrassed by the shameless political maneuvering of their representatives, resented the heavy-handed political interference of mainland authorities in Taiwan's free system, and feared China's barely hidden unification schemes. Beijing expected the KMT to perform far better than it did, not anticipating a big DPP victory. Of course, Beijing has dismissed the implications of this DPP success, ignoring any impulse toward greater flexibility on its part, preferring to continue to shun Chen and wait for him to be driven from office as a failure in 2004.

Perhaps Beijing's greatest worry is that the results of the LY elections will draw Washington yet closer to Taipei, making the United States even more sympathetic to Chen Shui-bian. Whereas Beijing perceived Clinton as a balancer who leaned too far toward Taipei when he sent aircraft carriers in 1996, they felt he ultimately recouped with the Shanghai Three No's, as well as facilitating WTO entry. In the end, he was a friend of China. But George W. Bush's interest in Taiwan has not, so far, been similarly balanced despite Beijing's hopes for the pro-China influence of his father. Bush and his closest advisors see China as a threat to be feared and Taiwan as a democracy to be admired. Elections that function smoothly despite economic and political strain confirm the positive image of a society striving to enjoy a system much like ours.

Indeed, the LY elections, coupled with the events of 9/11, did serve to activate two sectors of U.S. opinion makers—those who are sympathetic to Taiwan and those distraught that political developments in Taiwan are threatening yet again to set back the relationship with China—to try to bring pressure on the administration to devise new policies toward Taiwan and China. In each case the advocates wish to stimulate U.S. involvement at a new level of intensity in the cross-strait confrontation, seeking greater clarity and commitment from Washington. No one doubts that the Bush administration will remain supportive of and protective of Taipei. Beyond that, these groups are on the margins making demands that are not triggering policy responses—yet. But as the Afghan war wanes and Washington pays attention to issues beyond the hills of Tora Bora, it is clear there are opinion shapers who have Asia policies they are eager to press.

ADVOCATES OF A MORE SUPPORTIVE TAIWAN POLICY

The most public advocate of a series of stronger pro-Taiwan initiatives has been political commentator and columnist Bill Kristol—who made his points in *The Washington Post* on December 4, 2001, and reiterated many of them to Taiwan's president and other officials while on an election-monitoring delegation in Taipei.[1] His fundamental argument is that the United States ought to demonstrate political, economic, and military backing to match the Taiwan people's reaffirmation of democracy and disinclination to unify with the People's Republic of China as revealed in the election. Some of his policy prescriptions reach well beyond the scope of where the administration, any administration, will go, including the demand that Washington abandon the one-China policy and publicly acknowledge that there are two Chinas in the world. Others more closely reflect debate that has captured U.S. and China-watching circles for months and might be said to parallel policies the Bush administration has already moved toward, such as substitution of strategic clarity for traditional ambiguity; what Kristol termed an "unequivocal commitment" and President Bush called doing "whatever it took" for the defense of Taiwan.

Several other recommendations are hardly surprising. Kristol favors higher-level contacts between Taiwan and American officials, and Chen Shui-bian's New York transit surely fueled expectations. Subsequent lower-level visits have gone forward without fanfare, but there is still no access to the Department of State and the foreign minister is still barred from Washington and from shaking Colin Powell's hand. Such slights rankle.

There are also calls for more arms sales of bigger and better weapons systems, whether Taiwan wants them or not. Beijing has found it has cause for concern regarding diesel submarines, which last April Chinese leaders had concluded were offered as a political gesture. If, however, there may be manufacturers actually willing to build the boats, Beijing has seriously miscalculated, and that error may be as politically damaging in China as an actual sale. It is also impossible to predict at present, so long as Congress remains preoccupied with war and anthrax and the economy, what directions it might take on arms sales, but as the election season begins and with a new House Whip, Nancy Pelosi, who has a clear record as a China critic, support for Taiwan could grow. More importantly, and not prominent in Kristol's ruminations, the Bush administration has moved ahead briskly with the software initiatives begun in the Clinton years to increase military-to-military contacts and address deficits in Taiwan's military training, logistic capabilities, and strategic planning.

Finally Kristol talked about negotiating a U.S.-Taiwan free trade agreement to deal with the mounting threat of Taiwan's economic dependence upon China. Taiwan sympathizers in the United States find themselves in a quandary as Taiwan businesses increasingly invest on the mainland and move manufacturing to the lower-cost operating bases that China provides. Their desire to keep Taiwan prosperous runs up against concerns about (1) economic integration with and dependency upon China and (2) transfer of dual-use and military technology to China. The fact that the LY elections showed that voters in Taiwan appeared to continue to believe economic cooperation is possible without political entanglement obviated some concern that economic pressures could be furthering interest in political integration. But it also aroused fears regarding a Taiwanese sense of unreality and complacency as Beijing's leverage grows.

ADVOCATES OF RESTORING AND REVITALIZING SINO-AMERICAN RELATIONS

Many individuals, some prominent in opening the door to China in the 1970s, have watched with mounting dismay and apprehension as the relationship between Washington and Beijing has lost focus and become mired in the frictions and competing interests of security and political and economic competition. Ever since the end of the Cold War and the devastating events of the 1989 Tiananmen massacre, problems have proven more difficult to solve, and the very framework that bound China and the United States together has begun to crumble. Some of these observers in both the Democratic and Republican parties have argued that the time is long past, not simply for more talks about this or that issue, but for a fundamental restructuring.

The tragedy of 9/11 to them looms as an opportunity not to be lost. Finally, the war against terrorism provides a new common foe, a new campaign in which cooperation can blunt the edges of conflict and remind Americans and Chinese of the greater good of Sino-American friendship. The Taiwan election is not the source of their frustration, but the political developments on the island heighten the sense of events spinning out of control, of democracy unleashed and potentially irresponsible, that only magnifies the danger of allowing American policy to continue to drift.

Although several prominent exponents of this view have spoken on the subject, the most recent to link his name to the issue has been Richard Holbrooke, who, in a January 2, 2002, *Washington Post* op-ed piece, went public with the call for a fourth communiqué as a remedy for all that ails Chinese-American relations today.[2] Holbrooke correctly points out that the framework of the three existing communiqués is frayed—the August 1982 accord is almost 20 years old and no longer being observed—and he asserts that the effort to reach a new agreement by itself will build confidence between Washington and Beijing. Given that this is the single most important bilateral relationship the United States will have in the years ahead, Holbrooke asserts, we must try, and where agreement is impossible, we can adopt the model of previous communiqués in which each side simply stated its own view for the record.

Of course, the immediate contrast between Holbrooke's brief and Kristol's call to arms is the absence of an obvious echo from within the administration. Though some career diplomats might agree that damage has been done to U.S.-China ties since the Bush campaign labeled China a strategic competitor, it is clear that the urgency felt by advocates of a fourth communiqué is not shared by Bush, Rumsfeld, Cheney, Wolfowitz, Armitage, or Rice. Indeed, despite China's positive actions since 9/11, Jiang Zemin's supportive phone calls, and possibly even some intelligence sharing, the Bush administration remains wary and suspicious of Beijing. There were concerns to begin that Beijing would try to leverage assistance in Afghanistan for capitulation on Taiwan. To everyone's relief, that did not happen. But, relief did not translate into an enthusiastic embrace of a helpful friend.

Instead, the Bush administration will continue to do what it has been doing since the inauguration. Bush will refuse to go beyond Clinton's first No on Taiwan independence and will not accept the three no's as the basis for negotiating a fourth communiqué as Beijing would almost certainly demand. In fact, there is no reason to believe the administration sees any need to launch a process of negotiation that would require compromises and concessions to China on matters such as Taiwan. A strong Washington has no reason to be flexible or look weak on an issue it holds dear. Furthermore, Holbrooke is wrong to assume that Taiwan's anxieties about its security are exaggerated or that the Bush administration does not share Taipei's fear that Chinese missiles comprise a genuine threat. Moreover, China's continuing military modernization ensures that U.S. military assistance and arms sales will continue. Efforts to discuss a fourth communiqué in 1997 and 1998 broke down over precisely these issues—Beijing's demands that Washington end arms sales and oppose independence. It is simply impossible to imagine that the Bush White House would undertake a negotiation with Beijing that would fundamentally distress Taipei when this administration has not even been interested in encouraging cross-strait dialogue, as the Clinton administration did routinely.

Rather than anticipate startling new initiatives in the year ahead, it is far more likely that we are entering a period of quietude as all three actors become ever more preoccupied with their separate agendas. This is not necessarily a bad thing. The key will be for each party to resist the temptation to turn cross-strait problems into issues for domestic political gain at the risk of provoking a dangerous wider crisis.

NOTES

1. William Kristol, "Embrace Taiwan," *Washington Post*, 4 December, 2001, p. A25.

2. Richard Holbrooke, "A Defining Moment With China," *Washington Post*, 2 January, 2002, p. A13.

CHAPTER 15

Taiwan's Legislative and Local Elections: Their Meanings and Impacts

Xu Shiquan

On December 1, 2001, Taiwan held elections of its fifth Legislative Yuan and 23 local county commissioners and city mayors. As expected, no single party got an absolute majority in the legislature, but the voting results were full of surprises considering what the public opinion polls had predicted.

At the legislative election, the Kuomintang (KMT) suffered the second stunning setback since the general election held in March 2000, losing its half-century grip on the legislature. The Democratic Progressive Party (DPP) fulfilled its most optimistic expectations and emerged as the largest party. The People's First Party (PFP), a KMT splitter group formed barely a year and half ago, more than doubled its seats, becoming the decisive minority in the legislature. The New Party got only one seat, failing to meet the 5 percent threshold that allows it to claim legislator-at-large seats and campaign matching funds. The Taiwan Solidarity Union (TSU), with Mr. Lee Deng-hui as its patron, got 13 seats, falling behind its expected 25 seats. The non-partisan independents and fringe parties won the remaining 10 seats, only half of what they won in the previous election. The fundamentalist Taiwan Independence Party (TIP), which has one seat at the current legislature, became virtually extinct, only collecting a meaningless thousand ballots.

Meanwhile, the local county commissioners' and city mayors' elections presented a different picture. The KMT emerged as a moderate winner, gaining one more populous district on the island proper, whereas the DPP lost three, to its dismay. Now the DPP and KMT control equal numbers of nine counties and cities. The PFP conquered two counties whereas the New Party seized the offshore island of Kinmen. The remaining two counties fell into the hands of nonpartisans.

The December elections have no doubt redrawn the political map of Taiwan again and left strong impacts on the political, economic, and social development of the island and the future of its political parties. It has also further complicated the cross-strait relations at a time when they are already in a dangerous deadlock. This short chapter will try to examine these new developments.

ELECTION RESULTS

Because the elections were the first in the aftermath of the change of party in 2000, and the results would affect the political structure in Taiwan, all the six major parties went all out for the elections, and, as a result, the number of candidates reached an explosive extent. Four hundred fifty-five people were nominated to contend for the 176 constituency-elected legislative seats, while 88 people registered to contest the 23 county and city heads. However, in contrast, the turnout of the electorate was at a historical low. Among the 15,822,683 legitimate voters, only 66.16 percent cast their ballots for the legislative election and a few more voters participated in the local election. The low turnout was attributed to the economic recession and candidates' unclear platforms.

Legislative Election

To have a better understanding of the meaning of the election results, in particular the current balance of popularity between the major parties as reflected in the polls, it is necessary to go back to the elections of the fourth Legislative Yuan in 1998 and the third one in 1995 and compare the results with the recent poll. The seats and percentage of ballots garnered by the major parties in the three elections are shown in Table 15.1.

From Table 15.1, we can see clearly that in the past six years, DPP's popular basis has had little expansion. It bagged 33.38 percent of the votes last December, representing a 3.82 percent increase as compared with that of 1998 (It performed badly that year owing to campaign errors). Yet if compared with 1995, the increase is only 0.21 percent. That is to say that with basically the same degree of popular support, the DPP has managed to gain 17 seats more this time. Most analysts attribute this gain to DPP's successful election strategy. Knowing that none of the three major parties, the KMT, DPP, and PFP, would have a clear majority in the new legislature, the DPP put forward a short list of 83 candidates, avoiding suicidal fights among its own nominees. Taiwan's legislative election adopts the system of multimember-district, single nontransferable vote. Within one constituency, a party can

Table 15.1
The Last Three Legislative Elections

	Number of Seats	Percentage of Votes					
	Newly Elected	Current*	Elected in 1988	Elected in 1995	2001	1998	1995
KMT	68	115	123	85	28.56	46.43	46.06
DPP	87	67	70	54	33.38	29.56	33.17
NP	1	7	11	21	2.61	7.06	12.95
TIP	0	1	1	0	---	1.44	---
INDEP	10	16	20	4	9.12	15.51	7.82
PFP	46	19	---	---	18.57	---	---
TSU	13	---	---	---	7.76	---	---

nominate more that one candidate, so the nomination of their candidates is crucial to the success or failure of the contesting parties in the election. This tactics of the DPP obviously succeeded. As high as 83 percent of its candidates, that is, 69 out of 83, were elected. Meanwhile, the KMT nominated 98 candidates; only 53 were elected. The DPP also played to the full the tactics of vote-sharing, at which it is particularly good. This tactic was almost 100 percent effective in Taipei and Tainan counties and Kaosiung City. All 22 of its candidates were elected.

Another important point of observation regarding the legislative election is the new balance of power between the so-called pan-green and pan-blue blocks in the new legislature. The KMT suffered a devastating setback by loosing 47 seats. But where have these seats gone? Detailed analysis show that most of them went to the PFP, which increased its seats from 19 to 46. As a splinter group of the KMT, the PFP shares the same category of voters with the KMT, thus the success of PFP could only be achieved at the expense of the KMT. If we put combine the seats of the KMT and the PFP, they would reach 114 seats, 9 seats fewer than the KMT won in 1998. At that time, the PFP did not exist. With the New Party's one seat, the pan-blue camp have a total of 115 seats. The pan-green block, made up of DPP and TSU, has exactly 100 seats. As far as their popularity is concerned, the pan-green won 41.14 percent of the total ballots whereas the pan-blue won 49.74 percent. Comparing these figures with the average rates the pan-blue and pan-green had in the previous two legislative elections in 1995 and 1998, we will discover that the pan-blue's rate has decreased by about 6.5 percent whereas the pan-green (in 1995 and 1998 it was made up of the DPP and the TIP) has gained about 9.05 percent. As mentioned above, the December election did not show a marked expansion of DPP's popular base; the increase of pan-green's ballots could only be due to the advent of the TSU. Mr. Lee Deng-hui's added efforts to further split and weaken the KMT were successful in the southern counties and cities, where the TSU candidates won on average over 10 percent of the votes. Of the 7.76 percent ballots won by the TSU, some came from pro-Lee Deng-hui local factions that previously supported the KMT. The rest came from the supporters of nonpartisans whose voter support decreased from 15.51 percent of the electorate in 1998 to 7.82 percent last December.

From the above analysis, we can perhaps come to the following conclusion: The DPP is a clear winner of the legislative election, owing to successful campaign strategy. Being the largest party, Mr. Chen Shui-bian has earned an added legitimacy to form his cabinet. The possibility of a no-confidence vote against it by the opposition now becomes remote, and there is still less chance of an impeachment against Mr. Chen. However, the DPP is still a minority party, with only 38.67 percent of the legislative seats. It is going to be an arduous task if Mr. Chen wishes to have an absolute majority by formulating a "cross-party alliance of stability," for which he strongly lobbied before the elections. The success of such an alliance hinges very much on how many localized KMT lawmakers would defect to the DPP. Newspaper commentators in Taiwan give conflicting assessments about it. The formulation of the TSU represents the third split of the KMT following the NP and PFP. Most prominent pro-Lee Deng-hui localized politicians inside the KMT have joined the TSU. The question is how many more prolocalization KMT lawmakers the Bian-Lee mechanism could attract. Many observers focus their attention on Speaker Wang Jin-pyng and former premier Vincent Siew, both of them vice-chairmen of the KMT. A split of the KMT as serious as an open defection by two of its vice-chairmen does not look imminent. However, it could not be completely ruled out in the future, because the KMT has obviously not reached the bottom of its downhill slide. The KMT has the most spacious political territory in which the other parties could find room for expansion. True, the pan-blue opposition is not a solid block, but the pan-green Bian-Lee coalition is neither a piece of iron. A head-by-head count of the 13 TSU lawmakers would reveal that they are more or less a disorderly band. They have come together mainly for the sake of entering into the Legislative Yuan by the Lee Deng-hui gate. Only Lee could conduct this band, and there is no obvious successor to him in the foreseeable future. It would not be far-fetched to say that the TSU is a bubble blown up by Lee Deng-hui alone and the bubble would burst sooner than the New Party. Thus, in the political arena of Taiwan, the drama of horizontal alliances and vertical reformations among the parties will continue to be played. As one Taiwanese newspaper commentator put it, "Both the ruling party and the opposition have merely set their eyes on political booty-sharing" instead of establishing a functional and constitutional system of stability for Taiwan. "This legislative election in a sense has lost its function of articulating and aggregating popular will."[1] The political feuding that has been going on since the last general election will not come to an early end, and it will continue to be destructive.

County Commissioner and Mayoral Elections

Many observers have focused their attention on the legislative election and ignored the significance of the county commissioner and mayoral election. In fact, the latter has emitted important political messages as well. In contrast to a clear victory won by the DPP in the legislative election, the DPP suffered a setback at the local polls. The DPP-controlled districts decreased from 12 to 9, while those ruled by the KMT increased from 8 to 9. The PFP seized two counties. The NP won the offshore island of Kinmen. The other two were won by the independents, with one being pro-PFP and the other pro-DPP. As a result, 12 out of the 23 districts changed party colors and 8 out of the 14 incumbent local chiefs who sought second terms were defeated. In terms of pan-blue and pan-green blocks, 13 districts belong to the pan-blue and the remaining 10 are in pan-green hands. In terms of population ruled by the two camps, the pan-blue's share has enlarged from 28.4 percent at the last election in 1997 to 45.28 percent, whereas the pan-green's share dwindled from 71.5 percent to 54.72 percent. However, despite the setback, DPP's share of the votes has moderately increased from 1997's 43.32 percent to 45.27 percent, and the KMT's share slid from 42.12 percent to 35.15 percent. But in terms of the two contesting camps, the overall votes garnered by pan-blue candidates amount to about 51 percent of the total, and the pan-green share is about 47 percent. These and other figures can be compared in Table 15.2.

The most striking feature of the redrawn political map at the local level is that the political and ethnic divide between northern and southern Taiwan, which became so apparent at the March election in 2000, was further enhanced. The north further gravitated toward the pan-blue, whereas the south did so toward the pan-green. The offshore islands are, as in the past, controlled by the pan-blue. In the north, the KMT seized leadership from the DPP in six districts, including Keelung City, Taoyuan County, Hsinchu City, Hsinchu County, Taichung City, and Taichung County. Only Taipei County and Ilan County remained in the hands of the DPP. However, the battles in these two northern counties were extremely fierce. The incumbent DPP Commissioner of Taipei County, Mr. Su Tseng-chang, won his defensive battle narrowly by just over 50,000 ballots. Taipei County is the most populous district in Taiwan, with a population of over three million. His opponent, Mr. Wang Jian-hsuan, a New Party elder known as "Mr. Clean," went into the race barely two-and-half months before the election and took over 800,000 votes. He enjoyed the unanimous support of the pan-blue camp. The DPP has been ruling the Ilan County for over 12 years and cultivated the so-called

Table 15.2
The Last Two Local Elections

	1997	2001				
	Districts (number)	Population (%)	Votes (%)	Districts- (number)	Population (%)	Votes (%)
KMT	8	22.1*	42.22	9	41.4	35.15
DPP	12	71.5*	43.32	9	53.52	45.27
PFP	---	---	---	2	1.13	2.36
NP	---	---	1.65	1	0.24	0.1
INDEP	3	6.3	12.81	2	3.71	1.18
P.B.	9	24.7	48.17	13	45.28	51
P.G.	14	75.3	51.83	10	54.72	47

*They include the populations of Taipei under KMT and that of Kaosiung under DPP.
INDEP, independent; P.B., pan-blue, P.G., pan-green.

Ilan experience, that is "green governance, guarantee of quality." Yet, Commissioner Liu Shou-cheng escaped a disastrous defeat thanks to a few thousand more ballots than his KMT challenger.

In the south, from the central Taiwan's Nantou County down to the southern tip of the island, the DPP racked up victories in all the districts except Taichung County and City, Yunlin County, and Taitung County. The KMT lost Chiayi County and Changhua County to the DPP. The Daduhsi River that runs along the borders between Taichung and Changhua Counties marks the north-south divide.

In the legislative election, the bitter political mudslinging among the parties overshadowed the unprecedented economic recession. But in the local polls, the electorate was more conscious of the economic difficulties. The *Taipei Times* quoted political watchers as saying that the DPP's failure to deal with pressing economic issues had lost the party the support of many of its voters, citing the poor showing in Taichung County and Hsinchu City as examples. Former DPP Taichung County Commissioner Liao Yung-lai lost his leadership to his KMT opponent partly because of his opposition to a NT $50 billion investment proposal by the Bayer Group—a German health care and chemicals group—to establish operations in Taichung County in 1997. KMT officials said that the Bayer setback had repercussions in that other European companies that had shown interest in expanding their operations in Taiwan were now reluctant to do so. In Hsinchu City, DPP Mayor Tsai Jen-chien has experienced waning confidence among local residents after his failure last year to deal with environmental protection controversies linked to companies within the Hsinchu Science-based Industrial Park, the cradle of Taiwan's information technology industries.[2] According to these commentators, the DPP's impressive victory in southern Taiwan could be attributed to a close-knit relationship between local factions and the DPP-led central establishments. Some local factions, which had previously cooperated with the former KMT regime, have changed allegiance and thrown their support behind the new party in power. In addition to this, the so-called Taiwan Sadness complex in southern Taiwan is still stronger than in the north. The DPP and Lee Deng-hui strenuously fanned up the ethnic mistrust to its full. Some southerners were reported as saying, "even if I became a beggar, I would vote for A-Bian." Irrational sentiments have blurred real issues at the elections.

As it is known, northern Taiwan is the political, economic, and cultural center of the island, whereas the south is basically an area of agriculture and traditional industries. The economic gap between the north and south in recent years has been widening. Unemployment is most serious in southern districts, and agriculture is believed to be the sector that would be affected most negatively by Taiwan's entry into the WTO as a separate custom and tariff region. It is estimated that 100,000 jobs would be lost in the agricultural sector, and the agricultural output would be reduced by NT $60 billion. The south would be hit hardest by the negative impacts. History tells us that economic problems foster, in many cases, political extremism.

Among the seven major metropolitan areas on the island proper (Taipei and Kaosiung are under direct central administration and the remaining five are under direct provincial administration), those ruled by the DPP have decreased from five to two. Metropolitan areas are known to be centers of political dissent and reflections. If the DPP authorities fail to deal effectively with the pressing political, economic and social issues in the near future, the reshuffle of the local leadership last December would prove to be an early warning before a political earthquake in 2004.

IMPACTS ON CROSS-STRAIT RELATIONS

The December election's results have no doubt further complicated the already tense and difficult cross-strait relations. Mr. Chen Shui-bian's remarks made during the election campaigns concerning cross-strait relations have, in fact, dampened the prospect of an improved cross-strait relationship after the elections. His allegation that the 1992 Consensus was meant to "wipe out Taiwan," has destroyed the hard-won common ground between the two sides established to have contacts and dialogue. Meanwhile, DPP's improved position in the Legislative Yuan has obviously led the hardliners inside the DPP to believe that there is no need to moderate the party's independence platform. In addition, Mr. Lee Deng-hui will prove to be an added stumbling block to the DPP moderates' attempt to follow the middle road. Professor Wu Yu-shan, a political scientist at Taiwan University, was quoted as saying that Lee's remarks in the past three months had clearly shown that Lee was a fundamentalist advocate of Taiwan independence. "Lee will be an outspoken talker, much more so than Chen himself, to promote the issue because Chen has to be more reserved for fear of upsetting his neutral supporters. But Lee will have no restrictions in that regard."[3]

On the other hand, the DPP authorities are facing increasing pressures from the public in general and business circles in particular to lessen restrictions imposed on Taiwan's economic and trade exchanges with the mainland. These pressures have reached a degree that the DPP authorities could no longer ignore because of Taiwan's economic recession and the entry into the WTO by the two sides across the strait. Taiwan's economic future is becoming more and more linked with the mainland. The mainland is now the second-largest export market for Taiwan and the main source of its external trade surplus. The accumulated total in the past 10 years has exceeded U.S. $150 billion. Despite the political gridlock, Taiwanese investments on the mainland have been mounting with each passing year. There are about 50,000 pieces of Taiwanese investments on the mainland, with a realized input of about U.S. $30 billion. The entry into the WTO by the mainland has offered tremendous business opportunities, and practically no Taiwanese big business would let these opportunities slip away. According to the statistics of the mainland, in the period between January and October last year, the mainland approved 3,312 pieces of Taiwanese investments with a realized input of U.S. $2.398 billion, representing a 37.37 percent increase year on year.

In the face of the two-pronged pressures of conflicting nature, Chen Shui-bian is most likely to adopt what could be called tight-and-loose mainland policy in order to gain greater space to maneuver. Politically, he would harden his policies, refusing to accept the one-China principle and the 1992 Consensus. But he would continue to play the game of words, paying lip service to an improved cross-strait relationship in order to mislead public and international opinion. With DPP's gains in the legislative Yuan, it would be easier for Chen Shui-bian to have its policies passed in the legislature. It is expected that Chen would, more than ever, use the legislature to carry out his covert separatist designs, namely the so-called de-Chinese measures, such as changing the passport format from "Republic of China" to "Taiwan." Such maneuvers would no doubt be regarded by the mainland as provocative, thus leading to new rounds of tension across the strait. Economically, he would replace the go slow policy with an effective management policy for the sake of reducing the pressure from the public and business circles and reaping economic benefits from the mainland.

Under such circumstances, it could be expected that the political gridlock across the strait would continue with added potential dangers. The bilateral economic and trade exchanges would go on growing. It is becoming more and more apparent that Taiwan's refusal to have Three Direct Links (direct trade, shipping, and communications) with the mainland is a shot in its own foot. It is, in fact, one of the major reasons behind the flow of Taiwanese capital toward the mainland. For one thing, Taiwanese business has to pay U.S. $1.5 billion more shipping costs because shipping is indirect. So even for Taiwan's sake alone, expansion of cross-strait economic and trade cooperation is inevitable.

The mainland policy with regard to cross-strait relations will basically remain the same: peaceful reunification and one country, two systems, and the Eight-Point Proposal by Mr. Jiang Zemin. The mainland has been urged by some quarters to face the new reality in Taiwan following the elections. The new reality, as shown above, is that about 40 percent of the Taiwanese voted for the pan-green camp with a separatist platform, whereas about 50 percent of them voted for the pan-blue camp, which calls for a stable and mutually beneficial relationship across the strait on the basis of the 1992 Consensus. Professor Wang Yeh-lih of Taiwan's Tunghai University pointed out, "No significant structural change took place in Taiwan's last five legislative elections. In other words, the percentages of ballots cast for major parties have been the same. The 'pan-blue' camp attracted around 54 percent of the votes while the 'pan-green' camp attracted around 45 percent. Therefore, voter support for local parties is quite stable, as no structural 'political realignment' has occurred."[4] So the mainstream public opinion in Taiwan has remained supportive of a stable, positive cross-strait relationship within the framework of one China. The mainland has taken into account this reality in formulating its policy toward Taiwan. Neither government nor individual leader in Beijing could afford to betray the one-China principle. So long as the DPP refuses to accept the 1992 Consensus, the mainland will not deal with the DPP at official levels. However, if the DPP comes back to the 1992 Consensus, the mainland will not only immediately deal with it, but also being willing to resume cross-strait dialogues immediately. And the mainland is willing to discuss everything with the DPP, including military matters. As far as the mainland is concerned, as a Chinese saying goes, "everything is ready except the east wind." The east wind is the one-China principle from which the DPP is trying to shy away.

NOTES

1. *Taipei Times*, 2 December, 2001.
2. Ibid.
3. Ibid.
4. Ibid.

CHAPTER 16

Bush Administration's Taiwan Policy: Evolution and Trends

Jiemian Yang

In the past year, the Taiwan policy of the Bush administration has not fundamentally deviated from the one in the past three decades, but showed some interesting changes. It went from a cycle of noticeably tilting toward Taiwan at the beginning of the year, and then swinging toward the middle ground in the middle of the year, and finally adjusting to a nonconfrontational position with China over the Taiwan issue. The events of September 11, 2001, have made the United States deal with Sino-U.S. relations and the Taiwan issue based on a global strategic view. By the end of the year, the United States and China seemed to understand that it is in their best interests not to let the Taiwan issue get out of control.

INITIAL POLICY AND POLICY CONSIDERATIONS

During the presidential campaign in the year 2000 and its initial days in early 2001, the Bush administration emphasized the following three aspects in its policy toward Taiwan. First of all, the Bush administration tried hard to differentiate itself from its predecessor, the Clinton administration. The Bush administration criticized the Clinton administration for its engagement policy toward China by stressing that it was naive to believe that China can be changed through engagement. The United States should adopt a firmer and tougher policy toward China to prevent the latter from becoming a real threat or challenge to the United States. Secondly, the Bush administration was very ambiguous on the one-China principle, especially on the Taiwan independence issue. The Bush administration criticized the Clinton administration's

Three No's policy toward Taiwan. The Republican platform only acknowledged the one-China principle and did not go any further. Thirdly, in its actual dealings with Taiwan-related issues, the Bush administration was more inclined toward Taiwan. It announced a U.S. $4 billion arms sales to Taiwan and allowed Mr. Chen Shui-bian's "transit" in New York City and Houston, as compared with previous transits in Hawaii or Los Angeles for Taiwan leaders. Moreover, the Bush administration showed its readiness to go ahead with its missile defense program including its Theater Missile Defense, which would not only cover Taiwan but also make a quasi-military alliance between the two. President Bush himself even went so far as saying in a TV interview that his administration would "do whatever it takes to defend Taiwan."

However, one thing must be pointed out; it took quite some time to shape up Bush administration's foreign and security policy. The Taiwan issue's special timetable, for instance, for the annual arms sales decision at the end of April forced the Bush administration to make a decision while its overall foreign and security policy was not yet firm. Therefore, the administration's initial policy statements reflected only an ongoing process of policy debate and formation of the Bush administration. Having said so, we must fully understand that the above-mentioned policy statements or inclinations are not accidental. First, the Bush administration represents the right wing of the Republic Party and the conservative forces in the United States. These elements hold that the United States needs to readjust its global strategy in general and the Asian-Pacific one in particular. In the Asian-Pacific region the United States should focus on developing relations with its allies and friends, especially Japan. The four major existing or potential flashpoints in the region, the Korean Peninsula, the Taiwan issue, the South China Sea disputes, and nonproliferation are all related to China, especially the Taiwan issue. Second, these conservative elements at the Bush administration are still very much influenced by the Cold War mentality. They look at China through the prism of ideology and try to identify a new enemy in China to replace the former Soviet Union. Therefore, they want to contain China by elevating Taiwan's strategic importance. The mid-air collision on April 1 strengthened their belief about China. Third, part of the Bush administration is very hawkish. It believes that China has made the United States its enemy and that China would be its adversary in the future. Most importantly, China has stepped up its preparation to take over Taiwan by force and a head-on collision between the United States and China is inevitable. Therefore, the United States must adopt every means to counter this situation before it is too late. Fourth, the Bush administration stressed that Taiwan is a democracy and shares the same values with the United States. It also holds that the United States should prevent an "authoritarian" China from swallowing up the "democratic" Taiwan. Fifth, although it is always true that the military-industrial complex has a voice in the making and implementing of U.S. foreign and security policy, it is all the more true with the Bush administration.

This administration pays particular attention to expanding the U.S.-Taiwan military relationship. This also partly explains why it is enthusiastic to sell weaponry to Taiwan.

INTERIM CHANGES AND REASONS BEHIND THEM

In the middle of the year the Bush administration started to review its Taiwan policy. Logically, the Bush administration must review and make its China policy first. After the EP-3 incident in April 2001, both the United States and China went through a review of their policy toward each other. The Chinese government made it clear that it would not change its pre-EP-3 policy of stabilizing and developing the Sino-U.S. relations despite the incident. In the course of reviewing its policy, the Bush administration said that it would not oppose Beijing's bid for hosting Olympic Games in 2008. By the end of July, U.S. Secretary of State Colin Powell paid a one-day visit to Beijing, after which the Bush administration formally dropped the controversial term of "strategic competitor" and started to talk about a constructive relationship with China. On its Taiwan policy, the Bush administration still held a dichotomous position. On the one hand, the Bush administration does not want to reopen the wound of the Taiwan issue. The Bush administration repeatedly expressed its commitment to the one-China policy. On the other hand, the Bush administration tried to strengthen its relations with Taiwan. On many private occasions, its important figures still advocated China's threat to Taiwan, especially its missile deployment in the coastal provinces close to Taiwan. The Bush administration kept on calling on China to either remove or freeze these deployments.

There are many reasons to explain this duality of the Bush administration's policy toward Taiwan. First of all, in the transitional period of the new administration, the Bush administration learned through its dealings with China the importance and sensitivity of the Taiwan issue in Sino-U.S. relations. The United States must handle the Taiwan issue with care and caution. Second, the Bush administration also realized that being tough toward China simply would not work. It should seek a more balanced and workable relationship with China. Specifically on the Taiwan issue, this interim period saw no urgent and provocative events. Therefore, the Taiwan issue was not the focus of the Bush administration. Third, owing to make preparation for President Bush's meeting with his Chinese counterpart at the Shanghai APEC meeting, neither China nor the United States wanted the Taiwan issue to disrupt the planned summit. Fourth, most of American allies and friends want a stable Sino-U.S. relationship. They do not want to see the peace and stability being damaged by the Taiwan issue. They tried various channels to advise the Bush administration not to act in a rash way.

This interim and review period has once again proved that there is a great room for the two countries to match up in the transitional period. It also shows that there is a floor to slow or check the downslide of the Sino-U.S. relations and a limit for the U.S. relations with Taiwan. After all, the U.S. Taiwan policy should be governed by the overall and strategic considerations.

SEPTEMBER 11 EVENTS AND THEIR IMPACT

The September 11 Events and Sino-U.S. Relations

The unexpected events of September 11 have disrupted the strategic planning of the Bush administration. Before September 11, 2001, the Bush administration was working hard to shift its military focus from Europe to East Asia with a special attention on China. The Bush administration was also working to prevent China from adopting military measures to solve the Taiwan issue. However, the September 11 events have pulled its attention to the immediate and direct threat of terrorism.

The September 11 events have greatly changed the foreign and security policy of the Bush administration. Since its own territory now comes under direct threat, the United States has to make anti-terrorism the most important mission of its foreign and security policy. To deal with the most dangerous and urgent threat of terrorism, the United States must form a global coalition including as many friends as possible. The United States must readjust its relations with major powers such as Russia and China. The United States must create a favorable international environment.

As a result of September 11, the whole world, including the United States, came to understand that the humankind must seriously deal with the nontraditional threat and work for common security. The United States in particular is reviewing its former view of finding an enemy in a nation-state. The on-going antiterrorism struggle has shown that China is not an enemy to the United States, but an important partner. In the meantime, it began to realize that its unilateralism simply did not work.

The United States also learned through the experiences of the September 11 that in the Asia-Pacific region there are other places of concerns. The United States now is fighting in South Asia and central Asia area. It needs to form and maintain an antiterrorism coalition to sustain this war. To achieve this strategic goal, the United States must have an effective policy toward the Middle East, seek support from Russia and China, and keep good working relations with the central Asian countries and Pakistan.

In this context, the Bush administration is readjusting its China policy. First, although its fundamental strategy and policy toward China remain unchanged, its concrete policy and tactics are changing. As Professor David Lampton pointed out, "What has changed is that the United States is now more focused and disciplined in defining its interests with respect to China."[1] Second, the Bush administration has been emphasizing the importance of stabilizing and developing the Sino-U.S. relations. President Bush came to attend the APEC informal summit and met with the Chinese President Jiang Zemin. President Bush officially termed the Sino-U.S. relations as "constructive cooperation." This significant change has contributed to the improvement of the atmosphere first, with strengthening bilateral relations to follow. Third, both China and the United States used antiterrorism to enhance their cooperation. The Chinese side expressed its deep sympathy over the events and expressed its firm position to counter against all forms of terrorism. The United States and China cooperated at the United Nations to garner more international and legal support. In concrete dealings, the two countries have been working together in many aspects, including intelligence sharing and financial investigation. Fourth, in the United States there is seen an improvement of the general attitudes toward China. The anti-China voice is somewhat less vocal and Congress sees fewer anti-China bills submitted and passed. Besides, there are more people to come out to stress the importance of stabilizing and improving Sino-U.S. relations.

The September 11 Events and the U.S. Policy toward Taiwan

The September 11 events have profoundly changed the foreign and security policy of the Bush administration. Although the Taiwan issue is not directly related to the on-going struggle against terrorism, the following aspects of U.S. policy toward Taiwan merit our special attention. First and foremost, the United States is rethinking its world strategy. The Bush administration is beginning to realize the limits of the unilateralist foreign and security policy. The United States needs to readjust its relations with major powers in the world, especially Russia and China. Second, the Bush administration is reprioritizing its foreign and security policy. For the first time the United States has to care about the security of its own territory. Now its most urgent threat and enemy is terrorism. To foster a global coalition against terrorism, the United States needs assistance and cooperation from China. In the same line of thinking, the United States should concentrate its resources on the war against terrorism, not on curbing China. Third, the Bush administration is beginning to realize the new factors of the international affairs. The security issue has gone far beyond the traditional realm of a nation's physical and military security. It covers a wide range of aspects, including military, economic, information, and cultural realms. Increasingly, nonstate actors play an important role. Again, the United States needs China to cooperate to deal with this ramification. Fourth, the Bush administration has realized that, even though its basic interests concerning basic policy toward Taiwan will not change just because of the September 11 events, it has to be more cautious and careful in actual dealings with the Taiwan issue. In fact, the Bush administration has since tried hard not to be confrontational with China over the Taiwan issue.

TRENDS AND TENDENCIES

Given the past decades of experiences, one would not be so naive as to believe that the Taiwan issue would go away simply because of the September 11 events and/or a better Sino-U.S. relationship. The United States has a big stake in keeping the Taiwan issue a no unification, no independence, no war one. The Bush administration, like its predecessors, will continue the U.S. basic policy toward Taiwan. It should also not be ruled out that in the future there would be new and more troubles over the Taiwan issue. One also must realize that the post-Afghanistan policy of the United States would also exert a profound impact on the Sino-U.S. relations. Therefore, we must fully understand and prepare for the worst scenario to come.

But there are also reasons for one to make the following tentative predictions. First, both China and the United States will continue their limited but important strategic cooperation. The struggle against terrorism is a long and enduring one. It is in their fundamental national interests to cooperate to keep on fighting against terrorism. This is an overwhelming task to both, but especially to the United States. Second, the two countries cannot remove the root causes of their fundamental differences, yet they can put them under control. Their differences over the Taiwan issue were not made in one day, nor can they be solved overnight. Again, it is in their fundamental interests not to let it divert their attention, let alone make them confront each other. Thirdly, while the two countries are trying hard to prevent their differences from interfering with their overall relationship, there might be some chance that they could find ways to narrow their differences. Fourth, after a period of time, the Bush administration could understand better the delicacies and sensitivities of the Taiwan issue. The Bush administration will continue to walk on a thin line to balance on its relations with the Chinese mainland and Taiwan. Fifth, one must understand the political cycles in China and the United States. In China, there will be the 16th Party Congress to usher in a new generation of leaders. In the United States, there will be the election, a poll on the popularity of the Bush administration and the Republican Party. These political cycles will have some impact on their handling of the Taiwan issue.

NOTE

1. *The National Interest*, no. 66.

Conclusion

Donald S. Zagoria

The current political impasse between the People's Republic of China (PRC) and Taiwan over the issue of one China is unlikely to be solved in the near future. At its heart, the issue relates to the most sensitive problem between the PRC and Taiwan—the issue of sovereignty over Taiwan. The PRC continues to insist that the Taiwan authorities accept the principle of one China, with Taiwan a part of that China, while Taiwan, now led by President Chen Shui-bian, insists that although one China can be on the agenda for discussion, no prior conditions for dialogue should be set.

Many in Taiwan's ruling party, the Democratic Progressive Party (DPP), go even further than President Chen. A recent authoritative resolution on Taiwan's future by the DPP (see the appendices), says that Taiwan should renounce the PRC's one-China formula in order "to avoid international confusion" and to prevent the PRC from using that formula as a "pretext for forceful annexation."

Meanwhile, many in the PRC's leadership believe that the reason Chen Shui-bian refuses to accept the one-China formula is because he is determined to lead Taiwan toward independence. The mainland is extremely suspicious of Chen and the DPP, and there is very little confidence in them. The history of the DPP is well known on the mainland, and despite Chen's recent shifts from earlier policies relating to independence, these moves are viewed by Beijing as tactical.

Adding to the difficulties is China's formula of "one country, two systems," which is viewed by the PRC as generous in its provisions for Taiwan, but which is not acceptable to the overwhelming majority of Taiwan's citizens who are not prepared to become a province of 22 million in a country of 1.3 billion, even if guarantees of maximum autonomy were established. The

DPP's Resolution on Taiwan's Future says that both the PRC's one-China principle and the one country, two systems formula are "fundamentally inappropriate for Taiwan."

Over the longer run, it is possible that the two sides might eventually agree on a broader formula for establishing a loose association between the two sides, a formula such as confederation or commonwealth, but no PRC leader is now prepared to accept such an idea ,and in Taiwan itself, there is no clear consensus among the three major political parties on what kind of future association between Taiwan and the mainland is most appropriate.

In addition to the now unbridgeable gulf between the two sides on the issue of sovereignty, there is a basic lack of trust. Although President Chen, since his inauguration in May 2000, has repeatedly spoken of his desire to establish a stable and cooperative relationship with China, has removed barriers to direct trade and investment with the mainland, has talked of a shared history, and has referred vaguely to the possibility of a future one China, the PRC authorities remain extremely distrustful of Chen's intentions. They view his recent moves away from independence as merely tactical adjustments.

The Taiwan leader, on the other hand, and many others in the Taiwan political elite, view with equal suspicion some of the PRC's more flexible recent statements about one China—for example, that the one China the PRC has in mind is not the PRC and that China and Taiwan can negotiate as equals. Many in Taiwan believe that the PRC's ultimate intention is to delegitimize Taiwan's government and to subjugate Taiwan.

Adding to the problem is the continuing militarization of the cross-strait issue. The PRC continues to build up missiles opposite Taiwan and to modernize its military so as to pose a more credible threat to Taiwan. Taiwan, for its part, is also modernizing its military with help from the United States.

Perhaps the most worrisome of all aspects of the current situation is the complete absence of official dialogue since 1998, a situation that invites misunderstanding and suspicion on both sides.

Nor does the recent legislative election in Taiwan fundamentally alter the situation. The mainland's interpretation of that election, in which the DPP substantially improved its position in the legislature, is that it has led the hardliners in the DPP to believe that there is no need to modify the party's independence platform and that the DPP's new alliance with former president Lee Deng-hui will prove an added stumbling block to the DPP moderates' attempt to follow the middle road. (See Xu Shiquan's analysis in chapter 15.) Many on the mainland also seem to hope that the two major opposition parties—the Kuomintang and the People's First Party—will combine forces behind one presidential candidate in the 2004 presidential election and thereby be in a strong position to defeat Chen's bid for reelection. For these reasons, the PRC seems unlikely to abandon its present policy of refusing to deal with Chen unless he accepts the one-China formula, while at the same time courting the opposition.

Although the continuing political impasse between China and Taiwan is worrisome, the more serious risks are probably not in the next few years. There are a number of factors that diminish the risks of a military conflict in the short term. Three of them are of particular importance.

First, as the chapters by Clough, Yu, and Scalapino make clear, economic relations between China and Taiwan have increased dramatically in the recent past. Investment in China from Taiwan now totals some U.S. $60 billion, and some analysts regard the accurate figure as much larger. Cross-strait trade was nearly U.S. $15 billion for the first six months of 2001, and this trade represents a major factor in the Taiwan economy, since some 50 percent of Taiwan's gross domestic product comes from exports. Taiwan has become the fifth-largest trading partner for the mainland, and the mainland has become the second-largest export market for Taiwan.

It is likely, moreover, that cross-strait economic relations will continue to grow after both Beijing and Taipei adjust to their recent admission to the World Trade Organization. Business enterprises on both sides of the strait will find ways to expand economic relations, in anticipation of an upturn in the global economy in 2002.

Also, fundamental reasons are dictating the increase in cross-strait economic relations. Taiwan is in economic trouble. Taiwan's troubles are part of a broader picture in East Asia, which sees a number of smaller countries in difficulty because they face increased competition from the PRC with its low labor costs, increased productivity and quality, and export orientation. This forces the smaller countries to try to improve their competitive performances. In this situation, Taiwan is doing what is logical. The Taiwan business community has put pressure on the Chen Shui-bian government to legalize and encourage what is already its extensive investment on the mainland, to move production facilities to the mainland, and to use China's abundant and cheap labor force. As a result, a process of economic integration between China and Taiwan has begun despite the fears of many on Taiwan that this economic integration will give the PRC political leverage over Taiwan.

Perhaps most important, many analysts on the mainland seem to be betting that time is now on Beijing's side in its relations with Taiwan because growing economic interaction will eventually force Taiwan into a political accommodation with the PRC. Though this conclusion may turn out to be incorrect, it is positive in the sense that it is likely to steer the mainland into the direction of patience and away from trying to resolve the issue by force—at least in the short run.

The second positive trend has to do with Taiwan's politics and economics. With the decline of the Kuomintang now evident in recent elections, the DPP is becoming the single largest political party in Taiwan. And the DPP, now that it is in a position of power and responsibility, is moving away from its past advocacy of de jure independence to a more centrist position that—in tune with Taiwan public opinion—seeks neither independence nor reunification but maintenance of the status quo—that is, de facto independence. President Chen has made clear this new centrist stance of the DPP in a number of ways. He has declared and reiterated the Five No's—no declaration of Taiwan independence, no revision of the constitution, no change of the national title, no referendum on the question of independence, and no abolition of the Guidelines for National Unification and the National Unification Council, provided the mainland has no intention to use force against Taiwan. Thus, as Julian Kuo points out, President Chen has countered the continuing PRC threat to use force with the threat that Taiwan will declare independence only if the PRC uses or threatens force.

Perhaps equally significant, the DPP has come very close to formally abandoning its charter's call for independence. In its charter (see the appendices), the DPP originally called for amending the Republic of China (ROC) Constitution in order to change the official name of the island from the Republic of China to the Republic of Taiwan. But the DPP's 1999 Resolution on Taiwan's Future no longer calls for a Republic of Taiwan or for an amendment of the Constitution. Thus, both the DPP and President Chen have accepted the existing ROC Constitution, which, as Ma Ying-jeou points out, is a one-China constitution.

Also, President Chen has repeatedly stressed his desire to handle relations with China in a nonprovocative manner. And he has agreed to discuss the one-China issue, even though he refuses to accept it as a precondition for dialogue.

As a result of these important changes in the DPP approach to the mainland, there is, in fact, now little difference on cross-strait relations between the three major political parties in Taiwan. None of the three major parties stand either for reunification or for independence in the near term. All three want to maintain the status quo while deferring the issue of sovereignty and maintaining cooperative relations with the mainland. And influential leaders in all three parties are discussing a variety of formulas that could lay the basis for some kind of loose association with the mainland in the future—ideas such as confederation, commonwealth, a European Union–type arrangement, or a common market.

The DPP's move to the center is a positive development because it means that there is very little risk that President Chen will make any provocative moves toward independence while he is in office. Moreover, Taiwan's severe economic problems will require Chen to focus on economic recovery and domestic stability. To achieve these goals, some degree of stability in relations with the mainland is necessary.

The third important positive trend in cross-strait relations is that, for a variety of reasons, China is unlikely in the near future to want a confrontation with Taiwan. For the next few years, China will be faced with substantial challenges that occupy a higher priority than Taiwan—problems such as cushioning the adverse impact of China's entry into the World Trade Organization, maintaining political stability, dealing with corruption, reducing unemployment, phasing out inefficient state-owned enterprises, and reducing the gap in development between China's coastal and inland provinces. These problems, taken as a whole, are much more pressing than the Taiwan issue because, if they are not well managed, they could lead to substantial domestic unrest and a challenge to the legitimacy of the Chinese Communist Party. The PRC leaders are therefore likely to put Taiwan on the back burner while they deal with more urgent domestic problems.

China is also unlikely to ratchet up the tension with Taiwan in the near future because Beijing is becoming increasingly convinced that time is on its side as a result of growing economic and cultural interaction between the two sides of the strait.

Finally, as Scalapino points out, the PRC has gone to great lengths to improve its relations with all of its neighbors and with the United States. To undertake a conflict with Taiwan or to engage in ominous threats would endanger China's relations throughout East Asia and especially with the United States. The risks are too great.

Although a crisis in the Taiwan strait is not likely in the next several years, the long-range trends continue to be worrisome. Without a breakthrough on the critical political issues, the cross-strait relationship is likely to become increasingly militarized, the PRC may once again develop a sense of urgency about Taiwan drifting toward independence, and the lack of dialogue may increase each sides' worst fears.

The critical question over the longer run is whether economic integration will gradually lead to a reduction in political tensions and a resumption of the cross-strait political dialogue. If both Taipei and Beijing become more proactive and pragmatic in promoting economic exchanges, some reduction of tension is possible. They will need a mechanism to regulate the opening of the Taiwan market to mainland products, to allow Chinese investment in Taiwan, and to reassure Taiwan investors on the mainland. At the moment, each side is taking a variety of unilateral actions to increase economic and cultural interaction, but at some point they will need to sit down and discuss their differences and ways to overcome those differences. If the two sides can manage to increase trade and cultural exchanges, and to develop a mechanism for dealing with these issues, this could be a major step forward. And it might lead to an increase in mutual trust.

Still, economic integration will not automatically lead to political integration. Over the longer run, the PRC needs to think about formulas that set the sovereignty issue aside for the time being and that might be acceptable to the people of Taiwan. At the same time, the three major political parties in Taiwan need to develop a consensus on how to deal with the mainland. If, for example, the PRC were to develop a broader formula for one China that included the possibility of a confederation, and if the three major parties in Taiwan could agree on the desirability of such a confederation, the grounds for optimism would be substantially increased. But such developments will take time and a good deal of discussion in informal, track II–type dialogues, such as those the National Committee on American Foreign Policy has been conducting.

So far as the United States is concerned, it should continue to encourage by every means possible a peaceful resolution of the dispute, one that has the support of other Asia-Pacific nations as well as, we hope, China and Taiwan. The United States should therefore continue to oppose any declaration of independence by Taiwan and any use of force by China. And it should continue to uphold the thesis that any resolution of the issue must have the support of the Taiwan people.

Suggested Further Reading

Barnett, Doak A. *The FX Decision: Another Crucial Moment in U.S.-China-Taiwan Relations.* Washington, D.C.: Brookings Institution, 1982.

Barnett, Doak A., Donald S. Rice, Esq., William M. Rudolf, Dr. George D. Schwab, and Donald S. Zagoria. *Developing a Peaceful, Stable, and Cooperative Relationship with China.* New York: NCAFP, 1996.

Campbell, Kurt M. "New Directions in U.S. Policy toward Asia: The Initial Bush Approach." *American Foreign Policy Interests,* 23 (2001).

Chang, Charles Chi-Hsiang, Robert A. Scalapino, and Hung-Mao Tien. *Taiwan's Electoral Politics and Democratic Transition: Riding the Third Wave.* Armonk, N.Y.: M.E. Sharpe, 1997.

Chang, Parris H., and Dr. Martin L. Lasater. *If China Crosses the Taiwan Strait: The International Response.* Lanham, Md.: University Press of America, 1993.

Chen Qimao. "The Taiwan Factor in Sino-U.S. Relations: How to Keep the Situation Under Control?" *American Foreign Policy Interests,* 24 (2002).

Chen, York, Martin Edmonds, and Michael M. Tsai. *Taiwan's Maritime Security.* London: Routledge Curzon, 2003.

Cheng Tun-Jen, Chi Huang, and Samuel S.G. Wu. *Inherited Rivalry: Conflict across the Taiwan Straits.* Boulder, Colo.: Lynne Rienner Publishers, 1995.

Clough, Ralph N. *Cooperation or Conflict in the Taiwan Strait?* Lanham, Md.: Rowman & Littlefield Publishing, 1999.

———. "Cross-Strait Economic Relations." *American Foreign Policy Interests,* 21 (1999).

———. *Island China.* Replica Books, 2002.

———. "Managing the U.S.-PRC-Taiwan Relationship." *American Foreign Policy Interests,* 21 (1999).

———. "Negotiating an Interim Agreement Between Taiwan and the PRC." *American Foreign Policy Interests,* 22 (2000).

———. *Reaching Across the Taiwan Strait: People-to-People Diplomacy.* Boulder, Colo.: Westview Press, 1993.

Collins, Beverley, Inger Mess, and Suisheng Zhao. *Across the Taiwan Strait: Mainland China, Taiwan, and the 1995–1996 Crisis*. London: Routledge, 1999.
Copper, John F. *Taiwan in Troubled Times*. River Edge, N.J.: World Scientific Publishing Co., Inc., 2002.
———. *Taiwan: Nation State or Province?* Boulder, Colo.: Westview Press, 1999.
Edmonds, Martin, and Michael M. Tsai. *Defending Taiwan: The Future Vision of Taiwan's Defence Policy and Military Strategy*. London: Routledge Curzon, 2003.
Edmonds, Richard Louis, and Steven M. Goldstein. *Taiwan in the Twentieth Century: A Retrospective View*. Cambridge: Cambridge University Press, 2001.
Ferdinand, Peter. *Take-Off for Taiwan?* London: Continuum, 1996.
Fewsmith, Joseph. *China Since Tiananmen*. Cambridge: Cambridge University Press, 2001.
Finkelstein, David. *Washington's Taiwan Dilemma, 1949–1950*. Fairfax, Va.: George Mason University, 1993.
Garver, John W. *Face Off: China, the United States, and Taiwan's Democratization*. Seattle: University of Washington Press, 1997.
Glaser, Bonnie S. "China's Taiwan Policy in the Wake of 'One Country on Each Side.'" *American Foreign Policy Interests*, 24 (2002).
———. "Chinese Missiles and Taiwan Theater Missile Defense: Can a New Round in the Cross-Strait Arms Race Be Averted?" *American Foreign Policy Interests*, 21 (1999).
———. "Sino-American Relations Beyond September 11." *American Foreign Policy Interests*, 24 (2002).
———. "U.S.-China Relations: Moving Forward." *American Foreign Policy Interests*, 23 (2001).
Gold, Thomas. *State and Society in the Taiwan Miracle*. Armonk, N.Y.: M.E. Sharpe, 1986.
Gong, Gerrit W. *Taiwan Strait Dilemmas: China-Taiwan-U.S. Policies in the New Century*. Washington, D.C.: CSIS Press, 2000.
Hao, Yufan. "Dilemma and Decision: An Organizational Perspective on American China Policy Making." In *Research Papers and Policy Studies*, no. 40. Berkeley, Calif.: Institute of East Asian Studies, 1997.
Herschensohn, Bruce. *Across the Taiwan Strait: Democracy: The Bridge Between Mainland China and Taiwan*. Lanham, Md.: Lexington Books, 2002.
Hsing You-Tien. *Making Capitalism in China: The Taiwan Connection*. Oxford: Oxford University Press, 1998.
Hu Xiabo, Xiaobing Li, and Yang Zhong. *Interpreting U.S. China-Taiwan Relations*. Lanham, Md.: University Press of America, 1998.
Huang Chun-Chieh, Feng-Fu Tsao, and Chun-Kit Joseph Wong. *Postwar Taiwan in Historical Perspective*. Bethesda: University Press of Maryland, 1998.
Jefferson, Gary H. "Economic Scenarios for Cross-Strait Relations." *American Foreign Policy Interests*, 22 (2000).
Lampton, David M. "Recent U.S. Perspectives on Cross-Strait Relations." *American Foreign Policy Interests*, 21 (1999).
———. *Same Bed, Different Dreams: Managing U.S.-China Relations, 1989–2000*. Berkeley: University of California Press, 2002.
Lampton, David M., and Tadashi Yamamoto. *Major Power Relations in Northeast Asia: Win-Win or Zero-Sum Game?* Tokyo: Japan Center for International Exchange, 2002.

Lardy, Nicholas R. *Integrating China into the Global Economy.* Washington, D.C.: The Brookings Institution, 2002.

Lee, Bernice. "The Security Implications of the New Taiwan." In *Adelphi Papers,* no. 331. Oxford: Oxford University Press, 1999.

Lee, David Tawei. *The Making of the Taiwan Relations Act: Twenty Years in Retrospect.* Oxford: Oxford University Press, 2000.

Lin, Bih-Jaw, and James T. Myers. *Contemporary China in the Post-Cold War Era.* Columbia: University of South Carolina Press, 1996.

Lin, Cheng-yi. "Confidence Building Measures in the Taiwan Strait." *American Foreign Policy Interests,* 23 (2001).

Lin, Zhiling, Thomas G. Robinson, and Thomas W. Robinson. *The Chinese and Their Future: Beijing, Taipei, and Hong Kong.* Washington, D.C.: AEI Press, 1995.

Metzger, Thomas A. "The Unification of China and the Problem of Public Opinion in the Republic of China in Taiwan." In *Essays in Public Policy,* no. 32. Stanford, Calif.: Hoover Institution Press, 1992.

Mulvenon, James, and Michael Swaine. *Taiwan's Foreign and Defense Policies.* Santa Monica, Calif.: Rand Corporation, 2001.

Nathan, Andrew J., and Robert S. Ross. *The Great Wall and the Empty Fortress: China's Search for Security.* New York: W.W. Norton & Company, 1998.

NCAFP. "U.S.-China Policy and Cross-Strait Relations." *American Foreign Policy Interests,* 19 (1997).

———. "The Second Roundtable on U.S.-China Policy and Cross-Strait Relations." *American Foreign Policy Interests,* 20 (1998).

———. "The Third Roundtable on U.S.-China Policy and Cross-Strait Relations." *American Foreign Policy Interests,* vol. 20 (1998).

O'Hanlon, Michael. "Can China Conquer Taiwan?" *International Security,* 25 (2000).

Orletsky, David T., David A. Shlapak, and Barry A. Wilson. *Dire Strait?: Military Aspects of the China-Taiwan Confrontation and Options for U.S. Policy.* Santa Monica, Calif.: Rand Corporation, 2000.

Paal, Douglas H. "The U.S. Role in Cross-Strait Relations: Washington-Beijing-Taipei." *American Foreign Policy Interests,* 22 (2000).

Ravich, Samantha F. "Examining Trends of Convergence and Divergence across the Taiwan Strait: The NCAFP's Roundtable on U.S.-China Policy and Cross-Strait Relations." *American Foreign Policy Interests,* 21 (1999).

———. "U.S. Policy Toward the Taiwan Strait: A Historical Perspective." *American Foreign Policy Interests,* 21 (1999).

Rigger, Shelley. *From Opposition to Power: Taiwan's Democratic Progressive Party.* Boulder, Colo.: Lynne Reinner Publishers, 2001.

———. *Politics in Taiwan: Voting for Democracy.* London: Routledge, 1999.

Ross, Robert S. "The Stability of Deterrence in the Taiwan Strait." *The National Interest* (2001).

Rubinstein, Murray A. *Taiwan: A New History.* Armonk, N.Y.: M.E. Sharpe, 1999.

Scalapino, Robert A. "The United States and Asia: Challenges of the Twenty-First Century." *American Foreign Policy Interests,* 23 (2001).

Shambaugh, David. *Contemporary Taiwan.* Oxford: Oxford Press, 1998.

———. *The Modern Chinese State.* Cambridge: Cambridge University Press, 2000.

Song Yimin. "Relations between China and America Since President George W. Bush's Visit to China." *American Foreign Policy Interests,* 24 (2002).

Su, Chi. "Domestic Determinants of Taiwan's Mainland Policy." Paper presented at Oxford University Conference, Oxford, United Kingdom, May, 2002.

Sutter, Robert. *Taiwan in World Affairs.* Boulder, Colo.: Westview Press, 1994.

Swaine, Michael D. "Chinese Decision Making Toward Taiwan, 1979–1997." In *The Making of Chinese Foreign and Security Policy in the Era of Reform*, ed. David Lampton. Stanford, Calif.: Stanford University Press, 2001.

Swaine, Michael D., and Ashley J. Tellis. *Interpreting China's Grand Strategy: Past, Present and Future.* Santa Monica, Calif.: Rand Corporation, 2000.

Taylor, Jay. *The Generalissimo's Son: Chiang Ching-Kuo and the Revolutions in China and Taiwan.* Cambridge, Mass.: Harvard University Press, 2000.

Tien, Hung-Mao. *Taiwan's Electoral Politics and Democratic Transition: Riding the Third Wave.* Armonk, N.Y.: M.E. Sharpe, 1988.

———. "Taiwan's Perspective on Cross-Strait Relations and U.S. Policy." *American Foreign Policy Interests*, 21 (1999).

Tien, Hung-Mao, and Steve Yui-Sang Tsang. *Democratization in Taiwan: Implications for China.* Hampshire, England: Palgrave Macmillan, 1999.

Tucker, Nancy Bernkopf. *China Confidential.* New York: Columbia University Press, 2001.

———. "If Taiwan Chooses Unification, Should the United States Care?" *Washington Quarterly*, 25 (2002).

———. "Options for U.S. Policy Regarding U.S.-Taiwan Relations." *American Foreign Policy Interests*, 22 (2000).

———. "Taiwan, Hong Kong, and the United States, 1945–1992: Uncertain Friendships." In *Twayne's International History*, no. 14. Boston, Mass.: Twayne Publisher, 1994.

U.S. Department of Defense. "The Security Situation in the Taiwan Strait." Washington, D.C.: U.S. Department of Defense, 1999.

Van Kemenade, Willem. *China, Hong Kong, Taiwan, Inc.* Translated by Diane Webb. New York: Vintage Books, 1998.

Van Vranken Hickey, Dennis. *United States-Taiwan Security Ties: From Cold War to Beyond Containment.* Westport, Conn.: Praeger Publishers, 1994.

Wachman, Alan. *Taiwan: National Identity and Democratization.* Armonk, N.Y.: M.E. Sharpe, 1994.

Weller, Robert P. *Alternate Civilities: Democracy and Culture in China and Taiwan.* Boulder, Colo.: Westview Press, 2001.

Wheeler, Jimmy W. *Chinese Divide: Evolving Relations Between Taiwan and Mainland China.* Indianapolis, Ind.: Hudson Institute, 1996.

Wu, Hsin-Hsing. *Bridging the Strait: Taiwan, China, and the Prospects for Reunification.* Oxford: Oxford University Press, 1996.

Wu Xinbo. "The Taiwan Issue and U.S.-Asia/Pacific Security Strategy." *American Foreign Policy Interests*, 24 (2002).

Xu Shiquan. "The One-China Principle: The Positions of the Communist Party of China (CCP), the Kuomintang (KMT), and the Democratic Progressive Party (DPP)." *American Foreign Policy Interests*, 22 (2000).

Yang, Jemian. "U.S. Policy Toward Cross-Strait Relations: A Chinese Perspective." *American Foreign Policy Interests*, 21 (1999).

Zagoria, Donald S. *Cross-Strait Relations: Breaking the Impasse. An Interim Report (with Policy Recommendations) on U.S.-China Policy and Cross-Strait Relations.* New York: NCAFP, 2000.

———. "National Committee on American Foreign Policy's Project on U.S.-China Policy and Cross-Strait Relations." *American Foreign Policy Interests*, 21 (1999).

———. "Wanted: A Coherent U.S.-China Policy." *American Foreign Policy Interests*, 17 (1995).

Zi, Zhongyun. *No Exit: The Origin and Evolution of U.S. Policy Toward China, 1945–1950.* Santa Barbara, Calif.: Pacific Century Press, 2003.

APPENDIX 1

Excerpts from the Cairo Conference, Declaration of 1943, and Potsdam Statement, August 1, 1945

EXCERPT FROM THE CAIRO CONFERENCE, DECLARATION OF 1943

November, 1943
Released December 1, 1943

The Three Great Allies are fighting this war to restrain and punish the aggression of Japan. They covet no gain for themselves and have no thought of territorial expansion.

It is their purpose that Japan shall be stripped of all the islands in the Pacific which she has seized or occupied since the beginning of the first World War in 1914, and that all the territories Japan has stolen from the Chinese, such as Manchuria, Formosa, and the Pescadores, shall be restored to the Republic of China.

Source: http://www.yale.edu/lawweb/avalon/decade/decade17.htm.

EXCERPT FROM THE POTSDAM STATEMENT, AUGUST 1, 1945

Annex II (8): The terms of the Cairo Declaration shall be carried out and Japanese sovereignty shall be limited to the islands of Honshu, Hokkaido, Kyushu, Shikoku, and such minor islands as we determine.

Source: http://www.yale.edu/lawweb/avalon/decade/decade17.htm.

Appendix 2

Article 4 of the ROC Constitution, Effective December 25, 1947

CHAPTER I: GENERAL PROVISIONS

Article 4

The territory of Republic of China within its existing national boundaries shall not be altered except by a resolution of the National Assembly.

Source: http://wulaw.wustl.edu/Chinalaw/twguide.html.

Appendix 3

Excerpt from the Shanghai Communiqué on the Taiwan Issue, February 27, 1972

The two sides reviewed the long-standing serious disputes between China and the United States. China reaffirmed its position: The Taiwan question is the crucial question obstructing the normalization of relations between China and the United States; the Government of the People's Republic of China is the sole legal government of China; Taiwan is a province of China which has long been returned to the motherland; the liberation of Taiwan is China's internal affair in which no other country has the right to interfere; and all U.S. forces and military installations must be withdrawn from Taiwan. The Chinese Government firmly opposes any activities which aim at the creation of "one China, one Taiwan," "one China, two governments," "two Chinas," and "independent Taiwan" or advocate that "the status of Taiwan remains to be determined."

The U.S. side declared: The United States acknowledges that all Chinese on either side of the Taiwan Strait maintain there is but one China and that Taiwan is a part of China. The United States Government does not challenge that position. It reaffirms its interest in a peaceful settlement of the Taiwan question by the Chinese themselves. With this prospect in mind, it affirms the ultimate objective of the withdrawal of all U.S. forces and military installations from Taiwan. In the meantime, it will progressively reduce its forces and military installations on Taiwan as the tension in the area diminishes.

The two sides agreed that it is desirable to broaden the understanding between the two peoples. To this end, they discussed specific areas in such fields as science, technology, culture, sports and journalism, in which people-to-people contacts and exchanges would be mutually beneficial. Each side undertakes to facilitate the further development of such contacts and exchanges.

Both sides view bilateral trade as another area from which mutual benefit can be derived, and agreed that economic relations based on equality and mutual benefit are in the interest of the peoples of the two countries. They agree to facilitate the progressive development of trade between their two countries.

The two sides agreed that they will stay in contact through various channels, including the sending of a senior U.S. representative to Peking from time to time for concrete consultations to further the normalization of relations between the two countries and continue to exchange views on issues of common interest.

The two sides expressed the hope that the gains achieved during this visit would open up new prospects for the relations between the two countries. They believe that the normalization of relations between the two countries is not only in the interest of the Chinese and American peoples but also contributes to the relaxation of tension in Asia and the world.

President Nixon, Mrs. Nixon and the American party expressed their appreciation for the gracious hospitality shown them by the Government and people of the People's Republic of China.

Source: http://www.usconsulate.org.hk/uscn/docs/jc/720227.htm.

Appendix 4

Joint Communiqué on the Establishment of Diplomatic Relations between the United States of America and the People's Republic of China, January 1, 1979

(The communiqué was released on December 15, 1978, in Washington and Peking.)

The United States of America and the People's Republic of China have agreed to recognize each other and to establish diplomatic relations as of January 1, 1979.

The United States of America recognizes the Government of the People's Republic of China as the sole legal Government of China. Within this context, the people of the United States will maintain cultural, commercial, and other unofficial relations with the people of Taiwan.

The United States of America and the People's Republic of China reaffirm the principles agreed on by the two sides in the Shanghai Communiqué and emphasize once again that:

- Both wish to reduce the danger of international military conflict.
- Neither should seek hegemony in the Asia-Pacific region or in any other region of the world and each is opposed to efforts by any other country or group of countries to establish such hegemony.
- Neither is prepared to negotiate on behalf of any third party or to enter into agreements or understandings with the other directed at other states.

- The Government of the United States of America acknowledges the Chinese position that there is but one China and Taiwan is part of China.
- Both believe that normalization of Sino-American relations is not only in the interest of the Chinese and American peoples but also contributes to the cause of peace in Asia and the world.

The United States of America and the People's Republic of China will exchange Ambassadors and establish Embassies on March 1, 1979.

Source: http://www.usconsulate.org.hk/uscn/docs/jc/790101.htm.

Appendix 5

Taiwan Relations Act, April 10, 1979

Public Law 96-8 96th Congress
An Act
To help maintain peace, security, and stability in the Western Pacific and to promote the foreign policy of the United States by authorizing the continuation of commercial, cultural, and other relations between the people of the United States and the people on Taiwan, and for other purposes. Be it enacted by the Senate and House of Representatives of the United States of America in Congress assembled,

SHORT TITLE

SECTION 1. This Act may be cited as the "Taiwan Relations Act."

FINDINGS AND DECLARATION OF POLICY

SEC. 2. (a) The President—having terminated governmental relations between the United States and the governing authorities on Taiwan recognized by the United States as the Republic of China prior to January 1, 1979, the Congress finds that the enactment of this Act is necessary—

(1) to help maintain peace, security, and stability in the Western Pacific; and

(2) to promote the foreign policy of the United States by authorizing the continuation of commercial, cultural, and other relations between the people of the United States and the people on Taiwan.

(b) It is the policy of the United States—

(1) to preserve and promote extensive, close, and friendly commercial, cultural, and other relations between the people of the United States and the people on Taiwan, as well as the people on the China mainland and all other peoples of the Western Pacific area;

(2) to declare that peace and stability in the area are in the political, security, and economic interests of the United States, and are matters of international concern;

(3) to make clear that the United States decision to establish diplomatic relations with the People's Republic of China rests upon the expectation that the future of Taiwan will be determined by peaceful means;

(4) to consider any effort to determine the future of Taiwan by other than peaceful means, including by boycotts or embargoes, a threat to the peace and security of the Western Pacific area and of grave concern to the United States;

(5) to provide Taiwan with arms of a defensive character; and

(6) to maintain the capacity of the United States to resist any resort to force or other forms of coercion that would jeopardize the security, or the social or economic system, of the people on Taiwan.

(c) Nothing contained in this Act shall contravene the interest of the United States in human rights, especially with respect to the human rights of all the approximately eighteen million inhabitants of Taiwan. The preservation and enhancement of the human rights of all the people on Taiwan are hereby reaffirmed as objectives of the United States.

IMPLEMENTATION OF UNITED STATES POLICY WITH REGARD TO TAIWAN

SEC. 3. (a) In furtherance of the policy set forth in section 2 of this Act, the United States will make available to Taiwan such defense articles and defense services in such quantity as may be necessary to enable Taiwan to maintain a sufficient self-defense capability.

(b) The President and the Congress shall determine the nature and quantity of such defense articles and services based solely upon their judgment of the needs of Taiwan, in accordance with procedures established by law. Such determination of Taiwan's defense needs shall include review by United States military authorities in connection with recommendations to the President and the Congress.

(c) The President is directed to inform the Congress promptly of any threat to the security or the social or economic system of the people on Taiwan and any danger to the interests of the United States arising therefrom. The President and the Congress shall determine, in accordance with constitutional processes, appropriate action by the United States in response to any such danger.

APPLICATION OF LAWS; INTERNATIONAL AGREEMENTS

SEC. 4. (a) The absence of diplomatic relations or recognition shall not affect the application of the laws of the United States with respect to Taiwan, and the laws of the United States shall apply with respect to Taiwan in the manner that the laws of the United States applied with respect to Taiwan prior to January 1, 1979.

(b) The application of subsection (a) of this section shall include, but shall not be limited to, the following:

(1) Whenever the laws of the United States refer or relate to foreign countries, nations, states, governments, or similar entities, such terms shall include and such laws shall apply with such respect to Taiwan.

(2) Whenever authorized by or pursuant to the laws of the United States to conduct or carry out programs, transactions, or other relations with respect to foreign countries, nations, states, governments, or similar entities, the President or any agency of the United States Government is authorized to conduct and carry out, in accordance with section 6 of this Act, such programs, transactions, and other relations with respect to Taiwan (including, but not limited to, the performance of services for the United States through contracts with commercial entities on Taiwan), in accordance with the applicable laws of the United States.

(3) (A) The absence of diplomatic relations and recognition with respect to Taiwan shall not abrogate, infringe, modify, deny, or otherwise affect in any way any rights or obligations (including but not limited to those involving contracts, debts, or property interests of any kind) under the laws of the United States heretofore or hereafter acquired by or with respect to Taiwan.

(B) For all purposes under the laws of the United States, including actions in any court in the United States, recognition of the People's Republic of China shall not affect in any way the ownership of or other rights or interests in properties, tangible and intangible, and other things of value, owned or held on or prior to December 31, 1978, or thereafter acquired or earned by the governing authorities on Taiwan.

(4) Whenever the application of the laws of the United States depends upon the law that is or was applicable on Taiwan or compliance therewith, the law applied by the people on Taiwan shall be considered the applicable law for that purpose.

(5) Nothing in this Act, nor the facts of the President's action in extending diplomatic recognition to the People's Republic of China, the absence of diplomatic relations between the people on Taiwan and the United States, or the lack of recognition by the United States, and attendant circumstances thereto, shall be construed in any administrative or judicial proceeding as a basis for any United States Government agency, commission, or department to make a finding of fact or determination of law, under the Atomic Energy Act of 1954 and the Nuclear Non-Proliferation Act of 1978, to deny an export license application or to revoke an existing export license for nuclear exports to Taiwan.

(6) For purposes of the Immigration and Nationality Act, Taiwan may be treated in the manner specified in the first sentence of section 202(b) of that Act.

(7) The capacity of Taiwan to sue and be sued in courts in the United States, in accordance with the laws of the United States, shall not be abrogated, infringed, modified, denied, or otherwise affected in any way by the absence of diplomatic relations or recognition.

(8) No requirement, whether expressed or implied, under the laws of the United States with respect to maintenance of diplomatic relations or recognition shall be applicable with respect to Taiwan.

(c) For all purposes, including actions in any court in the United States, the Congress approves the continuation in force of all treaties and other international agreements, including multilateral conventions, entered into by the United States and the governing authorities on Taiwan recognized by the United States as the Republic of China prior to January 1, 1979, and in force between them on December 31, 1978, unless and until terminated in accordance with law.

(d) Nothing in this Act may be construed as a basis for supporting the exclusion or expulsion of Taiwan from continued membership in any international financial institution or any other international organization.

OVERSEAS PRIVATE INVESTMENT CORPORATION

SEC. 5. (a) During the three-year period beginning on the date of enactment of this Act, the $1,000 per capita income restriction in insurance, clause (2) of the second undesignated paragraph of section 231 of the reinsurance, Foreign Assistance Act of 1961 shall not restrict the activities of the Overseas Private Investment Corporation in determining whether to provide any insurance, reinsurance, loans, or guaranties with respect to investment projects on Taiwan.

(b) Except as provided in subsection (a) of this section, in issuing insurance, reinsurance, loans, or guaranties with respect to investment projects on Taiwan, the Overseas Private Insurance Corporation shall apply the same criteria as those applicable in other parts of the world.

THE AMERICAN INSTITUTE OF TAIWAN

SEC. 6. (a) Programs, transactions, and other relations conducted or carried out by the President or any agency of the United States Government with respect to Taiwan shall, in the manner and to the extent directed by the President, be conducted and carried out by or through—

(1) The American Institute in Taiwan, a nonprofit corporation incorporated under the laws of the District of Columbia, or

(2) such comparable successor nongovermental entity as the President may designate, (hereafter in this Act referred to as the "Institute").

(b) Whenever the President or any agency of the United States Government is authorized or required by or pursuant to the laws of the United States to enter into, perform, enforce, or have in force an agreement or transaction relative to Taiwan, such agreement or transaction shall be entered into, performed, and enforced, in the manner and to the extent directed by the President, by or through the Institute.

(c) To the extent that any law, rule, regulation, or ordinance of the District of Columbia, or of any State or political subdivision thereof in which the Institute is incorporated or doing business, impedes or otherwise interferes with the performance of the functions of the Institute pursuant to this Act; such law, rule, regulation, or ordinance shall be deemed to be preempted by this Act.

SERVICES BY THE INSTITUTE TO UNITED STATES CITIZENS ON TAIWAN

SEC. 7. (a) The Institute may authorize any of its employees on Taiwan—

(1) to administer to or take from any person an oath, affirmation, affidavit, or deposition, and to perform any notarial act which any notary public is required or authorized by law to perform within the United States;

(2) To act as provisional conservator of the personal estates of deceased United States citizens; and

(3) to assist and protect the interests of United States persons by performing other acts such as are authorized to be performed outside the United States for consular purposes by such laws of the United States as the President may specify.

(b) Acts performed by authorized employees of the Institute under this section shall be valid, and of like force and effect within the United States, as if performed by any other person authorized under the laws of the United States to perform such acts.

TAX EXEMPT STATUS OF THE INSTITUTE

SEC. 8. (a) The Institute, its property, and its income are exempt from all taxation now or hereafter imposed by the United States (except to the extent that section 11(a)(3) of this Act requires the imposition of taxes imposed under chapter 21 of the Internal Revenue Code of 1954, relating to the Federal Insurance Contributions Act) or by State or local taxing authority of the United States.

(b) For purposes of the Internal Revenue Code of 1954, the Institute shall be treated as an organization described in sections 170(b)(1)(A), 170(c), 2055(a), 2106(a)(2)(A), 2522(a), and 2522(b).

FURNISHING PROPERTY AND SERVICES TO AND OBTAINING SERVICES FROM THE INSTITUTE

SEC. 9. (a) Any agency of the United States Government is authorized to sell, loan, or lease property (including interests therein) to, and to perform administrative and technical support functions and services for the operations of, the Institute upon such terms and conditions as the President may direct. Reimbursements to agencies under this subsection shall be credited to the current applicable appropriation of the agency concerned.

(b) Any agency of the United States Government is authorized to acquire and accept services from the Institute upon such terms and conditions as the

President may direct. Whenever the President determines it to be in furtherance of the purposes of this Act, the procurement of services by such agencies from the Institute may be effected without regard to such laws of the United States normally applicable to the acquisition of services by such agencies as the President may specify by Executive order.

(c) Any agency of the United States Government making funds available to the Institute in accordance with this Act shall make arrangements with the Institute for the Comptroller General of the United States to have access to the books and records of the Institute and the opportunity to audit the operations of the Institute.

TAIWAN INSTRUMENTALITY

SEC. 10. (a) Whenever the President or any agency of the United States Government is authorized or required by or pursuant to the laws of the United States to render or provide to or to receive or accept from Taiwan, any performance, communication, assurance, undertaking, or other action, such action shall, in the manner and to the extent directed by the President, be rendered or Provided to, or received or accepted from, an instrumentality established by Taiwan which the President determines has the necessary authority under the laws applied by the people on Taiwan to provide assurances and take other actions on behalf of Taiwan in accordance with this Act.

(b) The President is requested to extend to the instrumentality established by Taiwan the same number of offices and complement of personnel as were previously operated in the United States by the governing authorities on Taiwan recognized as the Republic of China prior to January 1, 1979.

(c) Upon the granting by Taiwan of comparable privileges and immunities with respect to the Institute and its appropriate personnel, the President is authorized to extend with respect to the Taiwan instrumentality and its appropriate personnel, such privileges and immunities (subject to appropriate conditions and obligations) as may be necessary for the effective performance of their functions.

SEPARATION OF GOVERNMENT PERSONNEL FOR EMPLOYMENT WITH THE INSTITUTE

SEC. 11. (a)(1) Under such terms and conditions as the President may direct, any agency of the United States Government may separate from Government service for a specified period any officer or employee of that agency who accepts employment with the Institute.

(2) An officer or employee separated by an agency under paragraph (1) of this subsection for employment with the Institute shall be entitled upon termination of such employment to reemployment or reinstatement with such agency (or a successor agency) in an appropriate position with the attendant rights, privileges, and benefits with the officer or employee would have had or acquired had he or she not been so

separated, subject to such time period and other conditions as the President may prescribe.

(3) An officer or employee entitled to reemployment or reinstatement rights under paragraph (2) of this subsection shall, while continuously employed by the Institute with no break in continuity of service, continue to participate in any benefit program in which such officer or employee was participating prior to employment by the Institute, including programs for compensation for job-related death, injury, or illness; programs for health and life insurance; programs for annual, sick, and other statutory leave; and programs for retirement under any system established by the laws of the United States; except that employment with the Institute shall be the basis for participation in such programs only to the extent that employee deductions and employer contributions, as required, in payment for such participation for the period of employment with the Institute, are currently deposited in the program's or system's fund or depository. Death or retirement of any such officer or employee during approved service with the Institute and prior to reemployment or reinstatement shall be considered a death in or retirement from Government service for purposes of any employee or survivor benefits acquired by reason of service with an agency of the United States Government.

(4) Any officer or employee of an agency of the United States Government who entered into service with the Institute on approved leave of absence without pay prior to the enactment of this Act shall receive the benefits of this section for the period of such service.

(b) Any agency of the United States Government employing alien personnel on Taiwan may transfer such personnel, with accrued allowances, benefits, and rights, to the Institute without a break in service for purposes of retirement and other benefits, including continued participation in any system established by the laws of the United States for the retirement of employees in which the alien was participating prior to the transfer to the Institute, except that employment with the Institute shall be creditable for retirement purposes only to the extent that employee deductions and employer contributions as required, in payment for such participation for the period of employment with the Institute, are currently deposited in the system' s fund or depository.

(c) Employees of the Institute shall not be employees of the United States and, in representing the Institute, shall be exempt from section 207 of title 18, United States Code.

(d) (1) For purposes of sections 911 and 913 of the Internal Revenue Code of 1954, amounts paid by the Institute to its employees shall not be treated as earned income. Amounts received by employees of the Institute shall not be: included in gross income, and shall be exempt from taxation, to the extent that they are equivalent to amounts received by civilian officers and employees of the Government of the United States as allowances and benefits which are exempt from taxation under section 912 of such Code.

(2) Except to the extent required by subsection (a)(3) of this section, service performed in the employ of the Institute shall not constitute employment for purposes of chapter 21 of such Code and title II of the Social Security Act.

REPORTING REQUIREMENT

SEC. 12. (a) The Secretary of State shall transmit to the Congress the text of any agreement to which the Institute is a party. However, any such agreement the immediate public disclosure of which would, in the opinion of the President, be prejudicial to the national security of the United States shall not be so transmitted to the Congress but shall be transmitted to the Committee on Foreign Relations of the Senate and the Committee on Foreign Affairs of the House of Representatives under an appropriate injunction of secrecy to be removed only upon due notice from the President.

(b) For purposes of subsection (a), the term "agreement" includes—

(1) any agreement entered into between the Institute and the governing authorities on Taiwan or the instrumentality established by Taiwan; and

(2) any agreement entered into between the Institute and an agency of the United States Government.

(c) Agreements and transactions made or to be made by or through the Institute shall be subject to the same congressional notification, review, and approval requirements and procedures as if such agreements and transactions were made by or through the agency of the United States Government on behalf of which the Institute is acting.

(d) During the two-year period beginning on the effective date of this Act, the Secretary of State shall transmit to the Speaker of the House and Senate House of Representatives and the Committee on Foreign Relations of Foreign Relations the Senate, every six months, a report describing and reviewing economic relations between the United States and Taiwan, noting any interference with normal commercial relations.

RULES AND REGULATIONS

SEC. 13. The President is authorized to prescribe such rules and regulations as he may deem appropriate to carry out the purposes of this Act. During the three-year period beginning on the effective date of this Act, such rules and regulations shall be transmitted promptly to the Speaker of the House of Representatives and to the Committee on Foreign Relations of the Senate. Such action shall not, however, relieve the Institute of the responsibilities placed upon it by this Act.

CONGRESSIONAL OVERSIGHT

SEC. 14. (a) The Committee on Foreign Affairs of the House of Representatives, the Committee on Foreign Relations of the Senate, and other appropriate committees of the Congress shall monitor—

(1) the implementation of the provisions of this Act;
(2) the operation and procedures of the Institute;
(3) the legal and technical aspects of the continuing relationship between the United States and Taiwan; and
(4) the implementation of the policies of the United States concerning security and cooperation in East Asia.

(b) Such committees shall report, as appropriate, to their respective Houses on the results of their monitoring.

DEFINITIONS

SEC. 15. For purposes of this Act—

(1) the term "laws of the United States" includes any statute, rule, regulation, ordinance, order, or judicial rule of decision of the United States or any political subdivision thereof; and
(2) the term "Taiwan" includes, as the context may require, the islands of Taiwan and the Pescadores, the people on those islands, corporations and other entities and associations created or organized under the laws applied on those islands, and the governing authorities on Taiwan recognized by the United States as the Republic of China prior to January 1, 1979, and any successor governing authorities (including political subdivisions, agencies, and instrumentalities thereof).

AUTHORIZATION OF APPROPRIATIONS

SEC. 16. In addition to funds otherwise available to carry out the provisions of this Act, there are authorized to be appropriated to the Secretary of State for the fiscal year 1980 such funds as may be necessary to carry out such provisions. Such funds are authorized to remain available until expended.

SEVERABILITY OF PROVISIONS

SEC. 17. If any provision of this Act or the application thereof to any person or circumstance is held invalid, the remainder of the Act and the application of such provision to any other person or circumstance shall not be affected thereby.

EFFECTIVE DATE

SEC. 18. This Act shall be effective as of January 1, 1979. Approved April 10, 1979.

Source: http://ait.org.tw/ait/tra.html.

Appendix 6

U.S.-PRC Joint Communiqué, August 17, 1982

1. In the Joint Communiqué on the Establishment of Diplomatic Relations on January 1, 1979, issued by the Government of the United States of America and the Government of the People's Republic of China, the United States of America recognized the Government of the People's Republic of China as the sole legal government of China, and it acknowledged the Chinese position that there is but one China and Taiwan is part of China. Within that context, the two sides agreed that the people of the United States would continue to maintain cultural, commercial, and other unofficial relations with the people of Taiwan. On this basis, relations between the United States and China were normalized.

2. The question of United States arms sales to Taiwan was not settled in the course of negotiations between the two countries on establishing diplomatic relations. The two sides held differing positions, and the Chinese side stated that it would raise the issue again following normalization. Recognizing that this issue would seriously hamper the development of United States-China relations, they have held further discussions on it, during and since the meetings between President Ronald Reagan and Premier Zhao Ziyang and between Secretary of State Alexander M. Haig, Jr., and Vice Premier and Foreign Minister Huang Hua in October 1981.

3. Respect for each other's sovereignty and territorial integrity and non-interference each other's internal affairs constitute the fundamental principles guiding United States-China relations. These principles were confirmed in the Shanghai Communiqué of February 28, 1972 and reaffirmed in the Joint Communiqué on the Establishment of Diplomatic Relations which came into effect on January 1, 1973. Both sides emphatically state that these principles continue to govern all aspects of their relations.

4. The Chinese government reiterates that the question of Taiwan is China's internal affair. The Message to the Compatriots in Taiwan issued by China on January 1, 1979, promulgated a fundamental policy of striving for Peaceful reunification of the Motherland. The Nine-Point Proposal put forward by China on September 30, 1981 rep-

resented a Further major effort under this fundamental policy to strive for a peaceful solution to the Taiwan question.

5. The United States Government attaches great importance to its relations with China, and reiterates that it has no intention of infringing on Chinese sovereignty and territorial integrity, or interfering in China's internal affairs, or pursuing a policy of "two Chinas" or "one China, one Taiwan." The United States Government understands and appreciates the Chinese policy of striving for a peaceful resolution of the Taiwan question as indicated in China's Message to Compatriots in Taiwan issued on January 1, 1979 and the Nine-Point Proposal put forward by China on September 30, 1981. The new situation which has emerged with regard to the Taiwan question also provides favorable conditions for the settlement of United States-China differences over the question of United States arms sales to Taiwan.

6. Having in mind the foregoing statements of both sides, the United States Government states that it does not seek to carry out a long-term policy of arms sales to Taiwan, that its arms sales to Taiwan will not exceed, either in qualitative or in quantitative terms, the level of those supplied in recent years since the establishment of diplomatic relations between the United States and China, and that it intends to reduce gradually its sales of arms to Taiwan, leading over a period of time to a final resolution. In so stating, the United States acknowledges China's consistent position regarding the thorough settlement of this issue.

7. In order to bring about, over a period of time, a final settlement of the question of United States arms sales to Taiwan, which is an issue rooted in history, the two governments will make every effort to adopt measures and create conditions conducive to the thorough settlement of this issue.

8. The development of United States-China relations is not only in the interest of the two peoples but also conducive to peace and stability in the world. The two sides are determined, on the principle of equality and mutual benefit, to strengthen their ties to the economic, cultural, educational, scientific, technological and other fields and make strong, joint efforts for the continued development of relations between the governments and peoples of the United States and China.

9. In order to bring about the healthy development of United States China relations, maintain world peace and oppose aggression and expansion, the two governments reaffirm the principles agreed on by the two sides in the Shanghai Communiqué and the Joint Communiqué on the Establishment of Diplomatic Relations. The two sides will maintain contact and hold appropriate consultations on bilateral and international issues of common interest.

Source: http://www.usconsulate.org.hk/uscn/docs/jc/820817.htm.

Appendix 7

Ronald Reagan's Six Assurances to Taiwan, August 20, 1982

Washington:

1) has not agreed to set a date for ending arms sales to Taiwan;
2) has not agreed to hold prior consultations with the Chinese government on arms sales to the Republic of China on Taiwan;
3) will not play any mediation role between Taiwan and China;
4) has not agreed to revise the 1979 Taiwan Relations Act;
5) has not altered its position regarding sovereignty over Taiwan; and
6) will not exert pressure on the Republic of China on Taiwan to enter negotiations with the People's Republic of China.

Source: http://www.heritage.org/library/backgrounder/pdf/bg_1352.pdf.

APPENDIX 8

Excerpts from the DPP Platform, Adopted in the First National Congress, November 1986

1. The Establishment of a Sovereign and Independent Republic of Taiwan Territorial Sovereignty and nationality are the preconditions for modern sovereign nations to establish the rule of law and to develop international relations. The fact that Taiwan is sovereign and independent, that it does not belong to the People's Republic of China, and that the Sovereignty of Taiwan does not extend to mainland China, reflect historical realities as well as the present situation, and at the same time forms part of the consensus of the international community. According to this reality of sovereignty and independence, Taiwan should draw up a constitution and establish a nation. Only then is it possible to guarantee respect and security for Taiwanese society and for individual citizens, and to offer the people the opportunity to pursue freedom, democracy, prosperity, justice and self-realization.

Source: www.dpp.org.tw/.

APPENDIX 9

Guidelines for National Unification, March 14, 1991

Mainland Affairs Council, The Executive Yuan, Republic Of China.
Adopted by the National Unification Council at its third meeting on February 23, 1991, and by the Executive Yuan Council at its 2223rd meeting on March 14, 1991.

The unification of China is meant to bring about a strong and prosperous nation with a long-lasting, bright future for its people; it is the common wish of Chinese people at home and abroad. After an appropriate period of forthright exchange, cooperation, and consultation conducted under the principles of reason, peace, parity, and reciprocity, the two sides of the Taiwan Straits should foster a consensus of democracy, freedom and equal prosperity, and together build a new and unified China. Based on this understanding, these Guidelines have been specially formulated with the express hope that all Chinese throughout the world will work with one mind toward their fulfillment.

To establish a democratic, free and equitably prosperous China.

1. Both the mainland and Taiwan areas are parts of Chinese territory. Helping to bring about national unification should be the common responsibility of all Chinese people.
2. The unification of China should be for the welfare of all its people and not be subject to partisan conflict.
3. China's unification should aim at promoting Chinese culture, safeguarding human dignity, guaranteeing fundamental human rights, and practicing democracy and the rule of law.
4. The timing and manner of China's unification should first respect the rights and interests of the people in the Taiwan area, and protect their security and welfare. It should be achieved in gradual phases under the principles of reason, peace, parity, and reciprocity.

1. Short term—A phase of exchanges and reciprocity.
   (1) To enhance understanding through exchanges between the two sides of the Straits and eliminate hostility through reciprocity; and to establish a mutually benign relationship by not endangering each other's security and stability while in the midst of exchanges and not denying the other's existence as a political entity while in the midst of effecting reciprocity.
   (2) To set up an order for exchanges across the Straits, to draw up regulations for such exchanges, and to establish intermediary organizations so as to protect people's rights and interest on both sides of the Straits; to gradually ease various restrictions and expand people-to-people contacts so as to promote the social prosperity of both sides.
   (3) In order to improve the people's welfare on both sides of the Straits with the ultimate objective of unifying the nation, in the mainland area economic reform should be carried out forthrightly, the expression of public opinion there should gradually be allowed, and both democracy and the rule of law should be implemented; while in the Taiwan area efforts should be made to accelerate constitutional reform and promote national development to establish a society of equitable prosperity.
   (4) The two sides of the Straits should end the state of hostility and, under the principle of one China, solve all disputes through peaceful means, and furthermore respect—not reject—each other in the international community, so as to move toward a phase of mutual trust and cooperation.

2. Medium Term—A phase of mutual trust and cooperation.
   (1) Both sides of the Straits should establish official communication channels on equal footing.
   (2) Direct postal, transport and commercial links should be allowed, and both sides should jointly develop the southeastern coastal area of Chinese mainland and then gradually extend this development to other areas of the mainland in order to narrow the gap in living standards between the two sides.
   (3) Both sides of the Straits should work together and assist each other in taking part in international organizations and activities.
   (4) Mutual visits by high-ranking officials on both sides should be promoted to create favorable conditions for consultation and unification.

3. Long term—A phase of consultation and unification. A consultative organization for unification should be established through which both sides, in accordance with the will of the people in both the mainland and Taiwan areas, and while adhering to the goals of democracy, economic freedom, social justice and nationalization of the armed forces, jointly discuss the grand task of unification and map out a constitutional system to establish a democratic, free, and equitably prosperous China.

Source: http://wulaw.wustl.edu/Chinalaw/twguide.html.

APPENDIX 10

Jiang Zemin's Eight Points on Reunification, Excerpted from His Address of January 30, 1995

[FBIS Transcribed Text] Beijing, January 30 (XINHUA)—Jiang Zemin, General Secretary of the Central Committee of the Communist Party of China (CPC) and Chinese President, today made an important speech entitled "Continue to Promote the Reunification of the Motherland" and stated eight views and propositions on important questions that have a bearing on the development of relations between the two sides of the Taiwan Straits and the promotion of the peaceful reunification of the motherland.

Firstly, adherence to the principle of one China is the basis and premise for peaceful reunification. China's sovereignty and territory must never be allowed to suffer split. We must firmly oppose any words or actions aimed at creating an "independent Taiwan" and the propositions which are in contravention of the principle of one China.

Secondly, we do not challenge the development of non-governmental economic and cultural ties by Taiwan with other countries. However, we oppose Taiwan's activities in "expanding its living space internationally" which are aimed at creating "two Chinas" or "one China, one Taiwan." Only after the peaceful reunification is accomplished can the Taiwan compatriots and other Chinese people of all ethnic groups truly and fully share the dignity and honor attained by our great motherland internationally.

Thirdly, to hold negotiations between the two sides on the peaceful reunification of the motherland. Representatives from the various political parties and mass organizations on both sides of the Taiwan Straits can be invited to participate in such talks. On the premise that there is only one China, we are prepared to talk about any matter, including all matters of concern to the Taiwan authorities. As the first step, negotiations should be held and an agreement reached on officially ending the state of hostility between the two sides. On this basis, the two sides should undertake jointly to safeguard China's sovereignty and territorial integrity and map out plans for the future development of their relations.

Fourthly, we should strive for the peaceful reunification of the motherland since Chinese should not fight fellow Chinese. Our not undertaking to give up the use of force is not directed against our compatriots in Taiwan but against the schemes of foreign forces to interfere with China's reunification and to bring about the "independence of Taiwan".

Fifthly, Great efforts should be made to expand the economic exchanges and cooperation between the two sides of the Taiwan Straits so as to achieve prosperity on both sides to the benefit of the entire Chinese nation. We hold that political differences should not affect or interfere with the economic cooperation between the two sides. We are in favor of conducting the kind of negotiations on the basis of reciprocity and mutual benefit and signing non-governmental agreements on the protection of the rights and interests of industrialists and businessmen from Taiwan. Whatever the circumstances may be, we shall safeguard the legitimate rights and interests of industrialists and businessmen from Taiwan.

Sixthly, The splendid culture of Chinese nation has become ties keeping the entire Chinese people close at heart and constitutes an important basis for the peaceful reunification of the motherland. People on both sides of the Taiwan Straits should inherit and carry forward the fine traditions of the Chinese culture.

Seventhly, we should fully respect the life style of the compatriots in Taiwan and their wish to be the masters of our country and protect all their legitimate rights and interests. The relevant departments of our party and the government including the agencies stationed abroad should strengthen close ties with compatriots from Taiwan, listen to their views and demands, be concerned with and take into account their interest and make every effort to help them solve their problems. All parties and personages of all circles in Taiwan are welcome to exchange views with us on relations between the two sides and on peaceful reunification and are also welcome to pay a visit and tour places.

Eighthly, Leaders of the Taiwan authorities are welcome to pay visits in appropriate capacities. We are also ready to accept invitations from the Taiwan side to visit Taiwan. We can discuss state affairs, or exchange ideas on certain questions first. The affairs of Chinese people should be handled by ourselves, something that does not take an international occasion to accomplish.

Source: www.Lexis-Nexis.com.

APPENDIX 11

DPP's Resolution Regarding Taiwan's Future, Passed by the National Party Congress (8th Term, 2nd Meeting), May 8, 1999

I. PREFACE

Through years of hardship and trouble, the Democratic Progressive Party (DPP) and the people of Taiwan have compelled the Kuomintang (KMT) to accept democratic reforms by lifting Martial Law and terminating one-party authoritarian rule. Following the 1992 general elections of the national legislature, the 1996 direct presidential elections, and constitutional reform to abolish the provincial government, Taiwan has become a democratic and independent country.

In order to face the new environment and to create a vision for the future based on past accomplishments, the DPP continues to push for structural reforms in the state institutions while taking further steps to define Taiwan's status and the direction in which the nation is headed. This proclamation unequivocally clarifies the outlook of the DPP regarding Taiwan's future at this juncture in time. Our past experiences and achievements can be used as a foundation to face the challenges of the next century.

II. PROCLAMATION

1. Taiwan is a sovereign and independent country. Any change in the independent status quo must be decided by all the residents of Taiwan by means of plebiscite.

2. Taiwan is not a part of the People's Republic of China. China's unilateral advocacy of the One China Principle and One Country Two Systems is fundamentally inappropriate for Taiwan.
3. Taiwan should expand its role in the international community, seek international recognition, and pursue the goal of entry into the United Nations and other international organizations.
4. Taiwan should renounce the One China position to avoid international confusion and to prevent the position's use by China as a pretext for forceful annexation.
5. Taiwan should promptly complete the task of incorporating plebiscite into law in order to realize the people's rights. In time of need, it can be relied on to establish consensus of purpose, and allow the people to express their will.
6. Taiwan's government and opposition forces must establish bi-partisan consensus on foreign policy, integrating limited resources, to face China's aggression and ambition.
7. Taiwan and China should engage in comprehensive dialogue to seek mutual understanding and economic cooperation. Both sides should build a framework for long-term stability and peace.

III. EXPLANATION

Independent and autonomous sovereignty is the prerequisite for national security, social development and the people's welfare. Taiwan is a sovereign independent country, not subject to the jurisdiction of the People's Republic of China. This is both a historical fact and a reflection of the status quo. It is not only a condition indispensable to Taiwan's existence, but also a crucial element to the development of democratic political practices and the creation of economic miracles.

When the end of the cold war in 1991 marked a decisive victory for freedom, democracy, and self-determination, the DPP revised its party platform. The DPP advocated Taiwan's sovereign independence and proposed three areas of reform: Re-definition of national jurisdiction, structural revisions of the constitution, and the development of a new national identity. These positions were denigrated as heresy at the time, but in less than ten years, the notion of independent sovereignty has become the prevailing social consensus. Their ramifications have swiftly become the embodiment of Taiwan's constitutional and legal structure.

Taiwan is a sovereign and independent country. In accordance with international laws, Taiwan's jurisdiction covers Taiwan, Penghu, Kinmen, Matsu, its affiliated islands and territorial waters. Taiwan, although named the Republic of China under its current constitution, is not subject to the jurisdiction of the People's Republic of China. Any change in the independent status quo must be decided by all residents of Taiwan by means of plebiscite.

Under the current social consensus, externally, Taiwan no longer insists on using the Republic of China as the sole national name to participate in various governmental and non-governmental international organizations. Domestically, after breaking the KMT's mythical claim of being the sole legitimate government in all of China, we pushed for constitutional and political reforms which resulted in democratic national legislature elections, direct presidential elections, and the freezing of the provincial government. In developing a new national identity, we promoted the Taiwanization of public education to rebuild the awareness of Taiwanese history and culture. The enactment of the Law on Territorial Waters in early 1999 clearly defined the jurisdiction of national territory, and the government announced lifting the restriction on using the title Taiwan in national organizations. The principle of Taiwan's sovereign independence has comprehensively demonstrated its superiority and legitimacy in application. The forward-looking nature of the 1991 platform revision has been validated.

Today, in 1999, internal systemic reform is yet to be accomplished. Yet the confrontation and division between the ruling and opposition parties on the issue of national identity have been softened, opening up new opportunity for bi-partisan foreign policy. In facing the pressure from China, the divisions in values over national identity have given way to policy-level disagreements on how to ensure Taiwan's national security and independent sovereignty.

The DPP considers the following international elements favorable to the maintenance of Taiwan's independent sovereignty and international status: The end of the Cold War, victory of liberal and democratic ideas, Taiwan's democratization, and rising public opinion opposing reunification. However, the China's growing might and consistently stubborn hegemonic thinking presents the greatest obstacle to Taiwan's future. Given the unpredictability of international politics and the complicated web of interests, the DPP believes that Taiwan must take a safe, cautious, gradual, and well-examined approach to Taiwan.

It is the DPP's conviction that the cross-Strait relationship cannot stay outside of the global trend toward reconciliation, stability, and prosperity. Furthermore, it is impossible for two countries sharing geographic proximity, economic benefits and cultural origins to remain in a state of hostility and mutual isolation. The ultimate goal of the DPP's China policy is to establish a cross-Strait relationship that is mutually beneficial rather than discriminatory, peaceful rather than confrontational, and equal rather than subordinate to each other. The DPP asks the Chinese government to respect the will of the Taiwanese people and to accept the fact of Taiwan's independent sovereignty. Furthermore, we hope that China can abandon the outdated framework of nationalism and respect Taiwanese people's pursuit of independence, autonomy, and prosperous development under a free and democratic system. The DPP also hopes that in the coming century, China and Taiwan can abandon mutual suspicion and antagonism. Based on historical and cultural origins, and for the sake of geopolitical, regional stability and economic interests, both sides should work together towards a future of co-existence, co-prosperity, mutual trust and mutual benefits.

Source: www.dpp.org.tw/.

APPENDIX 12

DPP's China Policy, Content Compiled from the "Resolution Regarding Taiwan's Future," May 1999

The Democratic Progressive Party platform, originally adopted by the party's first national Congress in 1986, lists the establishment of a sovereign and independent Republic of Taiwan as the first among several goals of this property. However, recognizing Taiwan's responsibilities as a member of the global community and realities of the international political environment, the DPP has also adopted a realistic interpretation and pragmatic approach to China policy.

As the current ruling party in a maturing democracy, the DPP's priority on cross-Strait relations with China is the safeguarding of the sovereignty and rights of Taiwan's twenty-three million people, acting in the best interests of the island's security, and furthermore, undertaking Taiwan's responsibility in preserving stability in the East Asia-Pacific region.

The issue of Taiwan's relations with China is arguably the most emotionally provocative, controversial, and difficult to solve in Taiwan. Early in 1998, the DPP held a conference to discuss an appropriate China Policy. Through open debate, the differences were understood while a consensus was met. Among the agreed points, the DPP supports comprehensive dialogue and exchanges with China, with the goal of eventually achieving the normalization of cross-Strait relations. As for the issue of sovereignty, since under present international conditions, it is impossible for either side across the Strait to compromise on this matter, the DPP prefers to avoid discussion with China on this sensitive yet contentious topic while dealing with the more practical and functional matters first. Comprehensive dialogue may cover a wide range of practical issues, ranging from economic relations, cross-Strait trade and investment environment to fishing disputes and the three links—direct shipping, mailing, and transport. Only Taiwan's sovereignty is non-negotiable. National sovereignty is absolute and indivisible and not to be disposed of in negotiations.

During the National Party Congress in May 1999, the DPP amended its China Policy by passing the Resolution Regarding Taiwan's Future. It incorporated the changes to its China Policy by formally adopting them into the party platform. This resolution not only becomes the new foundation of the DPP's China Policy but it also reflects the willingness of the DPP to adjust and change its positions in accordance with the current trends and popular sentiment.

Source: www.dpp.org.tw/.

Appendix 13

Excerpt from President Chen's Inaugural Speech: The Five No's, May 20, 2000

"I fully understand that, as the popularly elected 10th-term president of the Republic of China, I must abide by the Constitution, maintain the sovereignty, dignity and security of our country, and ensure the well-being of all citizens. Therefore, as long as the CCP regime has no intention to use military force against Taiwan, I pledge that during my term in office, I will not declare independence, I will not change the national title, I will not push forth the inclusion of the so-called "state-to-state" description in the Constitution, and I will not promote a referendum to change the status quo in regard to the question of independence or unification. Furthermore, there is no question of abolishing the Guidelines for National Unification and the National Unification Council."

Source: http://www.mac.gov.tw/english/MacPolicy/cb0520e.htm.

Appendix 14

Excerpt from Chen Shui-bian's Address to the Economic Development Advisory Committee, August 26, 2001

[Point 5] With regard to the further development of cross-strait relations, the ROC government will use the four principles of "Taiwan first," "global perspectives," "mutually beneficial win-win situation," and "sound risk management" to replace the current "patience over haste" policy with one of "vigorous liberalization and effective management."

Consequently, we will establish a stable cross-strait policy. A flexible mechanism for the flow of capital between Taiwan and the mainland will be established, and the initiative will be taken in preparing for the opening of the "three links" and accession to the WTO by both sides. Tourist visits to Taiwan by people from the Chinese mainland will be promoted. Lastly, we will continue to push for dialogue between the two sides.

Source: http://www.gio.gov.tw/taiwan-website/4-oa/20010826/2001082601.html.

APPENDIX 15

Excerpt from Chen Shui-bian's National Day Message, October 10, 2001

IV. PURSUING CROSS-STRAIT RECONCILIATION

Although the Chinese mainland has not responded positively to our government's initiatives to normalize cross-strait relations since my inauguration on May 20 last year, we will continue to promote cross-strait reconciliation. The Economic Development Advisory Conference has reached a consensus on mainland relations that the "patience over haste" policy should be replaced by a policy of "proactive opening and effective management" under the principles of "Taiwan first, global perspectives, mutual benefit, and risk management."

In this regard, the ROC government will spare no effort to establish flexible mechanisms for cross-strait capital flow, cope with the challenges of our WTO accession and the "Three Links" across the Taiwan Strait, allow tourists from the Chinese mainland, and continue to promote cross-strait consultations.

I call on the leaders of the Chinese mainland to abandon obsolete and rigid thinking, raise their intellectual horizon in facing cross-Strait relations in the 21st century, considering themes such as humanitarianism to overcome the present impasse between the two sides. With the same cultural heritage, dedication to peace, and eagerness for mutually beneficial results, business, trade, and cultural exchanges will help remove political obstacles between the two sides. Only mutually supportive compassion will resolve unnecessary conflicts of opinion.

Pursuing a win-win result for the two sides and maintaining peace in the Asia-Pacific region are the unavoidable obligations of leaders on both sides of the Taiwan Strait; otherwise, we cannot face history or our people. We should be open and positive about developing a new era during our time.

Source: http://www.president.gov.tw/php-bin/docset/showenews.php4?_section=5&_rid=699.

Index

List of Contributors

Mr. RICHARD C. BUSH, Former Chairman of the Board, American Institute in Taiwan; Director, Center for Northeast Asian Policy Studies, The Brookings Institution

Prof. RALPH N. CLOUGH, School of Advanced International Studies, Johns Hopkins University

Ms. BONNIE S. GLASER, Consultant on Asian Affairs. Senior Associate, Pacific Forum/Center for Strategic and International Studies

Dr. JULIAN JENGLIANG KUO, Director, Policy Council and the Department of Propaganda, Democratic Progressive Party of Taiwan

Dr. DAVID M. LAMPTON, Director, China Studies, School of Advanced International Studies, Johns Hopkins University

The Hon. Dr. YING-JEOU MA, Mayor, Taipei City Government

Mr. ALAN D. ROMBERG, Senior Associate, Director, China Program, The Henry L. Stimson Center

Prof. ROBERT A. SCALAPINO, Robson Research Professor of Government Emeritus, Institute of East Asian Studies, University of California, Berkeley

Mr. DAVID A. SHLAPAK, Rand Corporation

Mr. WILSON TIEN, Former Director of International Affairs, Democratic Progressive Party of Taiwan

Prof. NANCY BERNKOPF TUCKER, Department of History, School of Foreign Service, Georgetown University

Mr. XU SHIQUAN, President, Institute of Taiwan Studies, Chinese Academy of Social Sciences

Prof. YU XINTIAN, President, Shanghai Institute for International Studies

Mr. JIEMIAN YANG, Vice President and Senior Fellow, Shanghai Institute for International Studies

About the Editors

DONALD S. ZAGORIA is Professor of Government at Hunter College. He wrote the seminal work on the Sino-Soviet conflict and has written numerous articles on U.S.-China, U.S.-Soviet, and Sino-Soviet relations.

CHRIS FUGARINO is a research assistant for the National Committee on American Foreign Policy and has participated in a number of conferences on international and security affairs, including the international Student Conference on United States Affairs (SCUSA-54), held at West Point, New York.